Five Roses
Cook Book

Being a Manual of Good Recipes

carefully chosen from the contributions of over two
thousand successful users of *Five Roses*
Flour throughout Canada

Also

Useful Notes on the various classes of good things
to eat, all of which have been carefully
checked and re-checked by
competent authority

D1081823

Issued by
Lake of the Woods Milling
Company Limited
Montreal

For my mother, Caroline Ada Richardson.
The Five Roses Cook Book *was given*
to my mother as a young bride.
Along with her love of cooking, she passed
her treasured copy of the book on to me.

— Carol Ann Shipman

Please note that the ingredients, methods and
cooking times listed in this book are consistent
with the kitchen appliances and techniques that
were in use in 1915. Current equipment and supplies may produce different results that are incon-
sistent with contemporary food safety theories.

Copyright © 1999 by Carol Ann Shipman
Whitecap Books
Vancouver/Toronto

First published in 1915 by Lake of the Woods Milling Company Limited.
Printed in Canada
Sixth Printing 2001

CANADIAN CATALOGUING IN PUBLICATION DATA

Main entry under title:
Five Roses cook book

Includes index.
ISBN 1-55110-995-6

1. Cookery.
TX714.F58 1999   641.5   C99-910831-X

The publisher acknowledges the support of the Canada Council for the Arts and the Cultural
Services Branch of the Government of British Columbia for our publishing program. We
acknowledge the financial support of the Government of Canada through the Book Industry
Development Program for our publishing activities.

FOREWORD

by Elizabeth Baird

Every year hundreds of new cookbooks arrive at Canadian bookstores from around the world. Nowadays, it is not uncommon for households to have dozens of culinary instruction tomes, souvenirs of travels to Nova Scotia or Provence, records of love affairs with pasta or cheesecakes, or virtuous attempts to stay slim. Some cookbook buyers admit to plunking down anywhere from $10 to $50, not necessarily to crack open their often lavishly illustrated purchase and actually cook, but simply to read it, to look at the pictures. For some, cookbooks are the bedtime reading of choice.

Now I can hardly grumble that consumers buy cookbooks for virtual cooking and eating, but I also can't help but reflect on this phenomenon when I look at the *Five Roses Cookbook*. I am the lucky owner of two editions, one, sadly coverless from 1913, cost 10 cents in silver or stamps, and the second just two years later. By the later edition, the price had risen to 30 cents and there were "nearly 650,000 copies of the book in daily use in Canadian Kitchens—practically one copy for every second Canadian Home." Note how the capitalization of "kitchen" and "home" imbue these places with emotion.

One of these books belonged to my maternal grandmother, who fed a husband, 8 children, plus threshers and seasonal helpers on a farm near Fullarton, Ontario. Her cookbook score? One—the *Five Roses Cookbook* was it. It hung handy, via the string looped through a hole punched conveniently near the binding, on a nail in her pantry. That's where she creamed the butter for the Burnt Sugar Cake (page 111), and where she separated the 11 eggs to whip up her Angel Food Cake (page 92). I don't know that she ever made the Hop Beer (page 129), but from the evidence of the drips and sticky bits, I suspect she made many a Mexican Date Pie (page 82). Second

to the family Bible, my grandmother's cookbook is like so many other women's stained records of the recipes that satisfied their families, and of their friendships and culinary experiences via the handwritten recipes, clippings from newspapers and pamphlets stuck in among the pages, to flutter out 20, 30, 40, 50 years after the last cookie was dropped onto the baking sheet.

There is much that is good about this original *Five Roses Cookbook*. It boasts a generous number of recipes, about 600, covering every dish from pancakes, gems (muffin-like quick breads), preserves, cookies, gingerbread, pies, cakes, cakes, and more cakes, and one of the earliest references to butter tarts in Canadian food literature. The recipes are presented in a very modern-looking style, mainly using volume measures as per the young home economics movement in North America. You will notice, though, that some list ingredients only. Well, the only thing you really had to know about a Christmas Pudding was how long to steam it. Like so many cookbooks of its era, recipes for vegetables or main courses are sparse. These were recipes considered so simple you didn't need a cookbook to tell you how. And if you didn't know, your mother, sister or neighbour would.

The *Five Roses Cookbook* played a very important role in forging a Canadian style of cooking. In creating a market for its flour, the company's cookbooks provided inspiration and instruction to generations of women so they could bake a variety of foods, and bake them well. We are the benefactors generations later of this skill as Canadians are among the premier home bakers in the world. Enjoy the *Five Roses Cookbook* as a charming glimpse into the past, and as my grandmother did, as a friend and helper.

Elizabeth Baird is the food director at Canadian Living Magazine.

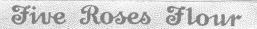

LIST OF RECIPES

◇ ◇

Arranged Alphabetically

LIST OF RECIPES—Continued

LIST OF RECIPES—Continued

A PAGE OF WEIGHTS AND MEASURES

BY using measures instead of weights considerable time can be saved the user of *Five Roses* Flour, and it is because the following equivalents have been of real use to many contributors that they are now added to the *Five Roses* Cook Book. All measures are level, unless otherwise specified. Due to the loss or gain of moisture constantly going on, no absolutely true measures can be given, but for ordinary purposes the following are approximately correct. Further hints and details dealing with the various classes of good things to eat will be found in their proper sections. Standard cups, spoons, etc., are used.

❖ ❖ ❖

2 saltspoons............1 coffeespoon
2 coffeespoons............1 teaspoon
55 drops................1 teaspoon
5 teaspoons (dry material)..1 tablespoon
4 teaspoons (liquid material) 1 tablespoon
4 tablespoons (liquid material)....½ cup
4 tablespoons (liq. material).1 wineglass
2 wineglasses................1 gill
14 tablespoons..........1 cup or ½ pint
2 gills......................1 cup
2 gills....................1 tumbler
2 cups.....................1 pint
2 pints....................1 quart
1 pint (liquid)..............1 pound
1 tablespoon (liquid)..........½ ounce
1 tablespoon (rounding) soft butter
................1 ounce
2 tablespoons melted butter....1 ounce
Soft butter size of walnut....1 ounce
Soft butter size of an egg....2 ounces
1 tablespoon (heaping) sugar or salt..............1 ounce
2 tablespoons (heaping) *Five Roses* flour................1 ounce
2 tablespoons (heaping) powdered sugar.................1 ounce
2 tablespoons (heaping) ground coffee..............1 ounce
1 square chocolate............1 ounce
1 cup butter or lard...........½ pound

1 cup granulated sugar (rounded)
................½ pound
1 " confectioner's sugar.....6 ounces
1 " brown sugar (heaping)...8 ounces
1 " sifted *Fives Roses* flour about.................4 ounces
1 quart or 4 cups sifted *Five Roses* flour....................1 pound
3 tablespoons (heaping) *Five Roses* flour....................1 cup
1 cup bread dough (rounded)... 6 to 8 oz.
1 " milk.................8 ounces
1 " tea..................4 ounces
1 " rice.................7 ounces
1 " bread crumbs (pressed in) 4 ounces
1 " suet (finely chopped)....4 ounces
2 cups minced beef (packed closely)
................1 pound
3 cups Indian Meal..........1 pound
1 cup (heaping) currants without stems.................6 ounces
1 cup (heaping) raisins without stems.................8 ounces
10 average sized eggs or 9 large eggs.................1 pound
1 cup egg whites or yolks......½ pound
10 whites or 13 yolks (average sized eggs)....................1 cup
2 yolks.......................1 egg
1 cup yolks..................7 eggs
5 average sized eggs...........1 cup

THE MAKING OF BREAD

(Editor's Note)

IN BREAD-MAKING there is no such thing as "luck." It is merely the effect that follows the use of the best flour, the best yeast and the proper method. The making of bread can now be made a simple, sanitary process involving little, if any, physical effort and very little time.

A chief purpose of the *Five Roses Cook Book* is to save the housewife baking worries, to indicate the proper methods, because nobody works so hard as the person who works badly.

Over two thousand of the very finest cooks in Canada have contributed their baking secrets to this book, and it is from these contributions that the following bread rules have been selected. Since it is a well-known fact that we have not all the same success with the same recipes, the wisdom of securing different methods for the same purpose is evident.

Each separate recipe having received careful checking at the hands of the *Five Roses* expert, there need be no fear of wasted material or disappointment, *if the rules be closely followed.*

The following pages reflect the various methods of bread-making in favour among users of *Five Roses* flour in every province of Canada. There is a sufficient variety at hand to suit all conditions which can possibly arise due to weather, convenience, economy, time, or object in view.

While each rule carries its own particular directions, yet a few general suggestions will prove worthy of attention.

❖ ❖ ❖

FLOUR

In cold weather, warm the flour. Put the dish on top of the stove and stir constantly with the hand from the bottom till the chill is off. Or, warm the jar or crock very hot, put the flour in and let stand some time before using. Besides making the flour more susceptible to yeast action, this dries it out and makes it a readier absorber of the liquid.

It is best, at all times, to have the flour at about 80 degrees Fahrenheit before mixing into either sponge or dough.

In fact, keep everything connected with bread-making at an even temperature.

YEAST

Due to varying conditions, housewives have different yeast preferences. Potato, home-made, dry or compressed yeast, whichever used should be fresh, lively and the best obtainable. It has a tremendous influence on the finished loaf.

All dry yeast should break brittle. If it crumbles in handling, do not use it. All compressed or fresh yeast should break apart. If soft and spongy, do not use it. The sweet, characteristic odour of sound yeast is a good sign. If it smells sour or musty, its use should be avoided.

If you make your own yeast, surgical cleanliness of materials and exact quantities should be observed, because the slightest impurity is multiplied to an incredible extent in the various stages of fermentation and baking.

Yeast is a cellular plant which grows and multiplies best at between 80 and 90 degrees Fahr., preferably 85 to 86 degrees. The ordinary dairy thermometer is very useful to insure right temperature, and costs very little. Over-heating the yeast is as fatal as chilling it.

Half a compressed yeast cake is equivalent to 1 cup liquid yeast or 1 whole dry yeast cake.

[*Making of Bread*]

MIXING

Use tepid water, and warm mixing bowl.

Never mix a sponge in a cold kitchen, for it will at once take on the temperature of the room, especially if a bread mixer be used which circulates air through the dough.

The best cooks use a wooden spoon.

Make your dough rather slack, just as soft as can be conveniently handled. Unlike weaker flours, *Five Roses* has a tendency to tighten up during the mixing and kneading. Less flour should be used, which means quite a saving.

A soft dough makes bread more tender and appetizing, and it keeps fresh longer than if made from a stiff dough. Of course, also avoid too light a dough, which is apt to make a coarse texture and spoil the appearance of the cut loaf.

KNEADING

Kneading is done to thoroughly mix the ingredients, to aerate the dough and supply air (its best food) to the yeast. It also softens the gluten and makes it elastic. Kneading distributes the gas bubbles evenly throughout the dough. The more thorough the kneading, the better these objects are attained.

After taking from mixing pan, knead the dough with the upper part of the palm near the wrist (the heel of the hand), not with the fingers. This should be done without flouring the hands or board—adding raw flour at this stage is poor policy.

The more you work the sponge or dough the whiter it gets, due to the action of the oxygen of the air. Lightness and whiteness depend a lot on the proper performance of this process.

Knead the dough to a smooth, velvety mass that does not stick to the board or fingers, and which, when cut with a sharp knife, shows the inside full of fine, even bubbles, without lumps or unmixed portions.

When sufficiently worked, return to well-greased earthen bowl which has previously been warmed. Let rise.

RISING

Always try to set your sponge at night (when the overnight process is used) at between 80 and 90 degrees Fahr.

Wrap up carefully in a warm bread cloth, put in a warm place free from draughts and where it will not be disturbed. Try to maintain a continuous even temperature.

Never expose a dough to an uncertain kitchen on a cold night. A good way to protect it is to simply place the bowl (or mixer) in a light paper box, insulated, and shut the lid. To chill the yeast cells at this stage may mean sour bread or other ills.

To keep bread dough from forming a crust or skin while rising, grease lightly bottom and sides of pan and roll dough over in it until outside is covered. Moistening with warm milk and water also checks a crust-forming tendency. A crust at this stage should be avoided, as it may leave a streak in the bread and also cause an unsightly crust in the baked loaf.

Dough is properly risen when it has doubled its original bulk. It is then ready to mould into loaves. Some housewives knock down the light dough and let it rise a second time, claiming thereby a finer texture; but one rising is sufficient for ordinary purposes.

An empty *Five Roses* flour barrel lined with 3 or 4 layers of newspaper pasted on makes an excellent place to set bread to rise overnight.

MOULDING

The less you handle the dough when shaping into loaves the better.

The less flour used at this stage the nicer the bread. In fact, particular housewives absolutely refuse to use dry, raw flour in moulding. To work in dry, unfermented flour after fermenting the dough for hours is really to court streaky bread, lumps of hard dough, holes, etc. They prefer to grease both board and fingers and, in this way, avoid using raw flour in moulding their bread.

[Making of Bread]

After shaping and placing in warm well-greased pans, cover with clean warm cloth and let rise again until twice original size. Avoid making loaves too large, **as it makes bread unwieldy and difficult to** bake properly.

BAKING

To get a golden crust **sweet as a nut,** with a tender elastic crumb, a steady *moderate* oven is required.

Too hot an oven prevents proper expansion of the loaves by forming a premature crust or even burning it, while at the same time leaving the crumb underbaked, resulting in a doughy centre. Bread should continue rising in the oven at least fifteen minutes before beginning to brown.

If you have an oven indicator, set the heat at about 350 degrees. The oven is right when the hand can be held in from 35 to 45 seconds. Burning flour is another test.

If you value light bread, never bang the oven door. Always close it gently.

If the oven is too hot, putting in a pan of boiling water will prevent burning and also improve the loaves.

Bread is done when the loaves sound hollow when tapped on bottom. Another sign is when it freely leaves the sides of the pan.

COOLING

Never leave hot bread in pans after taking from oven. Remove at once, turn on a wire rack or cloth to enable the air to cool it from every side, or stand on edge across top of pans.

If a soft crust be desired, rub with milk or melted butter. **If a hard crust,** cool uncovered.

When entirely cold, place in bread box. Bread is liable to become sodden when put away still warm.

BAKING BREAD IN GAS OVEN

Many housewives have wondered whether it is at all possible to bake bread in an oven which stands on top of gas rings. The principal thing to learn is just how high to have the gas: it must be kept rather low. While the top grate in the oven may be filled, two loaves can be baked on the under grate by having small pans. Place the length of the pan across the oven, shove the first one as far back as possible, and set the other one as close to the oven door as possible. The idea is *not* to have either of them immediately over the flame. Of course, they need to be closely watched and turned occasionally.

◇ ◇ ◇

*F*IVE ROSES *is the favorite in one million Canadian homes, not because it makes the most bread per sack or the best bread, but because it is steady, regular, dependable. Only one thing costs the miller more than quality, and that is the same quality all the time. Isn't it worth a lot to know that YOUR flour is sure, reliable, trouble-proof? Note the fourfold uniformity of FIVE ROSES flour, in strength, color, flavor and yield. It never fails.*

WHITE BREAD RECIPES

BREAD WITH COMPRESSED YEAST
(*Quick Method*)

1 cake compressed yeast (see note)
3 quarts *Five Roses* flour
1 tablespoon salt
2 tablespoons butter
1 quart lukewarm milk and water (or lukewarm water only)
2 tablespoons sugar.

Note—Two cakes of yeast may be used in this recipe with advantage to the bread and a saving of time.

Take the lukewarm milk and water, and put in a deep dish or pitcher. Add the yeast and sugar, and dissolve. Then take the flour (either all or part) and put in kneading pan. Add salt, mix thoroughly, and rub the butter well into the flour. Then mix in your yeast and knead to a nice soft dough that does not stick to the hands, adding more *Five Roses* flour if required. Let rise for about 2 or 3 hours. Then mould into loaves. Let rise in moderately warm place, free from draughts, until they are about half as big again as when you put them in the pans, and then bake for about ¾ hour. Turn upside down when done and tap bottom. If it sounds hollow, your bread is done.

When letting rise, cover with a lid or two or three thicknesses of cloth. This is the way to make quick bread. The entire process requires about 6 hours or less.

COMPRESSED YEAST RECIPE
(*Over Night*)

1 cake compressed yeast
2 quarts water
6 quarts sifted *Five Roses* flour
2 tablespoonfuls lard or butter, melted
2 tablespoonfuls sugar
2 tablespoonfuls salt.

Dissolve yeast and sugar in the water, which should be lukewarm in winter and cool in summer, add 2 tablespoonfuls lard or butter, and half the flour. Beat until smooth, then add balance of the flour, or enough to make moderately firm dough, and lastly, the salt. Knead until smooth and elastic. Place in well-greased bowl and cover. Set aside to rise over night, or about 9 hours. In the morning mould into loaves. Fill well-greased pans half full, cover and let rise until light, or until loaves have doubled in bulk, which will be in about 1½ hours. Bake 40 to 50 minutes.

This will make 6 large loaves. If this quantity of bread is not needed, the recipe can be divided very easily by taking just half of the ingredients called for above, as well as half the cake of yeast. The half cake of yeast, which you have left over, can be kept in good condition several days by re-wrapping it in the tinfoil and keeping it in a cool, dry place.

DRY YEAST BREAD

3 quarts *Five Roses* flour
1 tablespoon salt
4 cups lukewarm water
1 dry yeast cake.
Method:

Let the yeast cake dissolve in ¼ cup lukewarm water for about 10 minutes. Put the salt into mixing pan, add enough water and enough flour to make a stiff batter (about the consistency of pancake mixture). Add yeast and beat 2 or 3 minutes. Set in warm place to rise over-night.

In the morning, sponge should be twice its size. Add enough flour to make dough stiff enough not to stick to hands or board. After flour is mixed in, turn out on board and knead 2 or 3 minutes. Let rise again and put in pans. Cover well and let rise to 2½ times its size. Bake in moderate oven until it is nicely browned and feels light when taken out.

TWO-HOUR BREAD

Take **1** pint of lukewarm water and soak **4** Royal Yeast Cakes. Put in 4 tablespoons of *Five Roses* flour. Set in warm place to raise.

Cook **12** potatoes, mash and add to this 1 quart of warm water and 1 quart of cold water. Add 1 tablespoon salt and 1 tablespoon sugar. When lukewarm mix in the yeast and set away overnight.

Not Bleached ~ Not Blended

[*White Bread*]

In the morning, warm your flour and warm *half* your yeast. Mix into a stiff dough. Let rise, then add 1 tablespoon salt and work down stiff, or until the dough does not stick to the hands. Let rise again and then make into loaves.

Note—Many good bread makers claim that potatoes give to their bread a silkiness of texture not obtainable any other way.

BREAD WITH POTATO YEAST
POTATO YEAST

Materials:

8 large potatoes
4 tablespoons *Five Roses* flour
4 tablespoons salt
4 tablespoons granulated sugar
4 cups boiling water
4 quarts cold water
2 cakes Royal Yeast.

Method:

Peel and boil the potatoes, and mash in water boiled in. While boiling, pour this over the flour, salt and sugar (which have been previously stirred together). To this, add boiling water, mix well, then add the cold water. Dissolve the yeast cakes in $\frac{1}{2}$ cup lukewarm water, and mix with the above. Let this mixture remain in a warm place about 18 hours. Then it is ready for use. Keep in a cool place and use as required.

BREAD

Materials:

8 cups *Five Roses* flour (sifted)
1 tablespoon salt
1 tablespoon brown sugar
1 tablespoon butter
4 cups (1 quart) potato yeast.

Method:

Set the yeast on the stove and stir until it is at about blood-heat (98 degrees Fahr.). Then add the salt, sugar and butter. Mix in sufficient of the flour (previously warmed) to make a batter. This will require 3 to 4 cups to the quart of liquid used. Cover and set to rise. When light and frothy, add balance of the flour, or until the dough ceases to stick to the hands. Knead thoroughly for 15 minutes. Let rise again until double original size, when it may be gently moulded into loaves. Let rise again. Then bake 60 minutes in moderate oven.

Note—2 quarts of the liquid potato yeast in this recipe make 4 large loaves, so that the rule should be doubled for this quantity.

POTATO YEAST
(*With Mixer*)
YEAST

2 quarts potatoes
2 quarts boiling water
  Boil till tender and pour over
2 cups *Five Roses* flour
2 cups white sugar
$\frac{1}{2}$ cup salt
  Stir till smooth, then add
3 quarts cold water
2 quarts lukewarm water
$2\frac{1}{2}$ Royal Yeast cakes.

Let stand 24 hours in warm place. Then put away in air-tight jars in a cool place.

BREAD

For every loaf of bread take 2 cups of this yeast. Put in bread mixer set in pan of warm water. Heat stirring constantly to about 90 degrees. Allow about 3 cups sifted *Five Roses* flour to every cup of yeast. Have flour warm. Knead down hard and stand in warm place till risen about twice the size. Knead down well again—a long kneading improves it. Let rise again till light enough. Shape in loaves. Put on tins. Let rise till nice and light, then bake in moderate oven.

BREAD WITH POTATO YEAST
(*Short Process*)

N. B.—Many a batch of bread has been thrown to the pigs in this North-western country through some of the recipes calling for the yeast cake batter or even the dough to stand overnight, and it is not always successful this time of the year (January). This is a first class recipe: *Five Roses* flour at 12 noon and bread out of the oven at 5 P.M. is a pretty good record—5 hours in winter and 3 or 4 in summer.

[White Bread]

YEAST

Boil 8 large potatoes, mash in water boiled in, and when still boiling pour this over 4 tablespoons *Five Roses* flour. Then add 4 tablespoons each of salt and granulated sugar. To this add 1 quart of boiling and 4 quarts of cold water. Dissolve 2 yeast cakes of Royal Yeast in lukewarm water, and mix with the above. Let this mixture remain in a warm place for 18 hours. Then remove to a cool place and keep until required.

BREAD

1 quart of yeast for every 2 loaves. Set on stove and stir with hand till about blood-heat. Add 1 tablespoon each of salt, brown sugar and butter. Mix into a soft dough (having previously warmed the flour). Let rise for 30 minutes, then knead. When light enough again, mould into loaves. Put in a pan and allow to rise. Bake in moderate oven.

—*Mrs. J. L. Forrest, Naseby, Sask.*

QUICK BREAD
(*Without Yeast*)

1 quart *Five Roses* flour
1 teaspoon (heaping) cream of tartar
1 teaspoon (level) baking soda
$\frac{1}{2}$ teaspoon table salt
$\frac{1}{2}$ teacup shortening.

Work the above into a smooth dough with nearly 1 pint of milk or water.

Let stand for 10 minutes. Then mould into loaves. Put in tins and let rise for 10 minutes. Bake in brisk oven.

MILK BREAD

1 cake compressed yeast
1 quart milk (scalded, then cooled)
3 quarts *Five Roses* flour (sifted)
2 tablespoons sugar
2 tablespoons lard or melted butter
1 tablespoon salt.

Rule:

Dissolve the yeast and sugar in lukewarm liquid. Add 1$\frac{1}{2}$ quarts sifted *Five Roses*. Beat until smooth. Cover and set to rise in a warm place about 1$\frac{1}{2}$ hours.

When light, add lard or butter, the rest of the flour and the salt. Knead until smooth and elastic. Place in well-greased bowl. Cover and let rise again until double in bulk (about 2 hours).

Mould into loaves, place in well-greased bread pans, filling half full. Cover and let rise again until double in bulk (about 1 hour). Bake 40 to 50 minutes.

FIRST PRIZE AT COUNTY FAIR
(*Makes 8 Loaves*)
YEAST

1 cup *Five Roses* flour scalded with potato water at noon, and add 3 mashed potatoes. When cold, add 1$\frac{1}{2}$ cakes of Royal Yeast previously soaked in $\frac{1}{2}$ cup water, and set to rise in a warm place until bedtime.

BREAD

Strain the above through a sieve into a bread pan, and add 2 tablespoons salt, $\frac{1}{2}$ cup sugar, 4 quarts lukewarm water and enough *Five Roses* flour to make a stiff batter. Beat smoothly with spoon, and set to rise overnight in a warm place. In the morning, add enough flour to make stiff enough to knead on board. Set to rise again until light. Then mould into loaves, and let rise until light and up to top of pan. Bake 1 hour in steady oven.

—*Mary Hammond, Essex, Ont.*

POTATO YEAST BREAD
FIRST PRIZE FALL FAIR

I took 1st prize for my bread at the Fall Fair this year, also for plain biscuits.

At noon when getting dinner, pour the potato water over 2 tablespoons of *Five Roses* flour, 1 tablespoon salt, 1 tablespoon sugar. Add 2 boiled potatoes mashed and 1 dipper boiling water. Put this aside until it cools. Then I add 1 yeast cake which has been soaked for 20 minutes in a cup of lukewarm water, and stir well for 2 minutes. Then I cover it and set aside in a mdeerately warm place until 10 o'clock at night.

Put into bread tray 3 sifters *Five Roses* flour and pour the first mixture into it. Then work in all the flour for 20

minutes or more until it will not stick to the hands. Then cover up tight and warm. At 5 o'clock in the morning it is ready to mix down. Then cover up again for 1 hour. Form into loaves and set to rise for 1 hour. Then bake 1 hour in moderately hot oven.
—*Mrs. Andrew Henderson, Seaforth, Ont.*

EASY RECIPE FOR BEGINNERS
(*Over Night*)

Take a quart sealer. Put in 1 yeast cake, 2 tablespoons sugar and the water drained from the potatoes cooked at dinner-time (allowed to get lukewarm). Keep in a warm place to ferment. It will be ready for use in 5 or 6 hours. I then get about 5 lbs. or more of *Five Roses* flour and ½ tablespoon salt. Mix thoroughly. Then pour off the liquid in the sealer into the middle of the flour with as much warm water as it will take (a pint or more) to mix into a dough so that it does not stick to the hands. Allow to rise overnight.

In the morning, mould into loaves. Allow to rise again an hour or more. Bake as usual. This is an easy recipe for beginners, and a good one when made with *Five Roses* flour.

Note—The sediment in the sealer can be used for any length of time. It is called " a starter." Put 2 tablespoons sugar and the lukewarm potato water, and add a yeast cake occasionally.

HOMESTEADER'S PRIZE BREAD

Put a cup of loose hops in a muslin bag and boil them in 3 quarts of water for a few minutes. Have ready 1 quart of hot mashed potatoes. Add 1 cup of *Five Roses* flour, ½ cup sugar and 1 tablespoon salt. Over the latter mixture pour the boiling hop water. Add 2 cakes of yeast while it is warm and set in a warm place to rise.

Take 2 cups of mashed potatoes, 1 cup *Five Roses* flour, 1 cup hop yeast, and 1 cup warm water. Put in an 8 quart pail with a cover and mix well into a batter. Then add 4 more cups of warm water. Beat again to thoroughly incorporate the yeast with the mixture. Then add enough flour to make a stiff batter. Cover up and set in a warm place overnight.

[*White Bread*]

In the morning, sift 2 quarts of *Five Roses* flour in bread dish and take the cold chill out of it. Put in a handful of salt. Pour in the sponge and stiffen with flour a little and get it on the bread board as soon as possible, thoroughly mixing in a little flour at a time until it does not stick to the hands or board, which will require the better part of an hour. Roll with the heel of the hand, turning the right hand side farthest away from you—this is the best mixing process. Mould into loaves, bake.—*Thomas Orr, Beaver Creek, B.C.*

WHEY BREAD
(*8 Large Loaves*)
HOP YEAST

Peel and grate 8 medium-sized potatoes, then add ½ cup salt, ½ cup sugar (granulated), 3 tablespoons *Five Roses* flour. Take 4 quarts water and 1 large handful of hops. Put on to boil, and boil just 8 minutes. Pour this over the potatoes, sugar, salt and flour. Stir up well. Let cool. Put 2 yeast cakes in ¾ cup warm water. Add to the hop liquid when cool enough. Put in a warm place to rise. Then put in sealers to use as needed.

Rule:

Take 4 quarts sweet milk and 2 of buttermilk. Put on stove to boil, but do not let it scorch. Take off, dip the whey from the curd and let cool.

Put the flour in the bread dish. Make a hole in the centre, put in a ¼ cup salt, the same of sugar, 2 cups hop yeast and 4 quarts whey. This quantity will make 8 large loaves. Stir all together with a spoon until very stiff, then knead into stiff, solid bread about 10 o'clock at night. I get better bread this way than if made in a sponge. Cover up well and warm. In the morning, it will be up nice and light. Knead down, but do not add any more flour. It should be stiff enough not to stick to your hands. Let rise again, then knead into pans. Let rise 1 hour, or until very light. Then bake 1 hour. Be sure and use *Five Roses* flour: you can't miss but have beautiful light, white bread; it won't get hard and dry out like potato

[White Bread]

bread. If your bread has a tight skin on it and won't rise, wring a cloth out of very hot water, lay over the bread, then cover up for 5 minutes before you put it in the oven. That will take it off.

MAKING PULLED BREAD

Take a loaf of bread when it is cooled just enough to handle and remove the crust on all sides. Pull the loaf apart in halves with the fingers as lightly as possible. Then tear it into quarters and the quarters into small pieces, and keep on until the entire loaf is in pieces small enough to pack away. Place these in a pan and dry out the moisture in a slow oven. When the bread is dry, increase the heat until the bread is a very delicate amber color. If it is not eaten when perfectly fresh, reheat before serving.

BURSTING A LOAF RIGHT

There are three ways of getting the loaf to burst properly. First, we have the ordinary way, in which the knife is held perpendicularly over the loaf, exactly as we hold a knife in cutting a strip of paper, for instance. Now, this makes the loaf burst all right, but the burst goes *too deep* into the loaf, so that when the loaf is sliced the middle cut, instead of being oval, resembles half a moon or a cut from a melon. Yet if you don't cut fairly deep, the loaf may not be depended on to burst always. To get the same breadth of burst without the depth another way of cutting is adopted, but this requires a little more skill than the first. The knife is held slanting at an angle of about 45 degrees, and the cut made from point to point that way: that is, the knife penetrates the skin of the loaf in a way as if the operator was making a cut preliminary to skinning the loaf. This cut is made slightly *off the center,* because when the loaf bursts one side lifts up and opens more than the other. But the great point of the whole affair is that a beautiful break of equal size with the other is got without the drawback of depth. In fact, in this way the burst seems to be confined to the outside

layer of the loaf, and so it is we get good oval slices the whole way through. Bread to be treated in this way, however, must be properly fermented; underfermented dough often gives a blind loaf, i.e., the cut does not open. If there is a fair amount of moisture, however, in the oven the cut will *always* open.—*Bakers' Magazine.*

LEFT-OVER BREAD CRUSTS

Bread crusts added to a soup or stew and well-boiled will make the best of thickening, the whole being passed through a sieve to ensure evenness.

Croutons are stale pieces of bread, dipped a second in cold water, cut into neat squares, and either fried or browned in the oven with a dot of butter on each.

When kidneys are floured, browned in dripping and water added, if several crusts are broken in and allowed to simmer with the meat, then well beaten with a fork, the gravy will be found deliciously thick.

Crusts may also be used in scalloped dishes, as scalloped tomatoes, cabbage, etc.

Cut crusts into small squares. Then make ordinary lemon jelly and while still hot pour over the crusts. When cold, the whole is turned out and served with either custard or cream.

MAKING BREAD CRUMBS

Cut the soft part from a stale loaf, put it into a clean muslin bag, tie the bag at the top and gently rub it with the hands for a few minutes. The crumbs will then be fine enough for any purpose.

BREAD DUST

Two or three times weekly spread left-over scraps upon a tin plate or baking pan and dry perfectly in moderate oven. Throw out soft or soggy bits and keep the brown pieces separate from the white in a separate jar. While the dried bits are still warm, crush to powder on board with rolling-pin. Do this thoroughly, leaving no gritty particles. Keep in closed jar in dry place. Invaluable for breading croquettes, fried fish, chops, etc. Roll the article to be breaded first in a beaten egg, then in bread dust to which have been added a little salt and pepper.

RECIPES FOR FANCY BREAD

APPLE BREAD

Take a quantity of apples (fresh-gathered, if possible), and boil them to a pulp. Mix with double its weight of *Five Roses* flour. Little or no water is required. Yeast is employed in the same proportion as for ordinary bakings, and after being allowed to rise 10 hours (overnight), it is baked in long loaves. This bread is much eaten in France, and it is recommended for its light and agreeable properties.

—*Mrs. Mildred Linke, Trenton, Ont.*

BAKING POWDER BREAD

Sift together thoroughly 1 quart *Five Roses* flour, 1 teaspoon salt, ½ teaspoon sugar, and 8 teaspoons baking powder.

Add enough water to make a stiff dough (about 2 cups). Stir together quickly with a large spoon. Then turn it immediately into a well-greased brick-shaped baking pan, and bake at once for ¾ hour in a hot oven, covering with paper the first ¼ hour to prevent crusting too soon. Have the oven heated right before beginning to mix the bread, and have the pan greased and ready.

CURRANT LOAF

Take 1 quart bread sponge (made from *Five Roses* flour). Break and mix into it 2 eggs, 1 cup sugar, 1½ cup currants, ½ cup peel, 1 cup lard, with enough *Five Roses* flour to make stiff dough. Shape into loaf and place in pan you intend baking in which has been previously well-greased. Let rise once. Bake in slow oven 1 hour.

RHODE ISLAND BROWN BREAD

2½ cups corn meal
1½ cups rye meal
1 egg
1 cup molasses
2 teaspoons cream of tartar
1 teaspoon soda
½ teaspoon salt
1 quart milk.

Mix and bake in covered dish in moderately hot oven.

BROWN BREAD
(*Yeast*)

1 cup yeast or ¼ cake dissolved in 1 cup water (liquid yeast preferred)
3 cups scalded milk
1 or 2 tablespoons molasses
2 small teaspoons salt.
Equal parts Graham and *Five Roses* flour to make a dough as stiff as you can mix it with a strong spoon, but too soft to handle comfortably.

Cover and let rise to double its original size. Mix down and let rise again. Put in pans and when risen again, bake. Allow nearly as long again to bake as for white bread. Be careful to not let it overrise.

QUICK BROWN BREAD

1 egg
1 cup brown sugar
2 cups buttermilk (or sour milk)
1 teaspoon baking soda
½ teaspoon salt (small)
Graham flour

Mix stiff like Johnnie cake with Graham flour and bake like ordinary bread.

BROWN BRAN BREAD

Mix 1 or 2 yeast cakes with 1 pint warm water and *Five Roses* flour to batter same as for white bread. Let stand 3 hours or more to rise. Into bread mixer (about 9 o'clock) put

½ cup molasses
1 tablespoon brown sugar
1 teaspoon salt
Butter size of walnut
1 pint warm water
Add yeast and stir well
Add 2½ cups bran
3 cups Graham flour
2 cups (or more) *Five Roses*.

Mix and leave to rise in warm place overnight. In morning, shape into loaves, set to rise 1 hour, then bake 1 hour.

BROWN BREAD
(*Rolled Wheat*)

Scald 1 pint rolled wheat (or rolled oats). Let stand 1 hour, then mix and

[*Fancy Bread*]

knead with 3 pints *Five Roses* flour, 1 tablespoon salt, 1 cup yeast, $\frac{2}{3}$ cup molasses.

Set to rise overnight in a warm place. When risen to double original bulk in the morning, mould into loaves. Set to rise again and bake 1 hour and a half in slow oven.

BROWN RAISIN BREAD

1 tablespoon brown sugar.
1$\frac{1}{2}$ cups molasses (black)
1 egg
1 tablespoon butter (melted)
1 teaspoon salt
1$\frac{1}{2}$ cups sour milk
1 teaspoon soda (dissolved in hot water)
2 cups Graham flour
2 cups *Five Roses* flour
$\frac{1}{2}$ cup raisins.

Beat the white and yolk of egg separately and add the white last. Butter 1 lb. baking powder cans well and fill half full. Bake in moderate oven.

STEAMED BROWN BREAD

(*Home-made Boston Brown Bread*)

1 large tablespoon cooking molasses
2 tablespoons brown sugar
$\frac{1}{2}$ teaspoon salt
2 cups Graham flour
1 cup *Five Roses* flour
2 cups buttermilk (or sour milk)
2 teaspoons soda (dissolved in little hot water and then added to sour milk).

Mix well and put in a well-buttered pan. Steam 2$\frac{1}{2}$ hours. Then place in moderate oven for 15 minutes.

STEAMED BROWN BREAD

3 cups sour milk
1 cup molasses
1 egg
$\frac{1}{2}$ cup raisins
1 teaspoon salt
1 teaspoon (heaping) soda
1 cup Graham flour
1 cup Indian meal
1$\frac{3}{4}$ cups *Five Roses* flour
Steam 4 hours.

CORN BREAD

1 cup corn meal
1 cup *Five Roses* flour
2 teaspoons cream of tartar
1 teaspoon soda
$\frac{1}{2}$ teaspoon salt
2 tablespoons sugar
1 cup milk or water
1 egg
1 tablespoon butter.

Method:

Mix all the dry ingredients in a bowl. Sift the flour, soda and cream of tartar together. Beat egg till light, add it and the milk to the dry ingredients; lastly, add the butter which has previously been melted in the baking pan. Bake from 20 to 30 minutes in moderate oven.

N.B.—Sour milk can be used instead of sweet milk—1 cup with $\frac{1}{2}$ teaspoon soda omitting the cream of tartar.

DATE BREAD

1 egg
$\frac{1}{2}$ cup sugar
1$\frac{1}{2}$ cups sweet milk
4 cups *Five Roses* flour
1 teaspoon salt
2 teaspoons baking powder
1 lb. stoned dates
1 cup chopped walnuts.

Put in buttered loaf pan. Let rise $\frac{1}{2}$ hour, then bake in moderate oven.

FRUIT BREAD

2 cups sweet milk
2 cakes yeast
$\frac{1}{2}$ teaspoon salt
4 tablespoons lard
4 tablespoons sugar
1$\frac{1}{2}$ cups fruit cut fine
Five Roses flour.

Scald the milk and cool till lukewarm. Strain in the yeast dissolved in $\frac{1}{4}$ cup lukewarm water. Beat vigorously into liquid, and let sponge rise. Cream the lard and sugar. Dredge the fruit with *Five Roses* flour and add to the sponge. Add sufficient flour to make a soft dough. Knead thoroughly and set to rise. When light, divide, form into loaves and put in bread pans. When ready, bake in a

slightly cooler oven than is required for plain bread. For the fruit in this bread, use either raisins, currants, citron or dates.—*Miss Lumina Chaput,*
Paradise Hill, Sask.

GRIDDLE BREAD

1 pound *Five Roses* flour
1 tablespoon sugar
½ teaspoon soda
Pinch of salt
Sour milk.

Knead into stiff loaf and flatten on floured griddle. Cook slowly on top of fire ½ hour to each side.

HONEY BREAD

(*Boston Cooking School Recipe*)

1 yeast cake
1 cup scalded milk
¼ pound butter
¼ pound sugar
Pinch of salt
1 egg (well-beaten).

Dissolve yeast cake in scalded milk, then add butter, sugar, salt and well-beaten egg, then 3 cups *Five Roses* flour and beat 2 minutes. Add more flour (about 1 cup) to knead and let rise. Again knead, roll to ½ inch thick, spread with honey mixture, roll, let rise and bake in moderate oven.

HONEY MIXTURE

½ pound walnut meats (chopped finely)
¼ pound seeded raisins (cut finely)
1 cup honey.

NUT BREAD

4 cups *Five Roses* flour
4 teaspoons (heaping) baking powder
1 teaspoon salt
½ cup granulated sugar (or 1 cup brown)
1 cup chopped nut meats (walnuts or hickory)
2 cups sweet milk
1 egg (beaten).

Sift the flour, baking powder, salt and sugar together, and add the nut meats. Stir egg and milk together, and add to above. Let raise ¾ hour. Bake 1 hour

in hot oven. Don't have too stiff dough. Be sure to grease pans well. This makes 2 medium sized loaves. Thin buttered slices are delicious for picnics or luncheon.
—*Mrs. Dan Lynch, Esterhazy, Sask*

NUT BROWN BREAD

¾ cup Graham flour
¾ cup *Fives Roses* flour
1 teaspoon baking powder
½ cup brown sugar
⅓ cup chopped walnuts
1 cup sweet milk
Pinch of salt.

Mix all together and bake in baking powder can 40 minutes in a moderate oven.

OATMEAL BREAD

1 cup rolled oatmeal
1 pint boiling water
½ cup molasses
1 quart *Five Roses* flour
½ compressed yeast cake dissolved in ⅓ cup warm water or 1 cup home-made yeast
1 teaspoon lard or butter.

Pour boiling water over oatmeal and lard. Let stand 1 hour. Add molasses, salt, yeast and *Five Roses* flour. Let rise overnight. Shape in loaves, using as little flour as possible. Let rise until light, and bake 1 hour in quite hot oven.

Note—Might be used—1 pint warmed up or left-over porridge.

RICE BREAD

Simmer slowly, over a gentle fire, 1 lb. rice in 3 quarts of water till the rice has become perfectly soft and the water is either evaporated or absorbed by the rice. Let cool (not cold), and mix thoroughly with 4 pounds *Five Roses* flour. Add some fine salt and 4  tablespoons yeast (liquid). **Knead very** thoroughly. Let rise well before the fire. Make up into loaves with a little of the flour which you have reserved from your 4 pounds and bake rather long.
—*Mrs. A. C. Moffatt, Kilburn, N.B.*

[*Fancy Bread*]

SOUTHERN RICE BREAD

$\frac{2}{3}$ pint boiled rice
3 eggs
1 tablespoon butter and lard (mixed)
2 cups white corn meal
1 teaspoon baking powder
Sweet milk to make thin batter.

Bake in earthen pans or muffin rings.
—*Mrs. A. W. Fraser, Iron Springs, Alta.*

GOOD OLD-FASHIONED SCOTCH OAT BREAD

Take 1 cup standard oatmeal, 1 cup *Five Roses* flour, 1 small teaspoon salt, 1 teaspoon baking powder. Rub in butter size of an English walnut or more. Into this pour enough cold water to make a stiff dough as dry as possible, just as if you were trying to make good pie crust. Spread on board by hand pressure, and keep the edges from parting by the support of one hand while you spread with the other. At the last, roll your rolling pin over it to smoothen the surface. Get it $\frac{1}{4}$ inch thick, cut in squares, put in moderate oven and bake until it is quite hard through.

—*C. McGillivray, Mission City, B.C.*

PUMPKIN BREAD

$1\frac{1}{2}$ cups white corn meal
1 cup boiling water
1 cup sour milk
1 cup baked pumpkin or squash
1 egg (well-beaten)
1 teaspoon salt
1 teaspoon (level) soda
1 teaspoon (heaping) baking powder
1 teaspoon (heaping) sugar
1 teaspoon melted butter.

Scald $\frac{1}{2}$ cup meal with 1 cup boiling water. Add sour milk, baked pumpkin, beaten egg, salt, balance of cornmeal sifted twice with the soda and baking powder. Mix quickly and beat in well 1 heaping teaspoon sugar and 1 of melted butter. Stir and beat into a light batter. Pour into baking pan until it is about 1 inch in thickness. Bake quickly and serve hot.
—*Mrs. A. W. Fraser, Iron Springs, Alta.*

RYE BREAD

1 cup scalded milk
1 cup boiling water
1 tablespoon lard
1 tablespoon butter
$\frac{1}{3}$ cup brown sugar
$1\frac{1}{2}$ teaspoons salt
$\frac{1}{4}$ yeast cake dissolved in
$\frac{1}{4}$ cup lukewarm water
3 cups *Five Roses* flour
Rye meal to stiffen.

Dissolve lard, butter, sugar and salt in hot milk and water. When lukewarm, add dissolved yeast cake and flour. Beat thoroughly, cover and let rise until light. Add rye meal until dough is stiff enough to knead. Knead thoroughly, let rise, shape into loaves. Let rise again, and bake.

SALT-RISING BREAD

No. 1

At 6 o'clock a.m. mix 1 cup cornmeal with enough cold water to wet it. Stir this into 1 pint boiling water. Let boil 5 minutes, stirring constantly. Set off the fire and add 2 pints fresh sweet milk (yet warm from the cow), 1 tablespoon salt and 1 tablespoon sugar. Let cool, then stir in enough *Five Roses* flour to make a soft batter. Keep in warm place (should be kept lukewarm, for if it gets chilled it is ruined). At about 10 or 11 o'clock, when it seems thin, stir in $\frac{1}{2}$ pint more flour. It should be ready to finish mixing by 1 o'clock. Add 1 pint fresh thick buttermilk and 1 teaspoon soda, with enough flour to make a rather soft dough. Mould into loaves, put in greased pans, let rise 1 hour, then bake. I think *Five Roses* flour the best I've ever used.
—*Mrs. R. N. Lay, Sanderville, Alta.*

SALT-RISING BREAD

No. 2

(*Over Night*)

The night before you contemplate baking this bread, take $\frac{1}{2}$ cup cornmeal and a pinch of salt and sugar. Scald with *new* milk heated to boiling point, and mix to the thickness of mush. This can be made in a cup. Wrap in a clean cup and put in a warm place overnight. In the morning, when all is ready, take a one-gallon stone jar and into this put 1 scant cup new milk. Add a level teaspoon salt and one of sugar. Scald with 3 cups of water heated to boiling point. Reduce to a temperature of 108 degrees with cold water, using a thermometer to enable you to get the correct temperature. Then add *Five Roses* flour and mix to a good batter. After the batter is made, mix in the starter that was made the night before.

● Cover the stone jar with a plate, put the jar in a large kettle of water, and keep this water at a temperature of 108 degrees until the sponge rises. It should rise at least 1½ inches. When raised, mix to a stiff dough. Make into loaves and put into pans. Do not let the heat get out of the dough while working. Grease your loaves on top and set your bread where it will be warm and rise satisfactorily. Then bake in a medium oven, one hour and ten minutes. On removing from oven, wrap the loaves in a bread cloth.

—*Mrs. H. Johnson, Kindersley, Sask.*

UNLEAVENED BREAD

To 3 cups of *Five Roses* flour add 1 teaspoon salt. Mix into a stiff dough with milk or water. Roll out thin, and cut into rounds with a biscuit cutter. Roll these out again until they are not much thicker than paper. Bake quickly in floured pan.

—*Mrs. A. W. Fraser,
Iron Springs, Alta.*

WHOLE WHEAT BREAD

2 cups *Five Roses* flour
2 teaspoons soda
2 teaspoons salt
2 cups graham flour
4 cups whole wheat **meal**
½ cup molasses
Buttermilk.

Into a mixing pan sift the **flour, soda** and salt. Add the graham flour and meal. Sweeten with molasses and mix to a very stiff batter with buttermilk. Bake 1½ hours in moderate oven. Makes quite a large loaf. If preferred, rolled oats may be substituted in lieu of graham flour and sugar in place of molasses.

Note—In making whole wheat bread, it is preferable to make a sponge at first. Avoid too stiff a dough as it produces a tasteless loaf. Many housewvies use a bread mixer, and do not knead at all.

□ □ □

BREAD FROM FIVE ROSES BREAKFAST FOOD

(Makes 4 nice Loaves)

7 cups *Five Roses* Breakfast Food
4 cups *Five Roses* flour
4 cups sweet milk
2 cups water
3 teaspoons salt
1 cake compressed yeast
  Butter size of an egg.

Heat the milk to boiling point, stir in the salt and butter and pour over the breakfast food. Mix thoroughly. When cool, dissolve the cake of yeast in the two cups of water and add. Then gradually stir in the 4 cups flour. Knead well and cover. In the morning, stir or knead. Put in buttered bread pan and set to rise. Bake in a moderate oven for an hour. Sugar can be added, should a sweeter loaf be desired.

See also page 45 for further recipes with this delightful cereal.

*Avoid Stiff Doughs with
FIVE ROSES Flour*

What your own Friends and Neighbours say about *Five Roses* Flour

"I can say without contradiction that for the past twenty years I have used the best brands of flour manufactured in the U. S. and Canada and no other brand has given me the same satisfaction as FIVE ROSES."—Mrs. M. A. D., Roundwood, Ont.

"Since coming to Alberta three years ago I have always used your FIVE ROSES and think it is the best I ever used. It is known as the best in the West."
—Mrs. H. Y., Hindville, Alta.

"Well pleased with FIVE ROSES. It is a pleasure to think of bake-day when one knows that you have good flour."
—Miss C. M., Mildmay, Ont.

"We have been using FIVE ROSES as long as I can remember. I am seventeen years old now. As I am the oldest of the family of ten I have to be cook, and I find that FIVE ROSES flour is good."
—M. R. M., Rusagorish St., N.B.

"FIVE ROSES has a great reputation around here for making good bread."
—Mrs. L. B. H., Headford, Ont.

"I have used your FIVE ROSES and find it the best flour. Makes the most bread out of a barrel than any other. Have kept house for twenty years and it has given me the best satisfaction for bread and pastry."
—Mrs. J. E. L., Woodstock, N.B.

"Never had a failure with it yet."—Mrs. A. G., Weston, Ont.
"I use a barrel of FIVE ROSES every month. Have been using the same for twenty-one years and it beats all other flours for me."
—Mrs. H. J., Bridgetown, N.S.

PAGES of recommendations could be printed from experts, chefs of big hotels, clubs, steamship and railway companies, but they could not be so impressive nor would they bring home to you so vividly the perfect efficiency of *Five Roses* as the following simple, sincere commendations. These are taken from a few of many letters received from housewives throughout Canada who use *Five Roses* for their every-day purposes. Some of these are neighbours of yours. All opinions are *unsolicited*, and full names will be given on request.

"Being a user of FIVE ROSES flour for a number of years, I would like to speak of the priceless value it has been to me. In breadmaking it has worked wonders. Have also used it in pastry, proving it a success there."
—Mrs. J. G. P., Albury, Ont.

"Used FIVE ROSES for about ten years and find it the best flour for bread or any kind of pastry you would want."
—Mrs. S. F. O., Parry Sound, Ont.

"For bread and general cooking it is absolutely satisfactory. Since using it I have used no other."
—Mrs. A. L. C., Port Carling, Ont.

"A user of your flour for over twelve years."
—Mrs. A. J., Strathcona, Alta.

"FIVE ROSES beats them all in making whiter and lighter bread."
—Mrs. A. S. W., Bridgeport, Ont.

"Have used a great deal of your flour and breakfast food and would highly recommend them."
—Mrs. W. H. L., North Augusta, Ont.

"Find that it is all you claim it to be."
—Mrs. J. C. W., Fingal, Ont.

"FIVE ROSES makes good bread with very little trouble."
—Miss M. H., Ventry, Ont.

"Used FIVE ROSES for a number of years. Can guarantee its success both in bread and pastry."
—Miss E. H., Cushing, Que.

:: *Be sure you get FIVE ROSES Flour* ::

Milled by LAKE OF THE WOODS MILLING COMPANY LIMITED

Not Bleached - Not Blended

HOW TO MAKE DAINTY SANDWICHES

Specially prepared for Five Roses Cook Book
(For various bread recipes, see general index)

SANDWICHES are almost *perfect* food. They are made from bread, which is the great life-sustainer, and the filling supplies in tempting, digestible form the only food essential which bread lacks—*fat*.

Wishing to give your sandwiches the utmost food value, you should use *Five Roses* flour for bread. Made from the purest Manitoba wheat expertly ground, your bread necessarily possesses the energy-building and muscle-making constituents to be found at their best in this flour.

Besides being the picnic stand-by, sandwiches are deservedly popular in many emergencies, such as informal luncheons, or "muncheons," as a witty woman once called them.

Those whose folks are fond of bread will welcome the following sandwich suggestions.

❖ ❖ ❖

USE CLOSE-GRAINED BREAD

Coarse bread is apt to crumble and is not so tempting. If you use bread made from *Five Roses* flour, you will at once appreciate its fine texture and elasticity. Its peculiarly dainty flavor and healthy bloom will make your knack of sandwich-making an envied possession. Then, also, the moisture absorbing qualities of *Five Roses* cause your sandwiches to stay fresh and appetizing longer than is otherwise possible.

Bread baked in round tins is preferable to that cut into shape with a biscuit cutter, as the baked edges preserve the shape. Cutting the bread into fancy shapes, while more or less wasteful, will often make an invalid's tray more attractive and the food seem more appetizing. And, of course, the left-over pieces can be used for bread pudding, etc. Cooky cutters will give odd shapes to sandwiches.

FOR A CHANGE

One of the slices that form the sandwich may be of brown instead of white bread. Whole wheat or bread made from *Lake of the Woods* Breakfast Food, raisin bread or other fancy bread, might be used.

MOIST FILLINGS

Should be laid between fresh lettuce leaves, and by buttering the bread the moisture cannot penetrate it and make it soggy. Melted butter can be used when not soft enough to spread.

As many people cannot eat acids, the wise hostess should make two different kinds of sandwiches—some with the mixtures moistened with vinegar or lemon juice and others without.

HOW TO CUT FRESH BREAD

Getting the slices thin enough is undoubtedly the hardest part of making dainty sandwiches. The inexperienced say they cannot make sandwiches from fresh bread, because it goes all to pieces in the cutting. Many cookbooks advise using bread two days old, but the skilful person knows that fresh bread is always preferable. This is especially true when it is made from *Five Roses* flour, giving a close-grained crumb that slices practically without crumbling.

This is the way to handle a fresh loaf: *Always heat the knife blade and have edge rather keen. Turn the loaf on end and delicately pare off the crisp top crust in sections. Now remove the under crust in one slice. The side crusts must be left on as they help to hold the loaf together. As you begin to cut, hold on to the loaf by pinching it at the top as close as you can without breaking the texture of the bread, and cut while you pinch, so that the knife goes through a narrowed slice which opens out to its proper proportion as it drops to the board.*

MEAT SANDWICHES

Practically all meat sandwiches are extremely rich and strong condiments are noticeable in the fillings, especially mustard and catsup. While white meat makes a delicate sandwich, yet the *darker* meats, mixed with mayonnaise and other relishes are more appetizing.

To save tearing and preserve daintiness it is better to chop the meat exceedingly fine and make a paste of it and add to the following filling.

FILLING FOR MEAT SANDWICHES

Two cups cream or milk, 2 tablespoons (large) *Five Roses* flour, yolks of 4 eggs, butter size of an egg. Add 1 teaspoon salt, 1 teaspoon mixed mustard, black and red pepper to taste. Beat yolks well, mix in all other ingredients, put in double boiler and cook until thick, stirring constantly to prevent lumps. When cool, beat in $\frac{1}{2}$ cup lemon juice. Then add any finely-ground meat, such as veal, tongue, ham, chicken, etc. Fresh or potted meats may be used with this recipe. It may be varied by using finely-chopped watercress, lettuce, parsley, olives, etc.

TONGUE AND VEAL SANDWICHES

Remove from cold tongue and veal every scrap of fat, gristle and skin. Grind in your meat chopper, moisten just a trifle with soup stock and season highly with paprika and a mere dash of nutmeg. Spread lightly on thin white bread and serve very cold. A half warm meat sandwich is not appetizing. If you prefer a salad sandwich add to the ground tongue and veal a little mayonnaise. Another very dainty meat sandwich, which must be served crisp, is made from white *Five Roses* bread brushed lightly with butter, a crisp nasturtium leaf or sprig of watercress and a silver of highly seasoned cold chicken spread with a little mayonnaise.

PATE-DE-FOIE-GRAS SANDWICH

The mock pate de foie gras, which is difficult to distinguish from the real thing, is made by running boiled calf's liver through the meat chopper, reducing to a smooth paste and adding finely chopped mushrooms or truffles. Of course, genuine pate de foie gras can be used.

THE FAMOUS CLUB SANDWICH

Toast slices of *Five Roses* bread a nice brown, and while hot spread with butter and put between the slices a lettuce leaf, some cold baked chicken cut in thin slices, a few chopped olives and pickles, some slices of hot crisp bacon, a layer of salad dressing, another lettuce leaf and the other slice of toast. Slices of tomatoes are sometimes added. Delightful for Sunday evening supper.

OTHER MEAT FILLINGS

Equal parts chicken and ham, finely minced, and seasoned with curry powder.

One cup cold roast chicken, 3 olives, 1 pickle, 1 tablespoon capers. Mince fine and mix with mayonnaise.

Equal parts cold roast turkey, cold roast beef, boiled ham and tongue. Season with chopped pickles and mix with mayonnaise.

Not Bleached - Not Blended

Cold roast veal, chopped fine with hard-boiled eggs. Season with catsup.

Thin slices roast veal covered with chopped pickles.

Cold roast chicken and ¼ the quantity of blanched almonds, chopped fine and minced to a paste with cream.

FISH SANDWICHES

Fish used for filling should be pounded to a paste and then mixed with sufficient salad dressing to give it the proper consistency for spreading easily. The same filling as for meat sandwiches given above can be used. Fresh or salt fish may be used: roe, salmon, **sardines**, lobster, **shrimp**, etc.

HOT SARDINE SANDWICHES

Bone a number of sardines and rub a generous piece of butter to a smooth paste. Dust with cayenne pepper **or** add a dash of Worcestershire sauce. Heat well, spread on buttered toast and serve. Some like a little grated cheese sprinkled over the top. Do not put the pieces of toast together.

CAVIARE SANDWICHES

Mix half a can caviare, **1** teaspoon onion juice and lemon juice to taste. Cut thin rounds of bread, butter and spread.

RUSSIAN SANDWICHES

Chop olives fine and moisten with mayonnaise. Cut bread into thin narrow strips, spread half with chopped olives and the rest with caviare. Press together in pairs.

TARTAR SANDWICHES

Chop together **3** large sardines, **1** cup boiled ham (ground) and **3** small cucumber pickles. Add **1** teaspoon French mustard, or omit the cucumber pickles and add some chow-chow with a little mustard. Mix to a paste with a little catsup and vinegar or lemon juice.

OYSTER SANDWICHES

Cold fried oysters, chopped fine, lettuce leaves and French dressing.

CHEESE SANDWICHES

Use either Neufchatel (imported) or Canadian cream cheese. If the former is very hard, you must moisten it a trifle with sweet milk or cream. Add just a dash of paprika to give it a taste and a little salt. Finally, to each cheese add half a cup nut-meats ground in meat chopper. English walnuts are preferable. Almonds are flat **in** flavor. Spread mixture on thin slices of brown bread brushed with melted butter.

FILLING No. 2

To **2** tablespoons melted butter add **1** tablespoon and a half of *Five Roses* flour with half a pint of milk. Cook to a thick paste. Remove from fire and add salt and paprika to taste, also ¼ teaspoon French mustard. Work into this filling a large cup grated cheese. This will keep for a week.

MOCK CRAB SANDWICHES

Quarter cup grated cheese, ¼ teaspoon each salt, paprika and mustard, **1** teaspoon anchovy paste, **1** tablespoon chopped olives, **1** teaspoon lemon juice, **2** tablespoons creamed butter.

FRENCH SANDWICHES

With cooky cutter stamp out thin slices of white bread made with *Five Roses* flour. Spread half with cream cheese and currant jelly blended to a pink cream. On top of this spread a second round of bread lightly buttered and spread with chopped pistachio nuts.

SHERRY AND CHEESE SANDWICHES

Half pound Roquefort or other cheese, ¼ as much butter and half a teaspoon paprika. Mix to a paste with sherry wine. Spread on wafers or toasted rye bread.

[*Dainty Sandwiches*]

OTHER CHEESE FILLINGS

Cream cheese and minced walnuts.

Cream cheese and jam.

Cream cheese and olives partly chopped. Do not butter the bread for this recipe.

Cream cheese and peach marmalade.

Cream cheese and thin slices of preserved ginger. Lay the ginger over the cheese, not mixing the two together so as to confuse the flavors.

Crisp and tender radishes, chopped fine, chilled on ice and afterwards mixed with grated cheese.

Mince pineapple and cheese.

MUSHROOM SANDWICHES

Cut mushrooms into small pieces, cook in butter until tender, season with salt and paprika and cream to make of right consistency to spread. Let it just boil once. Add lemon juice and grated nutmeg. Spread on thin slices of whole wheat bread.

NASTURTIUM SANDWICHES

Wash the fresh flowers and lay the petals in ice water for a few minutes. Spread the bread with mayonnaise and place on a thick layer of the petals; or, omit the dressing and spread the petals on buttered slices. If possible, serve these sandwiches with a few of the fresh blossoms and leaves scattered loosely over the plate.

SWEET PICKLE SANDWICHES

Sweet pickles, chopped and spread between slices of nut or plain bread.

ONION SANDWICHES

 Eat this once properly prepared and never again turn up your nose at the name of onion. Soak for an hour finely cut Bermuda onions in ice water which is thoroughly sweetened with sugar and well salted; drain and mix with slightly sweetened mayonnaise. Serve in round slices without crust.

OLIVE SANDWICHES

Cut the meat off the stones and chop the olives very fine. Mix with mayonnaise dressing and spread on unbuttered white bread made with *Five Roses* flour and cut very thin.

NUT SALAD SANDWICHES

Grind English walnuts or hickory nuts in your meat grinder, mix with an equal quantity of celery chopped extremely fine and add to this mixture mayonnaise made with plenty of lemon juice. Have white bread made from *Five Roses* flour cut thin, brush lightly with melted butter, lay on a crisp lettuce leaf, spread this with the nut and celery mixture, lay the second slice of bread upon it and serve at once.

PEANUT SANDWICHES

One cup vinegar, 1 cup brown sugar, let boil then add 1 teaspoon *Five Roses* flour, 1 egg, $\frac{1}{4}$ teaspoon pepper, salt and mustard. Let cool, then add 1 cup crushed peanuts. Put between thin slices buttered bread.

FILLING FOR SWEET SANDWICHES
(*Keeps for a Week*)

Pint of milk, 1 cup sugar, 3 eggs, half a teacup of *Five Roses* flour. Mix sugar and flour thoroughly, then stir into the milk. Cook in double boiler to a thick paste. Add the eggs, well-beaten, just before removing from the fire. Let stand until cold. It is then ready for use for any kind of sweet sandwiches.

For instance, take a small portion of the paste and stir in a little vanilla and freshly-grated cocoanut, chocolate, preserved ginger or any kind of ground nuts. Black walnuts and roasted almonds are especially good. Jams, marmalade and orange may also be used in this way. Cocoanut and orange make a delicious combination. Raisins and chopped nuts also go well together. The sandwiches may be made of crackers and wafers or white and brown bread.

BANANA SANDWICHES

A very ripe banana mashed and put between slices of buttered *Five Roses* bread makes a very nutritious and appetizing sandwich.

COCOANUT SANDWICHES

A cup of freshly-grated cocoanut, half a cup of nuts ground fine, 1 teaspoon lemon juice, 2 teaspoons powdered sugar and 3 tablespoons thick cream worked in. Spread between wafers or between bread and butter.

SWEET WHOLE WHEAT SANDWICHES

Thin slices of whole wheat bread spread with unsalted butter and filled with a mixture of chopped raisins, almonds, orange juice, a little grated orange rind and enough olive oil to blend well together. Bread made with *Lake of the Woods* Breakfast Food could be used satisfactorily. *See Breakfast Food recipes.*

FIG PASTE FOR FILLING

Three-quarters of a pound of figs cut into small pieces, ¾ pound brown sugar, ¼ pound seeded raisins, 1 cup water and the juice of half a lemon. Stew on back of stove until very soft, remove and add a dessert-spoon vanilla. Then put all through meat-grinder, and to clear grinder use 2 or 3 crackers. If desired, the cracker dust may be stirred into the paste. It is then ready for use and will keep indefinitely. Delicious between thin, delicate crackers or thin slices of brown bread. It may also be put on thin slices of *Five Roses* bread buttered in layers and cut down like cake.—*Selected.*

SANDWICHES FROM ROLLS
(*See recipes for rolls*)

Unusually good picnic sandwiches can be made by baking a pan of little round rolls, cutting the tops neatly off when they are cold, scooping out some of the crumb, and filling them with chicken chopped and reduced to a stiff paste with cream. They must be seasoned highly with salt and black pepper. Other fillings, of course, may be used.

PEPPER SANDWICHES

Always a favorite with those who prefer dainties that are rather pungent.

Chop a pepper fine, removing all the seeds. Place in a saucepan with a tablespoon of butter and allow it to heat without browning. Stir briskly. Add a little salt and remove from the fire. When quite cold, spread between thin slices of *Five Roses* bread adding a little grated cheese before putting the slices together.
—*Mrs. Thos. Seli, Sunnyside Ave.,
Toronto, Ont.*

EGG SANDWICHES

Nice for lunches. Boil hard 1 egg for each person. Pulverize while hot. Add salt and pepper to taste and a dash of curry powder, ½ teaspoon melted butter to each egg, also 1 large pickled cucumber to each egg. Chop fine and mix well together. Spread on thin, well-buttered slices of *Five Roses* or graham bread.

LEFT-OVER SANDWICHES

After a party, luncheon or picnic, one may find oneself with sandwiches left over. An excellent plan to use these is the following: pass them through the mincing machine, mix with a good well-seasoned gravy, put in a pie dish and cover with mashed potato about an inch thick. This, baked in the oven, makes a delicious luncheon dish.

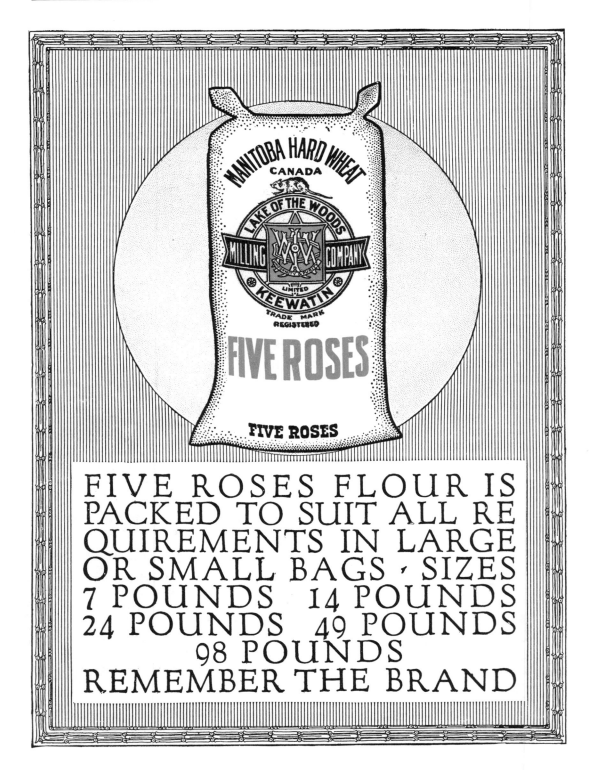

FIVE ROSES FLOUR IS PACKED TO SUIT ALL RE QUIREMENTS IN LARGE OR SMALL BAGS · SIZES 7 POUNDS   14 POUNDS 24 POUNDS   49 POUNDS 98 POUNDS REMEMBER THE BRAND

ROLLS AND RUSKS FOR BREAKFAST

ROLLS require a slightly better oven than for bread. Avoid too hot an oven at first, as it will prevent proper rising and proper baking of the centre.

Rolls should bake in from 10 to 30 minutes, rising for at least the first five minutes before beginning to brown.

Due to the remarkable expansion of *Five Roses* flour, shape your dough into rather small rolls, as they will swell greatly in size. Let rise to double original bulk in temperature of about 80 degrees Fahr. While rising moisten frequently with warm milk to prevent a skin forming on outer surface. If rolls stick to the pan, they can be put back on top of stove for a moment, when they will come out easily.

One pound of dough will make ten or twelve rolls.

❖ ❖ ❖

PLAIN ROLLS
(*Bread Dough*)

1 cup bread dough
½ cup butter
¼ cup sugar
1 cup lukewarm milk
Pinch of salt
Five Roses flour to make stiff dough.

Knead 20 minutes and put in a warm place to rise. Knead again very little, roll out and cut with biscuit cutter. Place in baking pan, let rise again and bake.

DELICIOUS ROLLS

1 pint milk
Butter size of an egg
Beaten white of 1 egg
½ cup white sugar
½ cup yeast
Five Roses flour to mould.

Boil the milk and while hot add the butter. When lukewarm, add the beaten white of egg, the sugar, yeast, and *Five Roses* flour enough to mould. Let rise overnight. Work down and let rise again, then roll out to the thickness of your finger. Cut the rolls the size you wish. Butter half very slightly and turn the other half over the buttered part. This keeps the rolls from sticking together and is the secret of retaining their shape. Place properly in baking tins and set in a warm place until very light. Then bake quickly.

If directions are closely followed, you will find these rolls will almost melt in the mouth.

Currants may be added, if desired.

BUTTER ROLLS
(*With Baking Powder*)

4 cups *Five Roses* flour
2 teaspoons baking powder
1 teaspoon salt
1 tablespoon butter
1 egg (beaten)
1 pint milk.

Sift the flour, salt and baking powder together. Rub in the butter and add the beaten egg. Mix with milk soft as possible. Roll out, cut and dip in melted butter. Fold over and bake quickly.

CINNAMON ROLLS

Take 1 quart of light bread sponge. Add 1 egg, a little mace, ½ cup sugar, ½ cup butter and ½ cup lard. Beat well with a wooden spoon and add *Five Roses* flour, but put it in slowly and do not mix too

[*Rolls and Rusks*]

stiff. Mix down twice, and the third time take out on board but do not knead—simply roll out thin, leaving the dough about 1 inch thick. Spread with soft butter till every part is covered, and sprinkle with about 1 cup sugar. Dust with cinnamon. Roll dough very tightly and pinch ends. Cut with sharp bread knife, and set closely together in pan. When light, put melted butter over them and bake 15 to 20 minutes in moderate oven, or till a light brown. Remove from oven, place on table and brush over with melted butter again. When cool (not cold) spread with thin icing made as follows: 1 cup sugar and $\frac{2}{3}$ cup milk or cream boiled till it threads. Let cool and apply as on cake.

BREAKFAST ROLLS

(*Yeast Cake*)

4 quarts *Five Roses* flour (sifted)
$\frac{1}{2}$ pint new milk
$1\frac{1}{2}$ pints water
2 tablespoons white sugar
1 teaspoon salt
$\frac{1}{2}$ yeast cake.

Make into soft sponge at night. Let rise. Roll and spread with melted butter and roll over. Make into rolls, let rise light, and bake $\frac{1}{2}$ hour.

FRENCH ROLLS

(*Eggless*)

2 quarts *Five Roses* flour
1 quart new milk (scalded)
$\frac{1}{2}$ cup sugar
1 teaspoon salt
1 tablespoon butter
$\frac{1}{2}$ cup yeast.

 Cool the milk and add 1 quart flour, the sugar, salt, butter and yeast. Mix in the other quart of flour and let rise overnight. In morning, mix twice, then cut in bun size and roll out. Rub over with melted butter and fold over once. Let rise and bake. When done, rub over with syrup of sugar and water and sprinkle with sugar.

RAISED FRENCH ROLLS

2 cups sweet milk
$\frac{3}{4}$ cup butter and lard (mixed)
$\frac{1}{2}$ cake yeast dissolved in
$\frac{1}{2}$ cup water
1 teaspoon salt.
Five Roses flour to make stiff dough.

Let rise overnight. In the morning, add 2 well-beaten eggs. Knead down and let rise again. Make balls size of an egg, and roll each one between the hands to make a long roll. Place close together in even rows on well-buttered pans. Cover and let rise again. Bake in quick oven to a delicate brown. Glaze the top with sweet milk before baking.

MILK ROLLS

(*Eggless*)

2 cups hot mashed potatoes
4 cups scalded milk
$\frac{1}{2}$ cup butter
$\frac{1}{2}$ cup white sugar
1 tablespoon (heaping) salt
1 yeast cake
Five Roses flour.

Pour scalded milk over mashed potatoes, then add butter, sugar and salt. Cool until lukewarm, then add yeast cake that has previously been soaked in a half cup of lukewarm water. Add flour until quite as stiff as bread dough. Let rise overnight. Roll until $\frac{1}{2}$ inch thick, cut with cake cutter, spread with melted butter and fold together. Let rise and bake about 20 minutes. If you use *Five Roses* flour, you will be surprised at the beauty as well as the quality of these rolls.

PARKER HOUSE ROLLS

2 cups scalded milk
3 tablespoons butter
2 tablespoons sugar
1 teaspoon salt
1 yeast cake dissolved in
$\frac{1}{4}$ cup warm water
Five Roses flour.

Add the butter, sugar, and salt to the milk. When lukewarm, add the dissolved yeast cake, and stir in 3 cups flour. Beat well, cover, and let rise until light; then add enough flour to knead (about $2\frac{1}{2}$ cups).

Let rise again, toss on to a lightly-floured board, knead and roll out to $\frac{1}{8}$ inch thickness. Shape with a round biscuit cutter dipped in flour. Then with the handle of a case knife make a crease through the centre of each round. Brush one half over with melted butter, fold and press the edges together. Place 1 inch apart in greased pan, cover, let rise, and then bake for about 15 minutes in a hot oven to a delicate brown.

SANDWICHES FROM PARKER HOUSE ROLLS

The soft interior of the rolls is removed and the cup-like cavity in each is filled with minced tongue and a little crisp bacon, a little chopped celery and Spanish peppers, and a dash of mustard. The combination of the sweet bread and the strongly flavored bacon and peppers is delectable.

CREAM FINGERS

1 cup cream
2 tablespoons sugar
$\frac{1}{4}$ tablespoon salt
1 yeast cake dissolved in
$\frac{1}{4}$ cup lukewarm water
Five Roses flour to knead.

Scald the cream, add sugar and salt. When lukewarm, add dissolved yeast cake and *Five Roses* flour enough to knead. Knead, cover and let rise until double original bulk. Toss onto floured board and roll dough to $\frac{1}{4}$ inch thickness. Shape with lady-finger cutter or with sharp knife. Cut strips $4\frac{1}{2}$ inches long by 1 inch wide, and round at corners. Cover again and let rise. Brush over with 2 tablespoons milk mixed with 1 tablespoon sugar. Bake in moderate oven. Delicious served with hot chocolate or coffee.
—*Mrs. E. Kelly, Naseby, Sask.*

RUSKS
(*Eggless*)

1 pound *Five Roses* flour
$\frac{1}{4}$ pound butter
$\frac{1}{4}$ pint boiling water
2 teaspoons baking powder

Slice the butter into the boiling water. Mix ingredients. Bake a nice brown. Take from oven, split open and then return to the oven to harden.

RUSKS
(*Yeast Recipe*)

1 pint milk
2 tablespoons yeast
2 tablespoons butter
1 cup sugar
2 eggs
2 teaspoons salt
Five Roses flour.

Prepare a sponge of yeast, milk and flour sufficient to make a thin batter, and let rise overnight.

Next morning, add eggs, butter, salt and sugar. Mix well together. Add flour enough to make soft dough. Shape into neat balls of equal size. Place in a pan and allow to rise until very light before baking.

Rusks require a long time for raising.

RUSKS
(*Bread Dough*)

2 cups raised dough
1 cup sugar
$\frac{1}{2}$ cup butter
2 eggs (well-beaten)
Five Roses flour.

Mix with enough flour to make stiff dough. Set to rise. When light, mould to high biscuit and let rise again. Add currants. Cover top with moistened sugar and cinnamon. Bake 20 minutes.

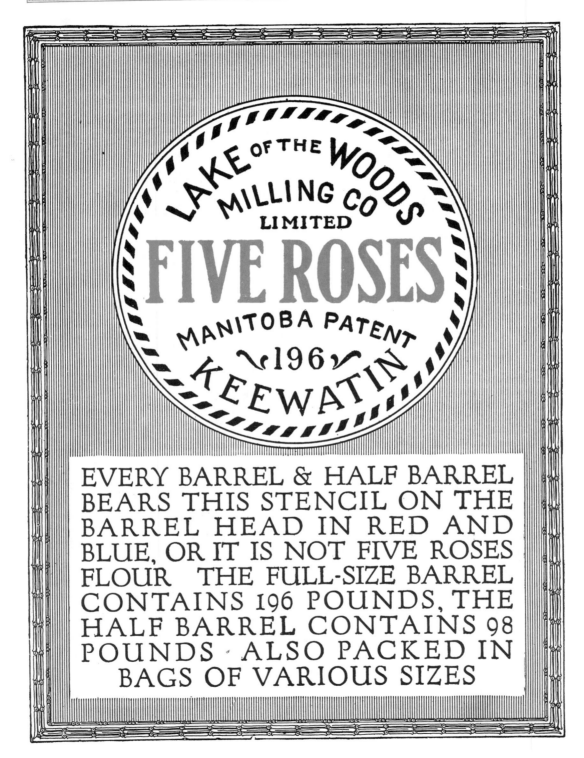

LAKE OF THE WOODS
MILLING CO
LIMITED

FIVE ROSES

MANITOBA PATENT
~196~
KEEWATIN

EVERY BARREL & HALF BARREL BEARS THIS STENCIL ON THE BARREL HEAD IN RED AND BLUE, OR IT IS NOT FIVE ROSES FLOUR THE FULL-SIZE BARREL CONTAINS 196 POUNDS, THE HALF BARREL CONTAINS 98 POUNDS · ALSO PACKED IN BAGS OF VARIOUS SIZES

BUNS OF ALL KINDS

DUE to the unusual expansion of *Five Roses* flour, slacker batters and doughs are advisable. Also mould your buns rather smaller than usual, as they will swell surprisingly.

Buns should bake in from 15 to 20 minutes. As in the case of bread, *Five Roses* flour produces a dough that is highly elastic and finely textured, so that the buns will continue to expand in your oven, if given the time and space to do so. Care should therefore be exercised that the oven is not too hot at first. The concentrated strength of *Five Roses*, an effect of its great gluten content, will keep your buns fresh and moist long after buns made from other flours have become harsh and tasteless.

❖ ❖ ❖

PLAIN BUNS
(*Yeast Recipes*)

1 compressed yeast cake
1 cup milk, scalded and cooled
1 tablespoonful sugar
$\frac{1}{2}$ teaspoonful salt
$\frac{1}{4}$ cup sugar
$\frac{1}{4}$ cup butter
3 cups sifted *Five Roses* flour.

Dissolve yeast and one tablespoonful sugar in lukewarm milk, add one and one-half cups of flour. Beat until smooth, then add butter and sugar creamed, the rest of the flour and salt. Knead lightly, keeping dough soft. Cover and set aside in warm place, free from draft, to rise until double in bulk—about one and one half hours. Mould into small round buns, place in well-greased pans, one inch apart. Cover, set aside to rise until light—about one hour. Brush with egg, diluted with water. Bake twenty minutes. Just before removing from the ovens, brush with sugar moistened with a little water.

PLAIN BUNS
(*Potato Yeast*)

Boil 2 medium sized potatoes. When done, put through a colander into a crock containing 2 cups white sugar and 1 tablespoon lard. Add enough water to make about 1 pint of mixture, 1 small cup homemade yeast and enough *Five Roses* flour to make a batter but not too stiff. Add 1 good teaspoon salt. Care must be taken taken not to have the mixture too hot

before adding the yeast. Set in warm place to rise. When nice and light, empty into your bread pan and add 1 pint of warm water and enough *Five Roses* flour to make a soft dough, but mix until it will not stick to the hands. Let stand until light. Make up into the pans and let get very light before baking.

ALMOND BUNS

2 ounces *Five Roses* flour
2 ounces cornstarch
2 ounces ground rice
2 ounces butter
3 ounces white sugar
2 eggs
1 teaspoon baking powder
$\frac{1}{4}$ teaspoon almond essence.

Cream butter and sugar, and beat in the eggs till quite smooth. Add dry ingredients and beat 5 minutes. Quite at the last add the baking powder and almond essence. Bake in small fancy bun tins.

BATH BUNS
(*Old English Recipe*)

1$\frac{1}{2}$ pounds *Five Roses* flour
$\frac{3}{4}$ pound butter
$\frac{3}{4}$ pound sugar
$\frac{1}{4}$ lemon peel (finely chopped)
$\frac{1}{4}$ yeast cake (or 2 ounces good liquid yeast)
6 eggs
Lemon or vanilla flavoring
1 pint warm milk (or milk and water)
1 teaspoon salt.

[Buns]

Dissolve the yeast in the warm milk, and make a sponge with ¼ pound *Five Roses* flour. Cover up and let rise for about 15 minutes. Rub the butter into the remainder of the flour. When sponge has risen, break in the eggs and stir well. Then add the salt, also the flour. Mix all together to a nice dough and set aside to rise well-covered. When well risen, spread the dough out on the board, add the peel, sugar and flavoring. Mix well and mould into buns of about 3 ounces each. Put in well-greased tin and set to rise. Then wash over with beaten egg, sprinkle with a little sugar and bake in moderate oven.

—*Mrs. W. A. Fraser, Iron Springs, Alta.*

CURRANT BUNS

(*Bread Dough*)

Use *Five Roses* flour for bread, and when your bread is ready to put in the pans reserve enough for a small loaf. Break an egg in a cup, put in a piece of butter the size of a small egg and 3 tablespoons sugar —beat to a cream, then fill up cup with sweet cream and mix all through your small loaf, adding ¼ cup currants. Do not use much flour, but keep your dough soft. After a thorough mixing, put away to rise. When risen to twice original bulk, make into small buns. When these have again risen, bake in a good hot oven. On removing from oven, gloss over with a little cream and sugar.

CHELSEA BUNS

Take bread dough that is ready for the oven. Roll thin and spread with butter  (or butter and lard). Sprinkle sugar over it. Do this 3 times. After the third time, sprinkle ground cinnamon over dough. Have currants washed and dried, and put over the cinnamon quite thick. Cut in strips about ¾ inch wide and roll each strip separately (make about the size of an ordinary bun). Stand these on end in a greased tin. Let stand until very light. Then bake.

CANADIAN BUNS

(*Over Night*)

Set a sponge overnight—½ a yeast cake dissolved in 1 cup lukewarm water stirred into 2 cups *Five Roses* flour. In the morning, add 2 eggs, a little salt, 1 tablespoon sugar. Beat all together with a spoon, then add flour to make stiff dough. Knead well 15 minutes, then stand in warm place and let rise till very light. Work in with the hands ½ cup soft butter, and let rise. When light, shape into buns. Put close together in baking pan, and put in a warm place to rise. When light, bake in moderate oven till a nice brown. Brush top with a little sugar dissolved in milk.

Note.—A pleasing variety may be obtained by adding ¼ pound of shredded cocoanut. This should be done when the eggs are being added and after the dough has risen—preferably in the morning. Or, if preferred, cinnamon, candied peel, raisins, or other fruit may be added to suit taste.

GERMAN BUNS

4 cups *Five Roses* flour (sifted)
1 small teaspoon salt
1 cup white sugar
½ cup butter
½ cup lard
1 egg (well beaten)
Mix up with milk and water (half each)
Add
1 teaspoon soda
2 teaspoons cream of tartar.

FILLING FOR GERMAN BUNS

1 egg
1 cup brown sugar
½ cup *Five Roses* flour.

Mix the above. Roll out your buns and spread on the filling. Then roll up and cut off in slices. Bake. Do not put the buns too close together, as they spread.

GRAHAM BUNS

2 cups graham flour.
2 cups *Five Roses* flour
¾ cup sugar
¾ cup lard and butter
1 cup currants
2 teaspoons cream of tartar

1 teaspoon soda
Pinch of salt
Sweet milk.

Mix with sweet milk, roll and cut out. Bake as usual.

GRANDMOTHERS' BUNS

(*3 dozen large or 4 dozen small*)

3 cups lukewarm water
½ cup lard
1 cup sugar
1 cup currants
1 tablespoon salt
1 Royal yeast cake
1½ or 2 quarts *Five Roses* flour.

Dissolve yeast cake in ¼ cup warm water for about 10 minutes. Melt the lard. Put water, sugar, salt and lard into mixing pan. Add dissolved yeast cake and *Five Roses* flour enough to make stiff batter. Beat hard, and let rise until light. This should be done in middle of afternoon. At bedtime, add the currants and flour, enough to make a dough stiff enough not to stick to the hands. Set in a warm place overnight. In the morning, dough should be twice original bulk. Knead lightly and let rise. Form into small buns, place in a buttered pan, and let rise again till almost treble their size. Brush the top with milk and sugar, and bake in medium hot oven ½ hour.

NUT BUNS

2 cups *Five Roses* flour
½ cup butter
¾ cup white sugar
½ cup chopped nuts
1 egg
Pinch of salt
1½ teaspoons baking powder
Little milk

Cream the butter and sugar in a basin, then add the well-beaten egg, then the nuts. Mix the baking powder well into the flour with the salt. Put the milk into the basin and stir well, then last the flour folded in. Have baking tins ready and drop the mixture on in teaspoonfuls, allowing enough room to rise. Bake about 15 minutes. Put a nut on top of each bun before putting in oven.

ORANGE BUNS

10 ounces *Five Roses* flour
¼ pound sugar
2 ounces butter
2 ounces lard
1 teaspoon baking powder
Rind of 1 orange (or lemon)
Pinch of salt
1 egg
Milk.

Rub the butter and lard into flour. Add sugar, baking powder, salt, orange rind. Mix to a stiff paste with the beaten egg and a little milk. Bake 10 minutes in a quick oven.

Strain juice of orange, add icing sugar, and ice the buns when cold.

ROCK BUNS

½ pound *Five Roses* flour
2 ounces sweet lard or butter
2 ounces granulated sugar
2 ounces currants
3 teaspoons baking powder
½ teaspoon salt
1 cup sweet milk.

Mix to a smooth batter, and drop in small spoonfuls on to a well-greased baking pan. Bake in moderately hot oven for 15 minutes or 20 minutes. Let cool in pan before breaking apart.

SCOTCH BLACK BUNS

½ pound *Five Roses* flour
1 pound raisins
1 pound currants
¼ pound sugar
2 ounces blanched almonds
2 ounces candied peel
1 teaspoon ginger
1 teaspoon cinnamon (or spices)
¼ teaspoon Jamaica pepper
½ teaspoon carraway seeds
½ teaspoon soda
½ teaspoon cream of tartar
1 teacup sweet milk (old ale may be used instead).

With the hand mix well in a basin all above ingredients. Line a cake tin with a plain short crust rolled out very thin, and put the mixture in this prepared tin, and roll out the scraps of paste to cover top.

[*Buns*]

Wet well the edges. Place top cover on and press well around the edges. Prick top with a fork, and brush over with sweet milk. Bake in moderate oven for at least 3 hours.

—*Mrs. J. W. McKendrick,*
Ladysmith, Vancouver Island, B. C.

YANKEE BUNS

Sift 3 cups *Five Roses* flour with 2 teaspoons cream of tartar and 1 teaspoon soda. Work ¼ lb. butter into the flour. Mix with the hands enough sweet milk to make a stiff dough. Roll ½ inch thick. Spread with ¾ cup butter and sugar creamed together. Roll up and cut in slices ¾ inch thick. Place in well-buttered pan and bake in moderate oven.

SPANISH BUN
No. 1

1 large tablespoon butter or shortening
1 cup brown sugar
2 eggs (save 1 white)
2 teaspoons cinnamon
½ cup sweet milk
2 teaspoons cream of tartar
1 teaspoon soda
1¼ cups *Five Roses* flour.

Note.—Butter and water may be used instead of shortening and milk.

Cream butter and sugar, then add eggs, then cinnamon, flour and cream of tartar.

Last of all the milk in which has been dissolved the soda. Take the white of egg, beat stiff, then add brown sugar enough to sweeten. Put on top of cake and brown in oven. This cake should be baked in small bread pan. I sometimes put nutmeg on the icing. If not, I put cocoanut on top.

SPANISH BUN
No. 2

4 eggs (reserve white of three for frosting)
2 cups baking sugar
¾ cup butter
1 cup sweet milk
1 teaspoon soda
2 teaspoons cream of tartar
1 teaspoon cloves
1 teaspoon cinnamon
1 teaspoon allspices
1 grated nutmeg
2½ cups *Five Roses* flour.

HOT CROSS BUNS

Take any ordinary bun dough and with a sharp knife slit top at right angles or press a cross on top of each with a long pencil. When nearly baked glaze, dredge the cross thus produced with granulated sugar, repeat glazing and dredging until the cross is filled with sugar. Complete baking. Cinnamon may be mixed with the sugar, or lemon extract.

□ □ □

*F*IVE ROSES is the only flour that is unreservedly and publicly guaranteed by its makers to be

Not Bleached—Not Blended

It is the pure extract of Manitoba's plump, sun-ripened wheat kernels milled by purely mechanical process. With no other flour are you so positive of the purity, strength and wholesomeness of all your bake things.

Not Bleached—Not Blended

BISCUITS

MIX the flour, baking powder and salt together and **dry thoroughly.** The best way to do this is to sift these ingredients together 2 or 3 times. Use cold milk or water, as the case may be.

After rolling out biscuit dough, if you let it stand a few minutes before and after cutting into shapes, it will considerably improve the texture and lightness.

Biscuits require from **10 to 20** minutes to bake properly.

Shortening may be sweet lard, or dripping, or butter, or a mixture. Vegetable lards and other shortenings are now being used considerably with some satisfaction. See that the shortening is soft enough to rub easily. Use broad, flexible knife for cutting and mixing.

Successful biscuits follow the use of *Five Roses* flour, a slack dough, quick mixing and as little handling as possible.

❖ ❖ ❖

PREPARED FLOUR FOR BISCUITS

Have the flour prepared in bulk as follows : To 16 lbs. of *Five Roses* flour, add ¼ lb. soda and ½ lb. cream of tartar and mix. Sift all together twice and put in an air-tight box.

PLAIN BISCUITS

(*Women's Institute Recipe*)

4 cups *Five Roses* flour (sifted)
2 teaspoons cream of tartar
1 teaspoon soda
2 dessert-spoons white sugar
1 (small) teaspoon salt
1 cup sweet milk
1 cup sweet cream.

Sift the cream of tartar and soda with the flour. Mix all with spoon, roll out and bake well in hot oven. A handful of currants is sometimes added. If no cream is at hand, substitute 1 tablespoon lard or butter.

PLAIN BISCUITS

(*First Prize Fall Fair*)

Into 1 sifter of *Five Roses* flour, put 1 teaspoon soda, 2 teaspoons baking powder, 1 teaspoon salt, 2 teaspoons sugar. Sift 2 or 3 three times, then mix with 2

cups cream and 2 of buttermilk. Roll out half an inch thick, put into smart oven and bake.

ARROWROOT BISCUITS

2 cups arrowroot
1 cup *Five Roses* flour
⅔ cup butter
Milk to stiffen.

Sift the arrowroot and flour. Rub the butter into the flour and stir in gradually sufficient milk to make a stiff dough. Roll out into a thick sheet, beat with a rolling pin, fold and roll out, and beat again, repeating this process 5 minutes. Roll the last time about an inch thick. Cut with round cutter. Brush with egg, and bake in a moderate oven.

BAKING POWDER BISCUITS

2 cups *Five Roses* flour
4 teaspoons baking powder
1 teaspoon salt
1 cup milk and water (half of each)
1 tablespoon butter
1 tablespoon lard.

Note—Currants may be added to taste.

Sift the flour, salt and baking powder twice together. Cream butter and lard and add to dry ingredients, using the tips

[*Biscuits*]

of your fingers. Then add the liquid, mixing with a knife until you have a very soft dough. Place on your mixing board but do not knead. Roll out lightly until ¾ inch thick. Cut out and bake in a hot oven for 15 minutes.

BUTTERMILK BISCUITS

2 cups *Five Roses* flour (sifted)
2 teaspoons cream of tartar
1 teaspoon soda
1 teaspoon salt
Lard size of walnut
Buttermilk (enough to make soft dough not thick enough to roll).

Mix together and empty on to well-floured board, smooth out a little and cut into size desired. Bake in hot oven.

LIGHT CREAM BISCUITS

4 cups *Five Roses* flour
2 eggs
1 cup sweet cream
2 teaspoons baking powder
Pinch of salt.
Note.—Ginger or other spice may be added to taste.

Beat eggs very light, and add to cream. Mix in the flour and baking powder, and make soft dough. Roll out and cut with small cutter. Bake in quick oven.

SWEET CREAM BISCUITS
(*Eggless*)

4 cups *Five Roses* flour
1 cup sweet cream
1 cup skimmed milk
2 teaspoons cream of tartar
1 teaspoon soda
1 teaspoon salt.

It is important to pay careful attention to the measurement of the materials. The cupfuls of cream and milk should be scant, but the cream should be rich. The cups of flour (measured before sifting) should be level. The teaspoons of cream of tartar and soda should be slightly rounded. The salt level. More-

over, the cups used should be the standard half-pint measure rather than the teacup or coffee cup.

Sift the salt, soda and cream of tartar with flour, and after putting the cream and milk together mix the ingredients just mentioned. Handle as quickly and as little as possible. Roll out without using any extra flour except a bare sprinkling on the board. Cut the biscuits ½ inch thick, put in warm pans and bake in a rather quick oven with a good bottom heat. The biscuits should rise to three times their original thickness before browning, and ought to be done in 20 minutes. The dough should be as soft as it is possible to handle—even slightly sticky. Success will depend mainly upon this and proper baking. Properly made, the biscuits will be as light as a feather.

DREAM BISCUITS

1 cup butter
1 cup sugar
1½ teaspoons baking powder
1 tablespoon cream
1 pinch soda in the cream
2 eggs (well-beaten)
Five Roses flour to roll.

These biscuits are delicious and dainty Should be cut with a tiny cake cutter. When baked, should be put togther with icing between and on top of them. Chocolate icing is also very good on top.

ICING FOR DREAM BISCUITS

1 tablespoon butter
1 tablespoon vanilla
3 tablespoons cream
Icing sugar to thicken.

HEATHER BISCUITS

2 cups brown sugar
3 eggs
Pinch of salt
1½ cups shortening
¾ cup water
3 teaspoons baking powder
3 cups oatmeal
1 cup *Five Roses* flour (or enough to make as thick as cookie dough).

[*Biscuits*]

LEMON BISCUITS

½ lb. butter
3 eggs
2 cups white sugar
1 pint sweet milk
5c. worth baking ammonia (pulverized)
5c. worth oil of lemon
6 cups *Five Roses* flour.

Cream the butter and sugar, add the eggs well-beaten. Sift the ammonia several times in the flour, then add. If not stiff enough, add more flour, as they should be quite stiff, and mix with the hands. Add the oil of lemon last. Cut in oblong shape about ¼ inch thick, and bake in rather hot oven. Will keep a long time.

This recipe makes feathery light, crisp and delicious little biscuits such as are commonly found only at the confectioner's.

LIGHT FOAM BISCUITS

1 quart *Five Roses* flour
1 tablespoon baking powder
1 tablespoon lard
1 tablespoon butter
1 cup (coffee cup) sweet milk
1 egg (beaten separately and mixed with milk)

Mix as usual, cut and bake 20 minutes in quick oven.

POTATO BISCUITS

2 cups *Five Roses* flour
2 teaspoons baking powder
2 cups finely mashed potatoes
1 tablespoon lard
Pinch of salt
Water to make biscuit dough.

Sift flour and baking powder together. Add finely mashed potatoes, lard, pinch of salt, and water to make biscuit dough. Roll and bake. A little ginger may be added if desired.

IRISH POTATO BISCUITS

Boil and mash six or eight potatoes. While warm, lay on a floured pastry-board and run the rolling-pin over and over them till they are free from lumps. Turn into a bowl, wet with a cup of sweet milk, add a teaspoon melted butter. When well mixed, work in ½ cup *Five Roses* flour

(salted) or just enough to make a soft dough. Return to the board, roll out quickly and lightly into a thin sheet, and cut into round cakes. Bake in a quick oven. Butter as soon as they are done, laying one on top of the other in a pile. Eat before they fall.

The excellence of potato biscuits depends very greatly upon the softness of the dough, light handling, and quick baking. If properly made, they will be found extremely nice. A favorite Irish dish.

—*Selected.*

PIN WHEELS

Put 2 teaspoons soda and 4 teaspoons cream tartar into 1 quart *Five Roses* flour. Sift twice. Add 2 large tablespoons lard and butter mixed, and enough milk to make a dough easily rolled. Roll about 1 inch thick, spread with a little melted butter, 1 cup of currants, and sprinkle over a little sugar. Roll up into a round loaf, cut into slices about 1 inch thick. Bake in moderate oven. This recipe, without the currants, makes an excellent biscuit recipe.

CARAWAY SEED BISCUITS

2 cups *Five Roses* flour
1 teaspoon (heaping) baking powder
½ teaspoon salt
2 teaspoons (heaping) caraway seed
4 teaspoons (heaping) sugar
Milk
1 tablespoon (heaping) butter.

Mix all together thoroughly, then wet with milk or water as moist as can be rolled out. Then cut into biscuits. Put in pans, sprinkle with sugar, and bake out in pans, sprinkle with sugar, and bake about 15 minutes in moderate oven.

FRENCH TEA BISCUITS

¼ cup sugar
1 egg (not beaten)
Piece of butter size of egg (melted)
1 cup sweet milk
1 nutmeg
2½ teaspoons baking powder
3 cups *Five Roses* flour (sifted with baking powder).

[*Biscuits*]

RICE BISCUITS

½ pound white sugar
½ pound ground rice
½ pound butter (or ¼ pound butter, ¼ pound lard)
½ pound *Five Roses* flour
½ teaspoon baking powder (or 1 teaspoon cream tartar and ½ teaspoon soda)
2 eggs.

Mix with sweet milk or water. Roll as for cookies. Cut in round or square cakes, and bake.

CREAM TEA BISCUITS

(*Makes 10 Biscuits*)

1 cup thin sweet cream
2 cups *Five Roses* flour (or enough to roll)
1 teaspoon baking powder to each cup of flour.

Put the cream in mixing bowl, add flour with baking powder gradually so as not to get the dough too stiff. Roll to ½ inch thick, cut, bake in oven not so hot as required for other biscuits.

CRUSHED WHEAT BISCUITS

3 cups crushed wheat flour
2 cups *Five Roses* flour
1 cup sugar
1 large tablespoon shortening
1 teaspoon soda
2 teaspoons baking powder
Pinch of salt
1 quart buttermilk.

(Instead of shortening and buttermilk, might use 1 quart cream.)

BANNOCK

1½ pounds *Five Roses* flour
½ pound butter or lard
½ pound raisins
½ pound currants
1 ounce candied peel
1 cup sugar
1 teaspoon carbonate of **soda**
1 teaspoon cream of tartar
Pinch of salt
Buttermilk.

Rub the shortening into the flour, add other ingredients and mix with enough buttermilk to make a nice light dough. Bake in moderate oven about 1 hour.

CHEESE ROLLS

Make a dough as for baking powder biscuit. Roll lightly with rolling pin until a little thicker than for pie crust. Spread liberally with grated cheese and roll over and over as for jelly roll. Cut the pieces about 1 inch thick. Place the cubes upright and bake until a light brown. Delicious with salad.

SAUSAGE ROLLS

Make a dough as for biscuits. Roll thin and cut into large rounds. Spread one-half thickly with sausage meat and turn the other side over. Pinch edges together and put in a baking pan. Bake half hour. Nice with meat course.

◇ ◇ ◇

*A*T *Fall Fairs throughout Canada, FIVE ROSES flour for many years has taken first and other prizes in open competition against all comers. Not only for breads, but for biscuits, cakes, pastry and all other forms of flour foods. Many of these prize recipes earned a place in the FIVE ROSES cook book.*

GEMS, SCONES AND MUFFINS

GRAHAM GEMS
No. 1

1 egg
1 cup of brown sugar
½ cup shortening
1 cup sour milk
⅓ cup *Five Roses* flour
½ teaspoon baking soda
½ teaspoon salt
Graham flour to make stiff batter.

Bake in buttered gem tins in quick oven.

GRAHAM GEMS
No. 2

2 eggs
2 cups sour milk
1 tablespoon butter or lard
Pinch of salt
2 tablespoons sugar
1 tablespoon molasses
1 teaspoon soda
1 teaspoon cream of tartar
3 cups graham flour
1 cup *Five Roses* flour.

CORN GEMS

⅓ cup butter
½ cup brown sugar
1 egg
¾ cup cornmeal
1½ cups *Five Roses* flour
1½ teaspoon baking powder.

BELFASTS

1 cup sugar
½ cup butter
1 cup buttermilk
1 egg
⅓ nutmeg
⅓ teaspoon cinnamon
1½ cups graham flour
¾ cup *Five Roses* flour
1 teaspoon soda
Pinch of salt
1 cup seeded raisins (optional).

Bake in gem rings in moderate oven.

PLUNKETS
(*To be eaten with Ice Cream*)

Cream 1 cup butter, and gradually beat in 1 cup sugar. Beat the yolks of 6 eggs until light, and the whites until firm. Then pour the yolks over the whites and beat both together. Pass through a sieve twice ½ cup *Five Roses* flour, ¾ cup cornstarch and 2 level teaspoons baking powder. Then add to other ingredients, adding 1 teaspoon vanilla extract. Bake in gem pans. Two scant cups *Five Roses* flour may be used, leaving out the cornstarch.

TEXTURE OF MUFFINS

For your own satisfaction, break apart a muffin or popover baked from *Five Roses*. Note the fine, silky texture, the evenly risen crumb. No other flour raises so uniformly.

BUTTERMILK SCONES

2 pounds *Five Roses* flour
¼ ounce carbonate of soda·
1 pint sour milk or buttermilk
Pinch of salt.

Mix to a light dough, roll out about ⅓ inch thick, and cut to desired shape. Bake 15 minutes.

SCOTCH SODA SCONES

1 quart *Five Roses* flour
1 teaspoon baking soda
2 teaspoons cream of tartar
A little lard or butter
Salt and sugar to taste.

Mix ingredients. Warm the flour. Add butter, milk or water to make consistent dough. Turn out on board and handle as little as possible. Turn out round, and bake in skillet, or on top of stove. When one side is done, turn over.

Note—Whole wheat flour can be used in the same way. A pint and a half of Lake of the Woods Breakfast Food instead of flour makes a very effective scone.

[*Gems, Scones and Muffins*]

RAISIN SCONES

3 cups *Five Roses* flour
2 teaspoons baking powder
1 cup butter
1 cup lightest yellow sugar
1 cup sweet milk (½ cream if desired)
1 cup chopped raisins
1 egg (white).

Mix and add raisins and well-beaten white of egg last. Roll about ½ inch thick, spread with the yolk of egg well-beaten. Cut into triangles or squares. Bake.

OATMEAL SCONES

1 cup baking oatmeal (standard variety)
1½ cups *Five Roses* flour
½ cup shortening
½ cup brown sugar
½ teaspoon soda
Sour cream to make firm dough (about ½ cup).

Do not roll but press with the hands into long strips about 2 inches wide and one-half inch thick. Hack with back of knife into deep ridges crosswise. Cut into 3-inch lengths and bake in hot oven.

Cold oat porridge is sometimes used instead of oatmeal.

POTATO CAKES

4 cups mashed potatoes
2 cups *Five Roses* flour
1 egg
1 tablespoon butter
Pinch of salt.

Mix the potatoes and flour together with the egg, adding first the salt. Roll out ⅓-inch thick. Cut in shapes and bake on baking sheet. When cooked, split and butter. Serve hot.

PLAIN MUFFINS

3 tablespoons sugar
3 tablespoons melted butter
2 eggs
1 cup sweet milk
2 cups *Five Roses* flour
3 teaspoons baking powder
½ teaspoon salt.

Melt butter, add sugar and mix well. Add eggs and beat. Add milk, sift in flour, salt and baking powder. Mix quickly to a smooth batter. Fill greased gem pans two-thirds full. Bake in a hot oven 20 to 25 minutes.

For *cornmeal* muffins, use 1 cup cornmeal and 1 cup *Five Roses* flour.

For *graham* muffins, use 1 cup graham flour and 1 cup *Five Roses* flour.

For *whole wheat* muffins, use 1 cup whole wheat flour and 1 cup *Five Roses* flour.

For *cocoanut* muffins, add 1 cup shredded cocoanut.

NELLIE'S MUFFINS

(*Eggless*)

2½ cups *Five Roses* flour
½ cup white sugar
2 tablespoons butter
2 tablespoons lard
2½ teaspoons cream of tartar
1¼ teaspoons soda
½ teaspoon salt
Sweet milk to make a soft dough.

Sift cream of tartar, soda and salt with the flour, rub butter and lard in flour, also sugar, and mix all together. Roll out about ¼-inch thick, spread thickly with butter and sugar, then begin at edge and roll up. Cut with a sharp knife into slices. Place slices in a buttered pan close together, sprinkle thickly with sugar, and bake. A little jelly placed on top of each before putting in oven improves them.

OATMEAL MUFFINS

½ cup sugar
1 tablespoon butter
2 eggs
2 cups buttermilk
1 teaspoon soda (dissolved in milk)
1 teaspoon (small) salt
2 handfuls (good) oatmeal
Five Roses flour to make stiff batter.

Drop from spoon in greased pan, and bake in moderate oven.

Not Bleached~Not Blended

BRAN MUFFINS

1 egg
½ cup brown sugar
1 cup buttermilk or sour milk
Butter size of an egg
1 teaspoon soda
1 cup *Five Roses* flour
2 cups bran (added last).

Bake in a square deep cake pan, and afterwards cut into squares.

CREAM MUFFINS

1 pint thin sweet cream
3 fresh eggs
2 teaspoons baking powder
1 teaspoon salt
2 tablespoons (level) sugar
Five Roses flour to make stiff batter.

Beat eggs light, add salt, sugar and cream. Add flour until it becomes a stiff batter. Grease muffin pans, fill and bake in quick oven.

Note on Muffins—Muffins may also be baked in rings on a griddle, and many prefer this method to baking in the oven. As the muffins cook and stiffen, slip off the rings and let them finish. Muffins with yeast recipe will take about 5 minutes longer to bake properly than with baking powder.

LEFT-OVER MUFFINS

Muffins left over from breakfast may be pulled, not cut apart, and toasted for luncheon or supper.

CRUMPETS

2 cups milk
3 cups *Five Roses* flour
2 tablespoons butter
1 teaspoon salt
¼ yeast cake.

Dissolve the yeast in warm water. Warm the milk, beat in the salted flour, the melted butter and the yeast. Let this sponge stand in a warm place until light. Bake in greased muffin rings on a hot griddle, or in patty pans in the oven. In either case, fill the pans or rings only half full, as the crumpets will rise in baking.

—*Mrs. James A. McIntyre,*
Owensville, Sask.

SALLY LUNN

(Always popular at tea during the cool months)

½ cup sugar
2 eggs
3 tablespoons butter
1 cup milk
2 cups *Five Roses* flour
1 teaspoon cream of tartar
½ teaspoon soda.

Bake in sheet or muffin pans good steady oven 20 to 30 minutes. When required for use, this tea cake might be cut into thick slices across, toasted, buttered and served very hot.

JOHNNY CAKE

No. 1

1 cup sour milk
½ cup molasses
1 egg
Pinch of salt
⅓ cup of melted lard
1 cup Indian meal
2 cups *Five Roses* flour
1 teaspoon soda.

Bake in hot oven.

JOHNNY CAKE

No. 2

Mix 3 cups buttermilk with 2 small teaspoons soda, 1 cup sugar, 2 eggs and 1 teaspoon salt. Add 3 cups cornmeal, 1½ cups *Five Roses* flour and 1 teaspoon cream tartar sifted with the flour. Heat 3 tablespoons shortening in baking pan and pour boiling hot over all. Beat well. Bake in hot oven.

JOHNNY CAKE WITHOUT EGGS

(Bachelors' Recipe)

2 cups cornmeal
1 cup *Five Roses* flour
2 cups sweet milk
2 tablespoons melted butter
2 tablespoons sugar
2 tablespoons baking powder.

—*Earl C. Tweedie, Macklin, Sask.*

[*Gems, Scones and Muffins*]

POPOVERS
No. 1

2 eggs (yolks)

1 tablespoon sugar
1 tablespoon melted butter
1 cup milk
1 cup *Five Roses* flour
1 teaspoon salt
2 teaspoons (heaping) baking
    powder.

Beat the whites of the 2 eggs perfectly stiff and add last of all. Bake in gem tins, filling each tin half full. Bake 10 minutes.

POPOVERS
No. 2

2 eggs
$\frac{1}{2}$ cup butter
$1\frac{1}{2}$ cups sugar
1 cup sweet milk
$\frac{1}{2}$ teaspoon soda
1 teaspoon cream of tartar
$\frac{1}{2}$ cup molasses
1 teaspoon mixed spices
Five Roses flour to stiffen.

Bake in moderate oven.

Note on Popovers—If a quick dessert is wanted, popovers may be readily used. As the batter is poured into the tins, add a piece of fruit to each. Served with a simple syrup, these popovers are delicious.

BREAKFAST PUFFS

1 egg
1 cup sweet milk
2 tablespoons melted butter
1 teaspoon soda
2 teaspoons cream of tartar
Five Roses flour to make drop batter.

TEA PUFFS

(*Bachelors' Recipe*)

$2\frac{1}{4}$ cups *Five Roses* flour
3 cups milk
3 eggs (beaten separately)
3 teaspoons melted butter
Pinch of salt.

Bake in muffin tins in hot oven.

BISCUITS, muffins, popovers, have you ever seen them at their best unless *Five Roses* flour was used? Tell your friends about your success; show them the delicate bread-morsels your folks enjoy for breakfast. Break the crisp, golden crust; show them the evenly risen inside, soft and porous. Tell them how appetizing and digestible *Five Roses* flour makes biscuits, rolls and other foodstuffs. Help your friends to better bake things. See that they also secure a copy of this cook book. But, above all, see that they also use *Five Roses*.

Not Bleached ~ Not Blended

A PURE WHEAT BREAKFAST FOOD

(Made by the Five Roses millers from the same wheat as the flour)

W E did not ourselves appreciate the delicacy of taste and nutritive value of the *Five Roses* Breakfast Food until its consistently increasing sales forced its merits upon our attention.

The really distinctive feature is the *natural* wheat flavor of this product. Made from identically the same splendid wheat as *Five Roses* flour, it is really nothing else but the plump Manitoba berry in its purest condition reduced expertly to an even granulation. Unlike other similar cereals, it is not roasted, baked, malted or otherwise prepared. There is therefore at your disposal in an attractive readily-prepared form all the nutrition and nutlike qualities peculiar to the sun-ripened wheat kernels grown in our North-West.

So far its sale has never been forced by advertising. It does not even possess a distinctive name or package.

If we had not been planning the *Five Roses* Cook Book you might never have heard of this good food. When we asked our expert to suggest a few recipes, she was truly amazed at the multitudinous uses of an article which so far we had regarded simply as a by-product. By merely substituting a cup of the Breakfast Food for every 1½ cups of *Five Roses* flour, any recipe contained in this book becomes completely changed, and the result is very original, appetizing and digestible. Try it for puddings, muffins, griddle cakes, fried cakes, cookies, rolls and dough nuts, and biscuits, etc., etc.

As a Breakfast Food, there is nothing so truly wholesome and easily prepared. And there is a certainty of digestion which creates confidence in the unfortunate possessor of a weak stomach. The Editor has seen children, just weaned, fed consistently on this cereal, and such happy, chubby babies are the very best advertisement the food can ever have. They never seem to tire of it. Ask your grocer for a trial package.

We append a few recipes which will suggest many other ways of using this delightful wheaten product. Each recipe has been tried and tested, and is guaranteed by the publishers of the *Five Roses* Cook Book.

◊ ◊ ◊

AS A BREAKFAST CEREAL

To **1** cup of the cereal add **4** cups of *cold* water and **1** level teaspoon of salt. Cook over rather slow fire, stir to keep from settling. If this is found thicker than desired, add *cold* water. Boil about **20** minutes. Or, it is at its best as a delicate nourishing breakfast dish, made in double boiler over night, simply bringing to boiling point and warming when required.

B. F. BREAD

7½ cups breakfast food
1 tablespoon brown sugar
1½ teaspoons salt
1 cake compressed yeast
1½ cups lukewarm water
1½ cups milk (scalded and cooled)
3 tablespoons lard or butter (melted).

Dissolve the yeast and sugar in lukewarm liquid. Add lard or butter, then the cereal gradually as it absorbs moisture rather slowly. Lastly, add the salt.

[*Breakfast Food*]

Knead thoroughly, being sure to keep dough soft. Place in well-greased bowl, cover and set aside in a warm place, to rise for about 2 hours. When double in bulk, turn out on kneading board. Mould into loaves, place in well-greased pans, cover and set to rise again for about one hour or until light. Bake 1 hour in a slower oven than for white bread.

If wanted for over-night, use ½ cake yeast and 1 extra teaspoon salt.

Note—As in the case of bread made from whole wheat meal, many prefer using a sponge at first. A sponge is a thick batter, not a dough—we knead a dough, but beat or mix a batter.

FOR SANDWICHES

A pleasing variation from the ordinary sandwich can readily be obtained by using slices of bread made with Lake of the Woods Breakfast Food. Also for a change one of the slices forming the sandwich may be made of the cereal and used instead of white bread.

For sandwich fillings, see pages 25-28.

B. F. BISCUITS

1½ cups *Five Roses* flour
1½ cups breakfast food
3 teaspoons (heaping) baking powder
1½ tablespoons lard or butter
1 teaspoon (scant) salt.

Sift the flour, cereal, baking powder and salt together thoroughly. Rub in the shortening and add enough *cold* water to make a dough, just stiff enough to roll and cut into biscuit. Bake in a good hot oven.

These are delicious eaten hot for breakfast, lunch or tea.

B. F. GEMS

2 cups *Five Roses* flour
1 cup breakfast food
1 egg
3 teaspoons baking powder
1 teaspoon salt
1 tablespoon melted butter.

Mix all together and add enough sweet milk to make a very soft batter. Bake in a quick oven in gem tins.

B. F. MUFFINS

1 cup hot milk
1 cup breakfast food
½ cup rolled oats
½ cup *Five Roses* flour (sifted)
1 cake compressed yeast
¼ cup lukewarm water
3 tablespoons sugar
2 tablespoons butter
1 teaspoon salt.

Boil oats and butter in a cup of milk one minute, let stand until lukewarm. Dissolve yeast and sugar in ¼ cup lukewarm water, and combine the two mixtures. Add cereal, flour and salt. Beat well. The batter should be thick enough to drop heavily from the spoon. Cover and let rise until light (about one hour) in a moderately warm place. Fill well-greased muffin pans two-thirds full. Let rise about 40 minutes, bake 24 minutes in moderately hot oven.

B. F. GRIDDLE CAKES

1½ cups breakfast food
1 cup sifted *Five Roses* flour
2 eggs
1 cake compressed yeast
2 cups milk (scalded and cooled)
2 tablespoons brown sugar or molasses
1 teaspoon salt.

Dissolve yeast and sugar (or molasses) in lukewarm milk. Cool and add flour, well-beaten eggs, breakfast cereal, salt, and beat until smooth. Cover and set aside to rise in a warm place for about 1 hour or until light. Stir well. Bake on hot griddle.

If wanted for over-night, use ¼ cake yeast and an extra half teaspoon salt. Cover and keep in cool place. See other griddle cake recipes on page 51.

B. F. PANCAKES

1 quart sour milk
2 teaspoons soda
1 teaspoon salt
2 eggs.

Mix with equal parts *Five Roses* flour and breakfast food to make smooth pancake batter. Beat well. Bake as usual. Serve hot with butter and syrup. See other pancake recipes page 49.

B. F. WAFFLES

Lake of the Woods Breakfast Food makes delectable waffles by substituting 1½ cups of the cereal for the 2 cups of *Five Roses* flour in the ordinary waffle recipe given on page 52. Mix with cold water.

A BREAKFAST COMBINATION

(*A welcome change from porridge*)

Mix together 1 cup of the cereal, 1 of oatmeal and 1 of barley. Rub in about 2 ounces of good dripping and 2 table-spoons soft brown sugar, a good pinch of salt and 1 heaping teaspoon baking powder Mix into a firm dough with milk or water, divide into two parts, roll out, prick it and bake until ready. Cut into thin slices and cook in a cooler part of the oven till thoroughly crisp and toasted throughout. Pound down with a rolling pin or, better still, put through the mincing machine twice. Put in an air-tight tin or bottle, and serve when wanted with boiling milk.

[Breakfast Food]

OTHER WAYS OF PREPARING THE CEREAL

A little ingenuity exercised in connection with the many favorite recipes enclosed in the *Five Roses* Cook Book will produce quite a variety of tasty desserts.

When making the morning meal, should you have any left over, pour the cereal into a deep dish to cool, and then, when required for lunch or tea, slice and fry. Very nice when served with fried bacon.

It can likewise be served as a dessert. Place in custard cups and serve with sweetened cream.

Note.—The Editor would welcome any new recipes dealing with this breakfast cereal not incorporated in the *Five Roses* Cook Book. Address your envelope: " Culinary Dept., Lake of the Woods Milling Company, Ltd., Montreal, Que."

❖ ❖ ❖

IT is from the great amount of phosphates and nitrates it contains that the Lake of the Woods Breakfast Food derives its high nutritive value. Phosphates build nerves and brain, nitrates produce muscle. The germ of the wheat, which is so rich in phosphates and other food values, adds a natural wheat flavor to this cereal that is very pleasing. Growing children, convalescents, all who require an easily digested food, full of wholesome, appetizing qualities and concentrated nutriment cannot help but find in this Breakfast Food the cereal best suited to their requirements.

N.B.—Since the publication of the first edition of this cook book. we have experimented with the Breakfast Food and have evolved a splendid recipe for bread-making with this Cereal. This can be found on page 21,

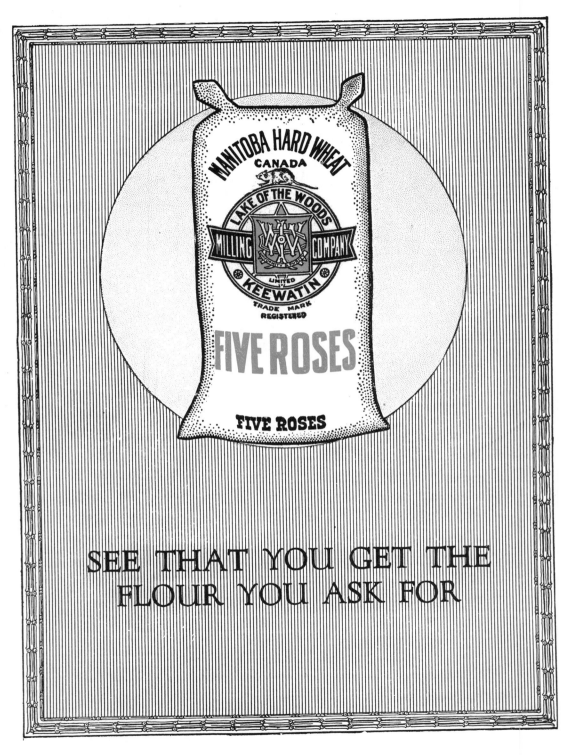

PANCAKES

WHEN using the yeast (overnight) batter, always keep at least one-third of the mixture as a "mother" for next day's cakes. Set in a cold place and keep well-covered. The evening before the cakes are required, add hot water, salt to taste and *Five Roses* flour to make thick batter.

Left-over batter should always be kept in a cool place in the same pitcher in which it was mixed. If kept cold, it will not spoil; in fact, freezing pancake batter adds to the quality of the cakes.

When the pancakes are sour, add a little soda, but limit this ingredient as much as possible. In using sweet milk, add baking powder in the morning instead of soda.

Delectable pancakes are readily made with Lake of the Woods Breakfast Food. Try it.

❖ ❖ ❖

PLAIN PANCAKES

2 cups sour milk
3 eggs (beaten separately)
1 teaspoon soda
1 teaspoon salt
Five Roses flour to thicken.

Mix as usual. Beat the whites of the 3 eggs and stir in slowly last thing before baking.

BUCKWHEAT PANCAKES
(*Over Night*)

1 quart water
½ yeast cake
1 teaspoon (heaping) salt
1 tablespoon brown sugar
Buckwheat to make stiff batter.

Let rise over night. In morning, dissolve 1 level teaspoon soda in a little water and add to the batter.

ENGLISH PANCAKES

1 pint milk
1 tablespoon sugar
2 eggs
1 cup *Five Roses* flour
1 teaspoon baking powder
Pinch of salt.

Sift the flour, salt and baking powder together. Add to this the well-beaten eggs and sugar, and mix all with the pint of milk. Mix all ingredients thoroughly. If too thick, add more milk. Put a small piece of butter in a hot frying pan, then spoonfuls of the batter. When lightly browned, turn over, then fold on hot dish. Serve with powdered sugar and a squeeze of lemon.

CORN PANCAKES

1 cup cornmeal
¾ cup *Five Roses* flour
½ teaspoon salt
1 teaspoon (heaping) soda
2 teaspoons (heaping) cream of tartar
Water to mix quite thin.

FRENCH PANCAKES

3 eggs (yolks)
1 cup milk
½ teaspoon salt
1 teaspoon sugar
Five Roses flour.

Mix yolks, milk, salt, sugar, and pour one-third of the mixture on ½ cup *Five Roses* flour and stir to a smooth paste; then add the remainder of the mixture and beat well. To this add ½ teaspoon of salad oil. Pour enough of the batter into a hot buttered frying-pan to cover the pan. When brown, turn and brown the other side. Spread with butter and jelly, roll up and sprinkle with powdered sugar.

[*Pancakes*]

DRY BREAD PANCAKES
(*For Four Persons*)

1 pint dry bread
1 pint milk or water
1 egg
1 cup sour milk
½ teaspoon soda
1 teaspoon cream of tartar
Pinch of salt
Five Roses flour.

Soak the bread in the milk or water for one hour. Beat up well with a kitchen spoon. Beat in 1 egg and the sour milk. Into this, sift a cup of flour into which have been mixed the soda, cream of tartar and salt. Add more flour, if necessary, to make a good pancake batter. Beat well. Bake on a hot greased griddle or frying pan. A good spoonful is enough for a cake. Serve hot with butter and syrup.

GRAHAM PANCAKES

1 egg (well-beaten)
1 cup sour milk
1 teaspoon baking soda
1 teaspoon salt (dissolved in warm water)
1 cup Graham flour
1½ cups *Five Roses* flour.

POTATO PANCAKES
No. 1

6 raw potatoes (grated)
1 egg.
1 tablespoon *Five Roses* flour
Salt and pepper.

Mix and fry the same as ordinary pancake. Fine with fried ham.

POTATO PANCAKES
No. 2

2 eggs
12 large grated potatoes
1½ cups *Five Roses* flour
⅓ cup sweet milk
1 tablespoon salt.

WHEAT PANCAKES

1 quart sour milk
2 teaspoons soda
1 teaspoon salt
2 eggs.

Mix with equal parts of *Five Roses* flour and wheatmeal to make batter.

◈ ◈ ◈

HOW TO KEEP FLOUR

BEING highly absorbent, flour should not be exposed to contact with other foods, vegetables, etc. It should be kept away from oils and odors of all sorts.

It should be scrupulously free from damp, otherwise it will quickly "work" and lose at least part of its baking qualities. When *Five Roses* is purchased by the barrel, elevate the barrel so that there may be a free current of air beneath it to prevent the flour at the bottom of the barrel from becoming musty.

A farmer's wife who stacked her flour bags upstairs beside the kitchen flue said that the last sacks used were very much whiter and made much better bread than the first bags. This is because the flour was gradually warmed through by the gentle heat, being aged and dried, which works considerable improvement in a sound flour, making it much whiter and livelier in the dough.

When mice become troublesome, a hint might be taken from the grocer who kept these household pests from his flour and cereals by using fine mesh steel wire to protect his bags and barrels.

Not Bleached ~ Not Blended

GRIDDLE CAKES AND WAFFLES

IF you can get a soapstone griddle, use no other. Cakes are baked—not fried—upon it, and are thereby made comparatively wholesome. Set the griddle at the side of the range and heat gradually at least one hour before you begin to bake. If heated suddenly it is liable to crack. Clean with dry salt, then wipe with a clean cloth and it is ready for use. *Never* allow a drop of grease to touch it.

If you have an iron griddle, lubricate with a bit of salt pork or ham, rind, leaving just enough grease on the surface to prevent sticking.

Soapstone and iron griddles alike need tempering or seasoning in order to do their work well. They are seldom just right at the first trial. Give them time and handle them patiently.—*The New Home.* Bake griddle cakes till porous and crinkly at the edges.

Many housewives avoid smoke and odour by *never* greasing their griddles at all, preferring to add a little more butter to the batter. Always clear the griddle between each baking.

Those seeking new effects in griddle cakes and waffles will be surprised agreeably by adapting Lake of the Woods Breakfast Food to their favorite recipe.

❖ ❖ ❖

PLAIN GRIDDLE CAKES

½ pint milk
2 eggs
½ teaspoon salt
1 teaspoon butter
2 teaspoons baking powder
Five Roses flour to make batter.

GRIDDLE CAKES WITH BREAD CRUMBS
(*Eggless*)

Cover bread crumbs with sour milk, and let soak until a pulpy mass.
1 cup soaked bread crumbs
1 cup *Five Roses* flour
1 teaspoon salt
1 teaspoon soda
Cold water to make thin batter.

Sift the flour, salt and soda into the bread crumbs. Add water gradually and beat well. Pour by spoonfuls on a slightly greased pan. When lightly browned on one side, turn and cook on the other. Serve in hot dish.

BUCKWHEAT GRIDDLE CAKES

1 cup *Five Roses* flour
1 cup buckwheat
½ cup sugar
½ teaspoon salt
2 teaspoons baking powder
¼ cup butter (melted)
1½ cups sweet milk.

GRIDDLE CAKES WITH BUTTERMILK
No. 1

2 cups *Five Roses* flour (see note)
½ teaspoon salt
1 teaspoon soda (level).
1¾ cups sour milk or buttermilk
1 tablespoon melted butter
1 tablespoon sugar.

Bake on good hot griddle and turn over.

Note—If the buttermilk is thick, measure the flour scant; if it is thin, let the measure be generous.

[Griddle Cakes and Waffles]

GRIDDLE CAKES WITH BUTTERMILK
No. 2

3 cups buttermilk
2 cups cream (not very thick)
5 eggs (1 egg to each cup)
2 teaspoons (rounded) cream of tartar
2 teaspoons (heaping) bicarbonate of soda
1 teaspoon salt
Flavor with nutmeg
Five Roses.

Bake on a smooth hot greased griddle. Use judgment in the use of soda; it depends on how sour the buttermilk is. If cakes are soggy or sticky, put in a little more flour or soda, or both. If cakes are too thick, add a little milk.

PLAIN WAFFLES

2 cups *Five Roses* flour
2 cups milk
$\frac{1}{2}$ cup melted butter
2 teaspoons sugar
2 teaspoons baking powder
1 teaspoon salt
2 eggs (beaten separately).
Have waffle iron hot and well-greased.

QUICK WAFFLES
(6 Eggs)

2 pints sweet milk
1 cup melted butter
6 eggs (beaten separately)
8 teaspoons (level) baking powder
Five Roses flour.

Mix the milk and butter together, and add enough sifted *Five Roses* flour to make a soft batter. Add the well-beaten yolks, then the beaten whites. Lastly, before baking, add 8 teaspoons baking powder. These are very good with 4 or 5 eggs, but much better as above.

CREAM WAFFLES

3 tablespoons cornstarch
1 cup *Five Roses* flour
1 teaspoon salt
1 pint sour milk
1 egg well (beaten)
1 teaspoon soda.

Stir the cornstarch and flour together until smooth, and add salt. Gradually mix in the sour milk, beaten egg and

small teaspoon of soda dissolved in water. Pour into hot waffle iron.

SOUTHERN WAFFLES

1 egg
1 teaspoon sugar
1 pint sweet milk
2 tablespoons (level) cornmeal
2 tablespoons melted butter
2 teaspoons baking powder
$\frac{1}{2}$ teaspoon salt
Five Roses flour to make thin batter.

Mix butter and sugar thoroughly, add egg and beat well. Then sift the cornmeal, flour, salt, baking powder into the sugar and butter, adding milk as required, using up the flour before the milk. Bake in hot waffle irons and serve at once with butter and syrup.

EGG TOAST
(For Breakfast or Supper)

4 eggs
$\frac{1}{2}$ pint milk
3 tablespoons *Five Roses* flour
Pinch of salt.

Mix the flour in just a little milk so as not to get lumpy. Add salt. Cut the bread in quarter slices and dip in above mixture. Have pan hot, put in butter and let melt until it turns a little brown. Put in bread and fry a golden brown. Turn over and brown. Good for supper instead of potatoes. Use stale bread.

CHEESE TOAST

Cut cheese up fine and mix it with 1 beaten egg, 1 tablespoon butter, $\frac{1}{2}$ cup new milk. Cook till smooth and pour over toast.

POTATO LOAF

3 cups mashed potatoes
1 egg (beaten)
1 cup bread crumbs
$\frac{1}{2}$ cup sweet cream
1 onion (chopped fine)
Pepper
Salt
Sage.

Mix and flavor to taste. Shape into loaf and place in cool spot. Cut into slices, dip in *Five Roses* flour and fry in a little butter.

Not Bleached - Not Blended

PUDDINGS OF ALL KINDS

(For Sauces, Custards, etc., see page 65)

ABOUT BOILED PUDDINGS

BEFORE attempting a boiled pudding, be sure that you have a good mold with a tightly-fitting cover in which to cook it. You may use such a substitute as a bowl with a floured cloth tied over the top, but this may allow the water to enter and ruin your dough. The best substitute for a mold is a lard pail with a top, which may be made more secure by tying it on. Always grease your mold thoroughly—top, bottom, and sides—and leave room for the swelling of the contents. Three hours will be, as a rule, the longest time required for the boiling of a pudding of ordinary size. All boiled puddings should be served as soon as they are cooked.

—Selected.

❖ ❖ ❖

APPLE PUDDING

Pare and slice a few nice cooking apples, and put into a pan to the depth of 2 or 3 inches. Add sugar to taste and any desired flavoring.

Make a batter of 1 cup sweet milk, a small teaspoon salt, 1 egg, 1 teaspoon soda and 2 teaspoons cream of tartar sifted with sufficient *Five Roses* flour to make a batter as stiff as for pound cake. Serve with cream.

Note on Apple Puddings—After paring fruit, drop it in cold water to prevent it changing color through contact with the air.

A good sauce for apple pudding is made by simply boiling good molasses with a little butter and serving hot.

APPLES IN AMBUSH

2 cups *Five Roses* flour.
½ cup butter
1 cup sugar
2 teaspoons baking powder
2 eggs
¾ cup milk
1 teaspoon vanilla
5 large tart apples.

Mix baking powder with the flour. Melt butter and sugar together, and add. Whip the eggs, and then put in milk and vanilla. Beat well as for a cake, but do not have too stiff. Add a little more milk if required.

Peel and cut up the apples, and mix with the batter. Butter a deep pudding dish and bake in a quick oven. Other fruit can be used instead of apples. Serve with any sweet sauce.

APPLE JACK

1 egg
1 cup buttermilk
1 teaspoon soda
Pinch of salt
1 tablespoon lard
Five Roses flour to thicken
Apples.

Cover bottom of pudding dish with apples. Sprinkle with sugar, then put in a layer of batter. Then another layer of apples, sugar and batter. Finish with apples sprinkled with sugar and little bits of butter.

AUSTRALIAN PUDDING

6 ounces *Five Roses* flour
4 ounces suet
4 ounces sugar
4 ounces sultanas
Mixed peel and ginger to taste
1 tablespoon baking soda
½ pint warm milk.

Not Bleached~Not Blended

[*Puddings*]

Mix all dry ingredients together, except the soda which is dissolved in the milk. Add latter to the mixture. Steam two hours.

BAKEWELL PUDDING

¼ pound puff paste (see pastry section)
¼ pound butter
6 ounces sugar
1 ounce almonds (chopped)
Yolks of 5 eggs and white of **1 egg**
Raspberry or strawberry jam.

Cover a dish with thin paste, and over this put a layer of jam (raspberry or strawberry preferred). Put the yolks of 5 eggs into a basin with the white of 1, and beat well. Add the sugar (sifted), butter and the almonds (well pounded). Now beat all together until well mixed. then pour into the dish over the jam. Bake for one hour in moderate oven.

BANANA PUDDING

1 quart milk
2 eggs
2 tablespoons **cornstarch**
1 cup sugar
Pinch of salt
Bananas.

Cook together the milk, eggs, cornstarch, salt and sugar. Color one-third with chocolate and one-third with fruit coloring. Line the bottom of pudding dish with bananas. Pour in the dark part, next the pink, and lastly the white part. Set on ice to get cold, and serve with whipped cream.

BARONCUP PUDDING

¾ pound chopped suet
¾ pound raisins
¾ pound *Five Roses* flour
½ pint milk
½ teaspoon salt

Mix all the dry ingredients and moisten with the milk. Place in buttered bowl, tie down with cloth and steam for four hours Serve with granulated sugar sprinkled over the pudding.

BATTER PUDDING

4 ounces *Five Roses* flour
2 drachms bicarbonate of **soda**
1 egg
A little sugar
Milk to make thin batter.

Mix to a thin batter and bake in a well-buttered tin in a brisk oven for ½ hour. Strew a few currants in the bottom of the tin.

ECONOMICAL BATTER PUDDING

4 tablespoons *Five Roses* flour
½ pint milk
Pinch of salt.

Place the flour and salt in a basin, make a hole in the centre of the flour and pour in half the milk. Work with a spoon, gradually getting the flour all mixed down in the milk. Beat the batter for about 10 minutes, or until a lot of little bubbles rise to the surface. Then add the remainder of the milk. Pour into a shallow, well-greased tin and bake about 20 minutes. If possible, make the batter an hour or two before baking, for the air to get well into it.

Note on Batter Puddings—Batter puddings of all kinds, especially when made with fruit, are more tasty steamed than baked.

BIRDS' NEST PUDDING

Take 8 apples, pare and core, leaving whole. Fill the cores with sugar and a little nutmeg. Place in a pudding dish. Now make a custard of 5 eggs to 1 quart of milk and sweeten to taste. Pour this around the apples, and bake in oven ½ hour. (See Paddy Bundles for slight variation of this recipe.)

BLACK PUDDING

1 egg
1 cup New Orleans molasses
1 cup warm water
1 teaspoon soda (dissolved in a little hot water)
½ teaspoon cinnamon
1 cup seeded raisins
2½ cups *Five Roses* flour
Pinch of salt
Steam 2½ to 3 hours.

SAUCE FOR BLACK PUDDING

For each person allow **1** egg beaten separately. For every **2** eggs allow ½ cup of pulverized sugar. Eggs should be beaten separately, whites and yolks. Add **2** tablespoons melted butter creamed. Beat all together.

BREAD PUDDING

1 cup stale bread crumbs (grated)
1 tablespoon (heaping) butter
½ cup white sugar
3 eggs
1 pint rich milk
Flavoring to taste.

Cream butter and sugar. Add 3 yolks and 1 white well beaten, then the milk and flavoring. Then add the crumbs. Beat well and bake in oven like a custard. To be served with a little sweet cream.

Note—A few shreds of candied orange peel will give a delicious flavor to a bread pudding.

BREAD AND FRUIT PUDDING

(*Old Country Favourite*)

Cut bread in slices of about ½ inch thick, remove the crust and line a pudding basin with the slices. Then place therein a layer of fresh fruit (blackberry, raspberry, currant, plum or other juicy fruit). Sprinkle over a little sugar, and place a slice of bread over alternating layers of fruit and bread sufficient to fill the basin. Tie up in a cloth and boil as usual. Makes an excellent dish served up cold with a coating of whipped white of egg and castor sugar.

BREAD AND BUTTER PUDDING

Butter stale bread (made from *Five Roses* flour). Place a layer of bread and butter in bottom of pudding dish. Strew raisins and currants over this, then lay another layer of bread and butter with another layer of fruit over it. Have bread and butter on top. Make a custard of **2** eggs to 3 cups of milk and ½ cup sugar. Pour this over pudding, and bake in slow oven for 1½ hours.

Note—When using stale bread for puddings, always soak it in *cold* liquid. Bread that has been soaked in cold milk or water will be crumbly and light, whereas if soaked in hot liquid it will be heavy.

BROWN BETTY

Into a buttered dish put a layer of sliced apples. Sprinkle with sugar and cinnamon, **and** cover with soft bread crumbs. Continue this process until the dish is filled, having bread crumbs as top layer. Dot all over with small pieces of butter. Add a few spoonfuls of hot water. Bake in moderate oven until apples are tender. Serve **hot** with vanilla sauce or cream.

CANARY PUDDING

3 eggs
Weight of 3 eggs in sugar
Weight of 2 eggs in *Five Roses* flour
Weight of 1 egg in butter
1 small lemon.

Melt the butter, stir in the sugar **and** add the juice of lemon and grated rind (being careful not to grate any of the inner white rind). Gradually add the flour and lastly the eggs beaten lightly (whites and yolks) separate. Pour in well-greased mould. Cover with lid and plunge into **a** pot of boiling water. Boil for **2** hours. Serve with lemon sauce or fruit sauce.

CARAMEL PUDDING

1 quart milk
1 cup brown sugar
2 tablespoons cornstarch
Pinch of salt
1 egg
Small piece of butter
Vanilla.

Put butter and brown sugar in a pan to brown. In another pan heat the milk, and when hot add the cornstarch dissolved in a little cold milk. Add the browned sugar and the egg. Cook until thick and set aside to cool. Serve with cream.

[*Puddings*]

CARROT PUDDING
No. 1

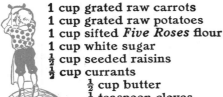

1 cup grated raw carrots
1 cup grated raw potatoes
1 cup sifted *Five Roses* flour
1 cup white sugar
½ cup seeded raisins
½ cup currants
½ cup butter
½ teaspoon cloves
½ teaspoon nutmeg
½ teaspoon cinnamon
1 teaspoon soda in ½ cup grated potato saved till last, and added last of all.

Flour the fruit well and steam 3 hours. Serve with maple syrup sauce.—See Pudding Sauces, page 65.

CARROT PUDDING
No. 2

1⅓ cups *Five Roses* flour
1 cup brown sugar
1 cup beef suet
1 cup stoned raisins
1 cup currants
1 cup grated raw potatoes
1 cup grated raw carrots
1 teaspoon soda.
Steam or boil for 3 hours.

ONE-EGG CARROT PUDDING

1 cup sugar
½ cup butter
1 cup grated carrots (raw)
1 cup grated potatoes (raw)
1 cup currants
1 cup raisins
1 egg
Pinch of salt
1 teaspoon soda
2 cups *Five Roses* flour.
Steam 3 hours. One cup molasses may be added to above.

CHICKEN PUDDING

4 cups *Five Roses* flour
2 teaspoons (large) baking powder
1 cup shortening
Salt to taste.
Shortening may be lard or butter, or half and half.

Wet and flour pudding cloth. Set in a deep dish to keep its shape. Put plate on bottom. Roll paste to thickness of about half an inch. Line cloth with it and fill paste with chicken cut small. Sprinkle with flour, pepper and salt to taste. Add a piece of butter the size of an egg. Tie up tight in cloth. Drop into boiling water, and keep boiling for 2½ hours. When done take pudding out of cloth and set on platter. Cut a round piece out of top, fill with water boiled in, loosen up chicken and serve. Fit for a king.
—*Mrs. H. Haryett, Fort Stewart, Ont.*

CHOCOLATE PUDDING

1 cup *Five Roses* flour
Pinch of salt
1 teaspoon baking powder
1 egg (beaten light)
2 tablespoons sugar
Butter, size of a walnut (melted)
½ cup milk
1¼ squares melted chocolate.
Stir all together. Add flour. Butter tin and steam 1 hour. Serve with sauce or whipped cream.

CHOCOLATE BREAD PUDDING

1 cup stale bread crumbs.
2 cups milk
1 tablespoon (heaping) butter
1 tablespoon (heaping) grated chocolate
½ cup sugar
1 teaspoon vanilla
3 eggs (beaten separately).
Put on fire and heat to boiling point the bread crumbs and milk; then add butter, grated chocolate, sugar and flavoring. Take from fire and cool. Stir in the beaten yolks and, lastly, fold in the stiff whites. Put in a buttered dish and bake. Serve with cream.

CHRISTMAS PUDDING
(*Old English Recipe*)

2 pounds bread crumbs
1 pound *Five Roses* flour (sifted)
1 teaspoon baking powder
1½ pounds beef suet (chopped finely)
1 pound currants
1½ pounds stoned raisins

[*Puddings*]

1 pound brown sugar
1 teaspoon allspice
½ pound ground ginger
1 ounce chopped almonds
¼ pound mixed peel
7 eggs
1 tablespoon syrup
½ teaspoon lemon essence
¼ cup brandy (or wine)
Milk to moisten dry ingredients.

More eggs may be added if richer pudding is desired. Mix dry ingredients in order given and let stand over night. In the morning, put into individual moulds (if so desired) and steam 8 hours, or even more. When about to be eaten, steam a couple of hours more, decorate with greens, pour over with a little cognac brandy and bring to the table blazing. Wine sauce is usually served with this pudding, although other sauces are often used. (See Pudding Sauces.)

CHRISTMAS PUDDING
No. 2

2 eggs
1½ cups currants
1½ cups raisins
1½ cups suet
½ cup sugar
1 cup molasses
½ cup milk
4 cups *Five Roses* flour
1 teaspoon soda
1 teaspoon cream of tartar
1 teaspoon mixed spice.

Boil or steam 3 hours. Sauce to taste.

CHRISTMAS PUDDING
No. 3

7 cups *Five Roses* flour
1 cup ground suet
1 cup sugar (white)
1 cup molasses
2 cups raisins
1½ cups currants
½ cup lemon peel
3 eggs
3 teaspoons (heaping) cream of tartar
4 teaspoons (heaping) soda
3 teaspoons (heaping) ginger
2 teaspoons salt
2 teaspoons lemon extract
Nutmeg and cinnamon to taste.

Steam 3 hours. Serve with any desired pudding sauce.

Note—See also plum puddings for further Christmas puddings.

GREEN CORN PUDDING

Grate the corn from the cobs, and put 1 cupful in a deep buttered baking dish. Cover this with milk, sprinkle in a little pepper and salt, add 1 tablespoon of butter and set in the oven for ½ hour. Now take out and stir in 1 egg well-beaten and return to oven, leaving it only until the custard has set. A few minutes will suffice. This is a delicious accompaniment to a meat course. What is left over can be warmed for breakfast by putting in a saucepan with a little butter and milk and stirring until it is smoking hot.

COTTAGE PUDDING

1 cup sugar
1 cup sweet milk
1 egg
Butter, size of a small egg
1½ cups *Five Roses* flour
2 teaspoons cream of tartar
1 teaspoon soda
Pinch of salt
1½ cups of any kind of fresh fruit.

Cream butter and sugar, add egg well-beaten. Beat well. Add flour and cream of tartar previously sifted together. Dissolve the soda in the milk. Add salt. Pour milk into dish just at side. Beat well. Into a pudding dish well buttered put a layer of batter, then a layer of fruit until all has been used up. Have batter on top. Serve with sweetened cream flavored to taste, or with cornstarch sauce. (See Sauces.)

COTTAGE PUDDING
(*Eggless*)

1 cup sugar
3 tablespoons melted butter
1 cup milk
2 cups (heaping) *Five Roses* flour
1 teaspoon soda
2 teaspoons cream of tartar

Bake in a pan about ½ hour. Add sliced apples if you like—quite an improvement. Any pudding sauce.

[*Puddings*]

CUP PUDDING

2 eggs
½ cup butter
¾ cup sugar
¾ cup *Five Roses* flour
¾ cup milk
1½ teaspoons baking powder
1 teaspoon extract of lemon
Fruit (fresh or preserved).

Fill cups ½ full of this batter after you have put in a small quantity of preserves. Steam ½ hour. Serve with either cream or sauce.

DATE PUDDING

2 cups bread crumbs
1 cup *Five Roses* flour
½ cup suet (chopped fine)
2 cups dates (chopped)
½ cup sugar
Pinch of salt
2 teaspoons baking powder
2 eggs (well beaten)
Milk to moisten.

Put in well-buttered bowl, and steam from 3 to 6 hours. Serve hot with cream or sweet sauce.

DATE WHIP

Beat stiff the whites of 6 eggs. When half whipped add ½ teaspoon cream of tartar and whip stiff. Add 1 cup sifted granulated sugar, 1 cup stoned and chopped dates, and 1 cup broken English walnuts. Bake in a loaf cake pan in moderately hot oven for ¾ hour. Serve with whipped cream. Can be served hot or cold.

FRUIT PUDDING
No. 1

(*Used by me for many years, and I can vouch for its deliciousness.*)

1 cup *Five Roses* flour
2 cups bread crumbs
½ lb. shredded suet
½ cup brown sugar
¼ pound mixed peel
Juice of 1 lemon
Peel of ½ lemon (shredded fine)
1 teaspoon (heaping) ginger
½ teaspoon cinnamon
½ teaspoon nutmeg
1 teaspoon baking powder
2 eggs (well-beaten).

Mix all dry ingredients together with the eggs, adding a small quantity of milk if too dry. Put in baking powder last. Place in mould or pudding cloth and boil 3 hours. Turn out and sprinkle top with white sugar.
—*Mrs. E. Wright, Holmstead Rd.,*
Langley, B.C.

Note—Always wet and flour well inside of pudding bags.

FRUIT PUDDING
No. 2

Fill a medium sized pudding dish ⅔ full of any raw fruit. Sprinkle slightly with sugar and spread on top the following: 1 egg well beaten, ½ cup sugar, 1 tablespoon butter, ½ cup milk, 1 cup *Five Roses* flour. Bake in moderate oven.

GINGER PUDDING

1 egg
1 cup sugar
⅔ cup sour milk
1 cup raisins
1 teaspoon ginger
2 tablespoons molasses
Butter size of a walnut
1 teaspoon soda
3 cups *Five Roses* flour.
Steam 1 hour.

HERBIE'S PUDDING

1½ cups bread crumbs
1 cup buttermilk
½ cup suet
1 cup sugar
1 cup raisins
1 cup currants
1 tablespoon cinnamon
1 teaspoon soda
1 cup *Five Roses* flour.
Steam 2½ hours.

LIGHT PUDDING

Butter size of an egg
1 cup sugar
2 eggs (small) or 1 large egg
2 cups *Five Roses* flour
2 teaspoons (level) cream of tartar.

1 teaspoon soda
1 cup sweet milk
1 cup raisins (floured).

Steam 1 hour over hot stove. Serve with plain sauce.

MADEIRA PUDDING

2 eggs
Weight of 2 eggs in *Five Roses* flour
Weight of 2 eggs in butter
½ teaspoon baking powder
Pinch of salt
2 tablespoons jam (any kind).

Cream butter and flour together, and work in the eggs. Then add baking powder and salt. Mix in the jam. Butter a mould and fill three parts with the mixture. Steam 1 hour. Serve with sweet sauce.

MAMMA'S FAVORITE PUDDING

(*Molasses*)

1 cup molasses
1 cup suet
1 cup currants and raisins (½ each)
2 teaspoons baking powder
Five Roses flour to make very stiff.

Put in a floured bag and steam constantly for 3 hours.

MAPLE CREAM PUDDING

1 pint milk
2 tablespoons cornstarch
½ teaspoon salt
2 eggs
¾ cup brown sugar.

Heat the milk, and when it comes to a boil thicken with cornstarch and eggs. Brown sugar in frying pan, then add the cream, beating all the time to prevent lumps. When sugar is all dissolved, pour in mould. Serve with whipped cream.

MARMALADE PUDDING

¼ pound *Five Roses* flour
2 ounces moist sugar
2 ounces suet (chopped finely)
3 ounces marmalade
1 egg
1 teaspoon baking powder
1 tablespoon milk.

Mix well together and boil in buttered mould 2½ hours.

[*Puddings*]

OYSTER LOAF

Take a large loaf of Vienna bread and cut off the top crust. Take out all the crumb and rub it up (as for dressing). Season with pepper, salt and butter. A dash of red pepper gives a finer flavor than black or white. Do not have the bread too fresh, as it will not crumb fine. Then take from a quart to three pints of well-drained oysters, putting in a layer of the seasoned crumb first, then a layer of oysters, till all is used up, keeping crumb for the top layer. When all is pressed in, generous pieces of butter are laid on. Replace top crust and bake for 40 minutes in a good oven. Try not to scorch the loaf, as many enjoy the crust. Serve hot with or without green peas and Saratoga chips. You will find this is a good dish for either supper or luncheon.

PADDY BUNDLES

6 tablespoons (heaping) *Five Roses* flour
1 teaspoon baking powder
3 dessertspoons (heaping) butter
Sweet milk (or cold water) to make soft dough.

Cut in 4 pieces. Do not roll, but on each piece put a peeled apple with core removed. With floured hands work the dough up around the apple. Fill the hole with sugar, butter and a couple of cloves. Work the dough right up over the hole. Brush over with sweet milk. Place in a pan, adding a little sweetened water. Bake 40 minutes. Serve with cream and sugar or the sauce in which they were cooked.

PINEAPPLE TAPIOCA PUDDING

¾ cup tapioca soaked over night in plenty of water. In the morning, drain off the water and add 1 can of pineapple (with syrup) and the juice of 1 lemon, also 1¾ cups sugar and salt to taste. Steam until clear (about 2 hours). Then add beaten whites of 3 eggs while hot. Set out until very cold. Serve with whipped or plain cream sweetened to taste.

[*Puddings*]

POOR MAN'S PUDDING

1 cup *Five Roses* flour
½ teaspoon soda

½ teaspoon cinnamon
½ teaspoon ginger
½ teaspoon allspice
½ teaspoon salt
¼ cup molasses
½ cup sweet milk
½ cup raisins.

Sift all dry ingredients together excepting the raisins. Add molasses, sweet milk and, lastly, the raisins. Steam 3 hours and serve warm with cream.

PLUM PUDDING

No. 1

1 pound *Five Roses* flour
1 pound suet
1 pound raisins
1 pound currants
½ pound bread crumbs
1 cup brown sugar
1 cup molasses
1 cup milk
5 eggs (more eggs may be added)
1 teaspoon soda
½ teaspoon salt
½ teaspoon spices
¼ pound citron
¼ pound orange peel.

Steam 5 hours. Serve hot with sauce.

Note—See Sponge Pudding No. 1 for substitute for the above.

PLUM PUDDING

No. 2

4 eggs
4 cups currants
4 cups raisins
4 cups sugar
1 cup molasses
1 pound chopped suet
1 pound chopped apples
3 cups sour milk
3 teaspoons soda
Spices to taste
Five Roses flour to stiffen.

Pack in a crock.

PLAIN PLUM PUDDING

(*Eggless*)

3 teacups *Five Roses* flour
1 teacup milk
1 teacup molasses
1 teacup chopped suet
1 teacup raisins
2 teaspoons cream of tartar
1 teaspoon soda
1 teaspoon cinnamon
1 teaspoon cloves
1 teaspoon nutmeg.

Boil or steam 3 to 4 hours.

PRUNE PUDDING

Cook prunes and mince. Soften ½ package gelatine in ¼ cup water, and add 1 cup of hot strained juice from the prunes, also 1 cup sugar, ½ cup mixed lemon and orange juice. Cool and add 1 pint whipped cream. Put in mould. May be used for charlotte or cake filling with whipped cream flavoured with almond essence.

RASPBERRY PUDDING

½ pound bread crumbs
3 ounces suet (chopped fine)
6 ounces raspberry jam
4 tablespoons sugar
¾ teaspoon soda
Buttermilk.

Put the soda, bread crumbs and suet into a basin. Add the jam and sufficient buttermilk to moisten (it must not be too moist). Put in a well-greased pudding basin. Cover with greased paper and steam 2 hours. Serve with melted jam for sauce.

RASPBERRY TAPIOCA PUDDING

Put ¾ cup tapioca into a kettle, cover with 4 cups boiling water and cook until transparent. Stir into this 1 pint of fresh berries, adding sugar to taste. Pour into a mould. Serve cold with cream.

QUICK PUDDING

Take dry cake enough to cover the bottom of a small basin. Beat 2 eggs in a bowl with **2 tablespoons** of sugar, a little salt and nutmeg. Fill up the bowl with sweet milk and turn over the cake. Put in oven just long enough to set the custard and it is ready to serve.

RICE PUDDING

3 tablespoons rice
1 pint milk
1 cup water
Butter size of an egg
$\frac{1}{2}$ cup sugar
$\frac{1}{2}$ teaspoon cinnamon (or nutmeg)
Pinch of salt.

Note—Raisins may be added.

Put in oven and bake 2 hours—don't disturb the rice. Take out and on top spread an icing made as follows:

ICING

2 eggs (whites)
1 cup sugar
1 cup raisins (chopped).

Put in oven to brown. Before putting the icing on top, remove the brown that forms over the rice.

ROLY-POLY

3 cups *Five Roses* flour
2 teaspoons baking powder
1 cup suet
$\frac{1}{2}$ teaspoon salt
Sweet milk to mix
Raspberry jam.

Mix with sweet milk and roll out. Spread with raspberry jam, roll in a cloth and steam 3 hours. Serve with sauce or cream and sugar.

ENGLISH ROLY-POLY

1 cup beef suet (finely chopped)
3 cups *Five Roses* flour
1 tablespoon sugar
Pinch of salt.

Mix salt into the dough, and roll out $\frac{1}{2}$ inch thick. Spread black currant preserves on the dough, roll up, tie in a cloth and boil $1\frac{1}{2}$ hours. Be sure to have the water boiling before putting the pudding in. Serve with sweet sauce.

SPONGE PUDDING

No. 1

1 cup chopped suet
1 cup molasses
1 cup milk
$3\frac{1}{2}$ cups *Five Roses* flour
2 eggs
1 cup raisins
1 cup currants
Citron and spice to taste
1 teaspoon soda (beaten in molasses).

Note—$\frac{1}{2}$ cup butter may be used instead of the suet in above recipe. Steam 3 hours, and serve with wine sauce. If suet is used, a pinch of salt should be added. Many prefer this to a plum pudding, because it is not so rich.

SPONGE PUDDING

No. 2

3 eggs
1 cup granulated sugar
1 cup *Five Roses* flour
2 teaspoons baking powder
3 tablespoons hot water.

Make 3 layers.

CUSTARD

1 quart milk
4 eggs
3 tablespoons granulated sugar.

Put between layers and on top. Whip **1 pint** cream for top.

SNOW PUDDING

1 pint boiling water
3 tablespoons cornstarch
2 tablespoons white sugar
Pinch of salt
2 eggs (whites beaten).

Stir cornstarch, boiling water, sugar and salt until it thickens. After it is cooked and while hot add the whites of **2 eggs** beaten to a stiff froth. Cornstarch sauce.

SNOWBALL PUDDING

$\frac{1}{3}$ cup butter
1 cup sugar
$\frac{1}{2}$ cup milk
$2\frac{1}{4}$ cups *Five Roses* flour
$3\frac{1}{2}$ teaspoons baking powder
4 eggs (whites).

Cream butter and add sugar. Cream again until sugar is dissolved, using a

[*Puddings*]

small quantity of hot water. Stir in milk. Sift in the flour and baking powder. Then fold in the stiffly beaten whites of 4 eggs Steam 35 minutes in buttered cups. Serve hot with canned fruit, lemon or chocolate sauce.

BREAD SPONGE PUDDING

2 eggs
1 cup currants (or raisins)
1 cup (small) brown sugar
½ teaspoon cinnamon
1 cup sour milk
1 teaspoon soda
Bread sponge.

Reserve a small bowl of bread sponge after mixing it down in the morning. When ready to make your pudding, chop the dough finely. Beat the eggs. Add all ingredients, also chopped dough. Beat together until smooth. Put in well-buttered dish, and steam.

SUET PUDDING

1 cup sour milk
½ cup molasses
1 cup suet
2 eggs
1 cup fruit
1 teaspoon soda
2 cups *Five Roses* flour.

Steam about 1 hour. Serve with currant and raisin sauce.

SUET PUDDING

(*Eggless*)

½ cup suet (chopped fine)
1½ cups *Five Roses* flour

1 teaspoon (heaping) baking powder
4 tablespoons molasses
½ cup raisins
1 teaspoon cinnamon
1 teaspoon cloves
1 teaspoon allspice
Sweet milk to make stiff batter.

Steam 1½ hours. This pudding is very nice by making it with sour milk and ½ teaspoon baking soda, instead of sweet milk and baking powder.

SUMMER PUDDING

1 quart boiling water
5 tablespoons (heaping) cornstarch
¾ cup granulated sugar
Grated rind and juice of 1 lemon.

Let this stand while you beat the whites of 2 eggs stiff, and add these to the cornstarch mixture.

Now heat 3 cups milk in double boiler until it boils, and then add ½ cup white sugar, the yolks of 2 eggs, 1 heaping tablespoon cornstarch, 1 teaspoon vanilla.

Let these 2 dishes stand until ice cold and serve putting part of the first mixture on dish with a large spoonful of the custard over it.

SUNSHINE PUDDING

Dissolve 5 scant teaspoons gelatine in 2½ cups boiling water, and strain. Beat the whites of 4 eggs with 2 cups granulated sugar, then beat with the gelatine for 15 or 20 minutes. Add 1 teaspoon cold water, a little vanilla, and set away to harden slightly. Very delicious.

SYRUP SPONGE

¼ pound *Five Roses* flour
¼ teaspoon ginger
¼ teaspoon baking soda
2 ounces suet
¼ teacup syrup
¼ teacup milk
1 egg.

Steam 1½ hours, and turn out on a plate. Sprinkle with sugar and pour melted syrup around it.

TOAST PUDDING

Take 3 slices of dry bread and toast to a nice brown, but do not burn. Butter each piece and put in a pudding dish. Make a custard of 4 eggs (reserve whites of 2 for frosting), ½ cup granulated sugar, 1 pint sweet milk, 1 pint water, a pinch of salt, 1 tablespoon vanilla (or ½ teaspoon nutmeg). Pour over toast and bake. When baked, beat well the 2 egg whites with 1 teaspoon sugar and spread over top. Put back in oven till a nice brown. Serve with milk or whipped cream.

Not Bleached~Not Blended

TRIFLE

Fill a glass bowl with a layer of sponge cake. Cover with red currant jelly or raspberry jam, then add more cake. Sprinkle over this a handful of shredded cocoanut and $\frac{1}{2}$ cup chopped nuts. Pour over all a custard made of 1 pint milk, 2 eggs, 2 tablespoons sugar. Boil custard till it thickens, and add a pinch of salt and vanilla. When cold serve with whipped cream.—*N. Hampson, Mount Forest, Ont.*

WHOLE WHEAT PUDDING

$\frac{1}{4}$ cup butter
$\frac{1}{2}$ cup molasses
$\frac{1}{2}$ cup milk
1 egg
$1\frac{1}{2}$ cups whole wheat flour
$\frac{1}{2}$ teaspoon soda
1 teaspoon salt
1 cup raisins (stoned and chopped).

Melt butter, add molasses, milk and well-beaten egg. Add dry ingredients mixed and sifted. Add raisins. Steam in buttered mould $2\frac{1}{2}$ hours. Serve with any pudding sauce.

SALMON LOAF

2 eggs (well beaten)
$\frac{1}{4}$ teaspoon pepper
$\frac{3}{4}$ teaspoon salt
1 cup (small) milk
6 biscuits (rolled fine)
1 can salmon (drained)
Flavour with sage or other flavouring.

Beat well, put in pan and steam 1 hour.

SALMON PUFFS

1 can salmon
2 eggs
3 tablespoons melted butter
2 tablespoons lemon juice
1 cup bread crumbs
Salt and pepper to taste.

Stir all together and put in mould. Steam 1 hour.

SAUCE

1 tablespoon *Five Roses* flour
2 tablespoons butter
1 cup milk
Salt and pepper.

Cook and pour over when ready to serve.

VANILLA SNOW PUDDING

1 cup rice
5 cups salted water.

Boil for 20 minutes, then add $\frac{1}{2}$ cup sweet cream, $\frac{1}{2}$ cup sugar, 1 tablespoon butter, and fold in the stiffly beaten whites of 2 eggs. Flavour with vanilla. Pile on dish and serve cold.

YORKSHIRE PUDDING

No. 1

1 pint milk
6 ounces *Five Roses* flour
2 eggs
$\frac{1}{4}$ teaspoon salt
$\frac{1}{2}$ teaspoon baking powder.

Put the flour in a basin with the salt, and stir in the milk gradually. Beat up the eggs and add to the batter when quite smooth. Allow to stand 2 hours, add the baking powder and pour into a well-greased baking pan. Bake $\frac{1}{2}$ hour.

YORKSHIRE SAVOURY PUDDING

No. 2

3 eggs
5 tablespoons *Five Roses* flour
1 pint milk
1 large onion
Pepper and salt to taste.

Beat the whites of the eggs to a stiff froth. Mix the yolks with the milk, flour and condiments. Lightly mix in the whites and pour into 1 or 2 well-greased pudding tins which have been made hot. Bake 20 minutes. The pudding should not be more than $\frac{3}{8}$ of an inch thick and should be of a nice brown colour.

—*Mrs. Thornton Blakely, Bloomfield, Ont.*

DUMPLINGS

BAKED APPLE DUMPLINGS
No. 1—Eggless
CRUST

4 cups *Five Roses* flour
8 level teaspoons baking powder
1 cup butter
1½ cups milk
Apples
Nutmeg, if desired.

Pare and quarter the apples. Sift flour and baking powder together. Mix in the butter. Add sufficient milk to make a stiff paste. Roll out ¼ inch thick, cut in large round pieces. Put several pieces of apple in each and fold into a ball. Bake in the following syrup:

SYRUP

3 cups water
1 cup sugar
1 tablespoon butter.

Put on stove and let come to a boil. Pour over the dumplings and bake in hot oven.

SAUCE TO SERVE WITH DUMP-LINGS

1½ cups water
½ cup sugar
1 teaspoon (large) cornstarch
Juice of 1 lemon
1 tablespoon butter.

Let come to a boil, and thicken with the cornstarch.

APPLE DUMPLINGS
No. 2—Eggless

Take 3 apples (rather tart), pare, halve and core.

CRUST

2 cups *Five Roses* flour
1 teaspoon (heaping) baking powder
Pinch of salt
2 tablespoons (heaping) fresh lard and butter
Sweet milk to make a dough.

Sift flour, baking powder and salt together. Cut in shortening and stir in milk. Roll to about ¼ inch thick and wrap each half of apple and put in rather deep pan.

SYRUP

4 cups sugar
1 tablespoon *Five Roses* flour
1 tablespoon butter
Nutmeg to taste.

Mix and add 1 quart boiling water, stirring while adding. Pour over the dumplings in pan, and bake ½ to ¾ hour in rather hot oven. Baste dumplings with the sauce when half done and bake a nice brown. Serve with whipped or plain cream.

PLAIN DUMPLINGS

1 teacup milk
1 egg (large)
Pinch of salt
2 tablespoons butter
2 teaspoons baking powder
Five Roses flour to make very stiff batter.

Beat well, and drop a spoonful at a time in boiling hot stew.

APPLE SUGAR DUMPLINGS

Sift an even quart of *Five Roses* flour twice with 1½ teaspoons baking powder, and ½ teaspoon salt. Chop into this a tablespoon cottolene or other fat and one of butter. Mix into a soft dough with 2 cups milk; roll out into a sheet a scant ½ inch thick, and cut into squares about 5 inches each way. Lay in centre of each a large tart apple, pared and cored. Fill space left by coring with sugar, fold the corners together, enveloping the apple, tie up in cheese cloth squares, dipped into hot water, and well floured on the inside. Have ready a pot of boiling water. Drop in the dumplings and cook fast one hour. Dip each for one second in cold water to loosen the cloth, turn out upon a hot dish and eat with hard sauce.—*Selected.*

DUMPLINGS
(*Eggless*)

2 cups *Five Roses* flour
½ teaspoon salt
1 teaspoon soda
2 teaspoons cream of tartar
Cold water to make very stiff batter.

Drop into boiling water and cool 20 minutes without raising lid of kettle.

[*Dumplings*]

LIGHT DUMPLINGS

Four eggs beaten very light. Add a pinch of salt, 6 tablespoons sweet milk or water, 1 teaspoon baking powder, 1 cup *Five Roses* flour, or enough to make a batter thick enough to drop from spoon.

DUMPLINGS WITH ROAST BEEF

Take beef out of dripping pan. Put in water to make about 2 quarts of gravy. Wet about 2 tablespoons *Five Roses* flour and put in dripping pan. Take 2 eggs, ¾ cup milk or water, pinch of salt, baking powder (1 teaspoon per cup of flour) and *Five Roses* enough to make a stiff batter. Drop by spoonfuls in the gravy and boil

15 to 20 minutes, or till done. Arrange neatly around meat on platter. Serve with plenty of gravy.

DUMPLINGS WITH STEWS

Ten minutes before the stew is done, put half a pint of flour into a bowl, add ½ teaspoon salt and a teaspoon baking powder; sift, and add sufficient milk just to moisten. Drop by spoonfuls on top of the stew; cover and cook 10 minutes without lifting the lid. Dish the dumplings around the edge of the platter, fill the stew into the centre, and serve.

—*Selected.*

◇ ◇ ◇

PUDDING SAUCES
CREAMS—CUSTARDS—DESSERTS

(*Measurements level unless otherwise specified*)

PLAIN SAUCE

1 cup sugar
1 tablespoon *Five Roses* flour
Water (about 1 pint—boiling)
Pinch of salt
2 tablespoons butter
Nutmeg or lemon.

Mix sugar, flour and salt with a little water. Over this pour the pint of boiling water and let boil a few minutes. Just before removing, add the butter, then the flavouring. Wine or vinegar is sometimes added to season.

BANANA SALAD

Cut bananas in half crosswise, roll in white of egg, then in finely chopped walnuts. Serve with following dressing: ¾ cup milk, 1 tablespoon sugar, 2 small tablespoons *Five Roses* flour, ½ cup vinegar. After it is cooked, add a small lump of butter, ½ teaspoon salt and 8 walnuts rolled fine.

BREAD SAUCE

Sufficient bread crumbs to fill a small tureen, ½ pint milk, 1 small onion, cayenne or white pepper and salt. Peel the onion and put it with mace into the milk, in which boil for a few minutes till the milk is flavoured. Then remove, put in the crumbs and seasoning and serve hot.

CARAMEL SAUCE

Burn 1 cup sugar in the spider, stirring all the time. Then add 1 pint hot milk and 2 tablespoons cornstarch stirred together, also ½ cup hickory nutmeats.

CHOCOLATE SAUCE NO. 1

2 tablespoons butter
1 tablespoon *Five Roses* flour
Pinch of salt
1 cup boiling water
1 square chocolate
4 tablespoons sugar
1 teaspoon vanilla

[*Pudding Sauces*]

Melt butter in saucepan, add dry flour and salt. Mix until smooth, then add slowly the hot water, beating well. Add the square of chocolate and sugar, and stir until melted. Add vanilla just before serving.

CHOCOLATE SAUCE NO. 2

1 pint milk
Yolks of 2 eggs
½ cup sugar
1 square chocolate

Put the milk to scald in top of double boiler, and add chocolate and sugar. Beat eggs till light and pour over them the scalded milk. Return to boiler and cook till it thickens and coats the spoon, stirring constantly. Serve hot.

MILK CHOCOLATE

1 cup rich milk
4 teaspoons cocoa or grated chocolate.
1 tablespoon butter
2 cups granulated sugar
1 teaspoon vanilla extract

Mix well together milk, sugar and cocoa, and boil until a small quantity stirred in a saucer becomes a creamy substance. Remove from the fire and add a tablespoon good butter and a teaspoon vanilla. Beat thoroughly until cool, and pour into a pie tin.

CORNSTARCH SAUCE NO. 1

2 cups boiling water
¾ cup sugar
Butter size of walnut
2 heaping teaspoons cornstarch
Pinch of salt.

CORNSTARCH SAUCE NO. 2

1 cup sweet milk
1 teaspoon cornstarch
3 teaspoons white sugar
2 eggs (yolks only)

Stir until cooked, then add the yolks of the 2 eggs. After it is cooked and while it is hot, add vanilla and other flavouring.

ECLAIR CUSTARD

1 ounce sugar
1½ gills milk
½ ounce ground almonds
2 eggs (yolks)
½ ounce corn flour
Grated lemon rind

Mix the corn flour with a half gill cold water to a smooth paste. Boil remainder of milk and add to mixture. Returning to saucepan, stir till it becomes thick, then add almonds and lemon rind. Use cold.

ORANGE CUSTARD

Strain the juice of 5 oranges and sweeten with powdered loaf sugar. Stir it over the fire until quite hot, then remove and allow to cool. When nearly cold, add the well-beaten yolks of 5 eggs, ½ pint milk and a few drops of ratafia. Put the whole into a saucepan and stir over a clear fire until it thickens. Pour into custard glasses and serve cold.

FRUIT SAUCE

1 cup raisins and currants (chopped finely)
1¼ cups boiling water
1 cup sugar
½ cup butter
Vanilla

Bring to a boil and flavor with vanilla. Any fruit may be used in above recipe instead of raisins and currants.

A nice fruit sauce is made by melting a glass of quince jelly, to which add the same quantity of water and a little butter, also a pinch of cinnamon.

FRUIT JUICE SAUCE

Take ½ pint of any kind of fruit juice (apricot, peach, etc.) and add 1 teaspoon *Five Roses* flour and ½ cup sugar. Mix well, boil 5 minutes and strain.

HARD SAUCE

½ cup butter
1 cup sugar (fruit sugar)

Cream together and flavor to taste. Keep cold.

Not Bleached - Not Blended

LEMON SAUCE

1 lemon
1 cup sugar
4 tablespoons water
4 teaspoons cornstarch
1 tablespoon butter.

Boil sugar, then add cornstarch and butter, lastly the lemon, also grated rind. Serve at once. Vinegar is sometimes added to season.

GERMAN SAUCE

To the whites of 2 eggs add the juice of 1 lemon and sugar enough to beat up to a proper consistency for serving.

HOW TO PEEL LEMONS

Peel with a sharp knife clear to the white skin before putting in squeezer. The work is easier and more juice is thereby obtained.

MAPLE SYRUP SAUCE

1 tablespoon melted butter
1 tablespoon (heaping) *Five Roses* flour
$\frac{1}{2}$ cup brown sugar
$\frac{1}{2}$ cup maple syrup
2 cups boiling water.

Boil till clear.

RHUBARB SAUCE

4 pounds rhubarb (cut in squares)
2 pounds brown sugar
$\frac{1}{4}$ cup vinegar
1 teaspoon cinnamon
1 teaspoon cloves
1 teaspoon allspice
1 teaspoon salt
Red pepper to taste.

SPANISH CREAM

$\frac{1}{4}$ package gelatine
2 eggs
4 tablespoons sugar
1 pint milk
1 teaspoon vanilla.

Soak gelatine in milk, put on fire and stir until dissolved. Add yolks of eggs well beaten with 2 tablespoons sugar. Stir until it reaches boiling point. Re-move from stove. Have whites of eggs beaten stiff with 2 tablespoons sugar and add to mixture. stirring briskly until well mixed. Flavour and turn into mould. Serve with whipped cream or custard sauce.

TAPIOCA CREAM

Soak 1 cup tapioca over night in 2 cups milk, then add 4 cups milk. Boil till clear, then add salt, yolks of 4 eggs, 1 cup sugar, vanilla flavour to taste. Bake in oven. When done, spread whites of eggs beaten stiff with $\frac{1}{2}$ cup sugar on top and brown.

WINE SAUCE NO. 1

1 pint white sugar
$\frac{1}{4}$ pound (scant) butter
1 glass wine
1 nutmeg
1 tablespoon warm water.

Beat steadily for $\frac{1}{2}$ hour. Put sauce-pan on fire with about a gill of water in it. When it boils, put in sugar, etc., but do not stir or let boil. Let simmer gently until all is dissolved. Pour into tureen and let get cold.

WINE SAUCE NO. 2

2 cups white sugar
2 eggs
Butter size of egg
$\frac{1}{2}$ cup wine
2 tablespoons sweet cream.

Beat sugar, eggs and butter to a cream. Add wine and sweet cream, and it is ready for use. Vanilla is sometimes added.

MOCK MAPLE SYRUP

Take 2 quarts very small potatoes. Wash very clean, without breaking skins. Cover with water and boil till done, but be sure to drain before the potatoes break. Take 1 cup sugar to every one of potato water and boil 15 minutes. Season with vanilla.

[*Pudding Sauces*]

PUMPKIN SYRUP

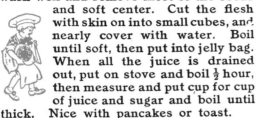

Take **1** good-sized pumpkin (ripe), wash well and remove most of the seeds and soft center. Cut the flesh with skin on into small cubes, and nearly cover with water. Boil until soft, then put into jelly bag. When all the juice is drained out, put on stove and boil ½ hour, then measure and put cup for cup of juice and sugar and boil until thick. Nice with pancakes or toast.

MAPLE MOUSSE

1 cup maple syrup
1 pint whipped cream
Yolks of 4 eggs (or 2 whole eggs)

Boil the syrup and pour it over the well-beaten eggs. When cold, add the whipped cream. Pour into mould and set on ice for 3 or 4 hours.

ORANGE FLOAT

1 quart water
Juice of 2 lemons
1 cup sugar
4 tablespoons cornstarch
Oranges

Boil the water, lemon juice and sugar. While boiling, add the cornstarch and boil for 15 minutes. When cool, pour it over 5 sliced oranges. Spread meringue over top.

RASPBERRY CROWN

2 tablespoons water
2 tablespoons cornstarch
1 cup boiling raspberry juice
1 egg
Pinch of salt
Lemon extract

Cook until creamy. Put into mould. When cold, serve with raspberries or whipped cream.

RED CURRANT SNOW

2 cups boiling water
1 cup sugar
2 tablespoons cornstarch
2 eggs (whites)

When cooked thick, remove from fire and add the juice of 2 cups red currants crushed and pressed through a colander. Beat the whites of 2 eggs, add a little sugar and pour over all.

Raspberries, strawberries and other fruits can be treated in the same way. This recipe came from Women's Institute Branch of Department of Agriculture.

APPLE SNOW

Take 2 cups of apple sauce cooked as dry as possible. Press through sieve and sweeten. Add the white of 1 egg beaten stiff, and beat briskly. Heap in a dish and heap whipped cream around it or boiled custard.

CHEESE ENTREE

1 tablespoon butter
1 tablespoon *Five Roses* flour
1 cup cream
Salt and pepper
3 eggs (beaten separately)
1 cup grated cheese

Put the butter into saucepan on the stove and stir in the flour, cream or milk, salt and pepper to taste. Beat the yolks and grated cheese and add to mixture. When it is cool, add the whites beaten to a stiff froth. Bake about 20 minutes in quite hot oven. Serve hot. May be served in individual dishes.

LEMON FOAM

2 cups hot water
1 cup sugar
2 tablespoons (rounding) cornstarch
1 lemon
3 eggs (whites)

Put the hot water and sugar into double boiler or saucepan. When it boils, add the cornstarch moistened with a little cold water and stir. After cooking 4 or 5 minutes, squeeze in the juice of 1 lemon (or lemon extract) stirring steadily. Now whip to a stiff froth with wire spoon the whites of 3 eggs in a large earthen dish. By this time the cooked cornstarch, which has been stirred constantly, is cool enough to be poured over the egg whites. Beat rapidly, and in a

Not Bleached - Not Blended

few minutes the whole mass will be light and foamy and ready to be set away to cool. The colder it can be kept the better. Serve with custard. Very good as summer dessert.

CHARLOTTE RUSSE

Make a custard of ½ pint milk and 3 eggs, adding a pinch of salt. When cold, dissolve nearly half a package jello (or like product) in a little boiling water and stir in the custard. Sweeten, flavour and whip 1 pint cream and stir in custard. Pineapple or lemon flavouring.

COCOANUT SOUFFLE

1 cup milk
Pinch of salt
3 tablespoons *Five Roses* flour
2 tablespoons butter
4 eggs
4 tablespoons sugar
1 teaspoon vanilla
1 cup shredded cocoanut

[Pudding Sauces]

Heat the milk, add salt and flour (which has been softened in a little milk) and cook 10 minutes after it has thickened. Mix together butter, sugar and yolks of eggs. Pour hot mixture over, stirring well, and set aside to cool. Add vanilla and cocoanut. Lastly, fold in the stiffly beaten whites. Bake in buttered pan in moderate oven till firm. Serve with hot chocolate sauce No. 1.

OMELET SOUFFLE

Yolks of 7 eggs
Whites of 8 eggs
¼ pound sugar
2 dessertspoons *Five Roses* flour
Vanilla extract
Pinch of salt

Beat the yolks with the flour rubbed smooth in a spoonful of milk. Add sugar, vanilla and pinch of salt. Beat all well together and stir in lightly egg whites whisked very stiff. Put souffle in centre of a dish and bake in moderate oven 15 minutes. When done, sift over with sugar and serve quickly.

◇ ◇ ◇

*Y*OUR hands are the first that touch *Five Roses* flour. From the sun-flooded prairie lands of Western Canada, through the eighty elevators of the Lake of the Woods, cleaned, scoured, ground gradually by modern process, bolted many times through silk, packed automatically into absolutely new full-weight bags and barrels—*Five Roses* comes to particular housewives immaculate, untouched by human hands. Where else can you get so pure a flour?

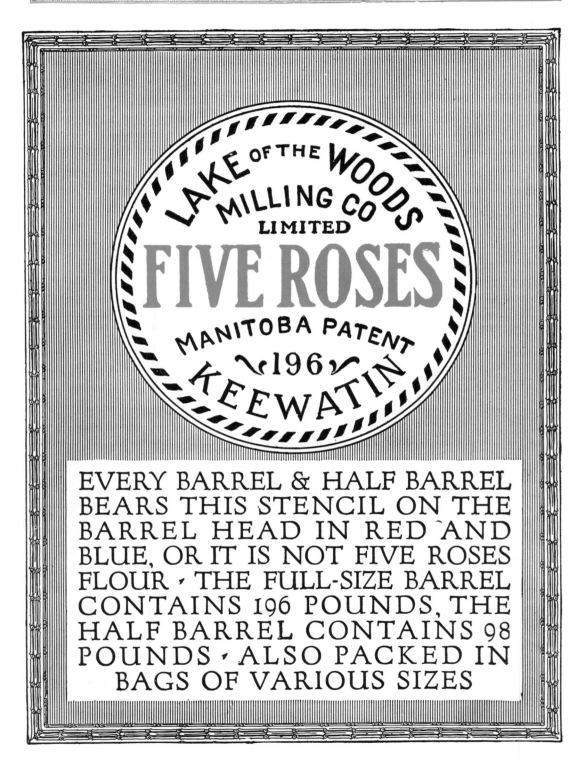

LAKE OF THE WOODS MILLING CO LIMITED

FIVE ROSES

MANITOBA PATENT ~196~

KEEWATIN

EVERY BARREL & HALF BARREL BEARS THIS STENCIL ON THE BARREL HEAD IN RED AND BLUE, OR IT IS NOT FIVE ROSES FLOUR · THE FULL-SIZE BARREL CONTAINS 196 POUNDS, THE HALF BARREL CONTAINS 98 POUNDS · ALSO PACKED IN BAGS OF VARIOUS SIZES

Not Bleached - Not Blended

PASTRY BAKING AND CRUST MAKING

Specially prepared for the Five Roses Cook Book

PERFECT PASTE requires few ingredients: flour, fat, water and COLD. The last is *not* the least important. Everything connected with the making of pastry should be thoroughly chilled, even the board and rolling-pin should be clean, smooth and cool. If, however, the housewife can work in a very cool temperature, it will save a lot of troublesome chilling of materials.

Unless the hands are cool and dry, the shortening should not be rubbed into the flour, not even with the tips of the fingers. A flexible, broad-bladed knife should be used for cutting and rubbing in the fat and mixing in the paste with the ice water. Handle paste as little as possible.

The shortening may be butter or lard, or half and half, or any of the vegetable shortening compounds now on the market. Of course, nothing can replace the flavor or texture obtainable from the use of the best butter, but economy and convenience are often factors requiring attention. Beef suet, dripping, meat fats are also used.

Keep your shortening firm and dry—butter that has been mellowed by heat loses strength, and the paste cannot spring and puff in the oven as it should. One very useful pointer in making puff paste is to have the dough of the same consistency as the butter, so that in summer it is necessary to have it much softer than in winter.

Too much water toughens pastry, fat makes it tender; therefore fat rather than water should predominate in the mixture. Use only sufficient water to hold it together. It should be a smooth, dry mass easily lifted from the bowl; if it sticks or adheres at any point, too much water has been added.

Sprinkle board and rolling pin with flour and roll lightly and evenly from front to back of board, then lift roller and begin again. Rolling in one direction and then in another is sure to toughen the paste.

Sometimes, as will be seen from the various recipes given in the following pages, a little baking powder is added to make the crust lighter, some sugar to improve the color, lemon juice to season slightly, white of egg to improve the texture, or yolk of egg to give it a golden hue or gloss the outside surfaces. If the butter has been washed free of salt, a little of the latter is sometimes added. These, however, are merely tricks of the trade and not essential to a well-made paste.

MIXING AND BAKING

It is preferable to mix pastry several hours before it is to be rolled out. Keep on ice until required. Before baking, pastry will likewise improve considerably if set aside for some time in a cool place. The basic idea of good pastry is COLD. In folding the fat over and over again considerable air is enclosed between the various layers. If everything is as cold as possible, the air in the dough will be chilled, and the colder that is the more it will expand when heated. This lifts up the greased layers of crust, then the heat penetrates and cooks the moistened flour.

Often a crust is so thick that it is not readily baked. One-eighth to one-fourth of an inch is quite thick enough. Heat the oven for some time before baking the paste. An oven that has just baked a batch of bread is hot enough to bake puff paste. The

[*Pastry Baking and Crust Making*]

heat should be greater at first in order to puff the layers well, and then reduced slightly to thoroughly bake the paste. All paste should be thoroughly baked, even colored—it is more digestible and crisp when over-baked than when under-baked. To prevent pastry from burning while baking, a pan of water may be set in the oven.

The pastry recipes in the *Five Roses* cook book have all been thoroughly checked by an expert in that line. Sufficient variety is offered to please any taste and condition.

Measurements are level, unless otherwise specified. Always sift the flour.

◆ ◆ ◆

SHORT PASTRY

1 pound *Five Roses* flour
½ pound shortening
Ice-cold water

Mix flour and shortening into dough with ice-cold water, using only enough to hold it together. It should be so dry that it will not stick to the bowl anywhere. Turn out on board, and knead only enough to make the ball smooth. It is then ready to put into pie plates. The quantity of shortening is lessened for plainer pastry.

SHORT PIE CRUST

1 pound *Five Roses* flour
¼ pound butter
¼ pound lard
2 ounces fine sugar
1 teaspoon (small) **salt**
1 Egg
2 teaspoons baking powder
Water.

Sift flour, sugar, salt and baking powder together. Rub butter and lard lightly into the flour, etc. Beat the egg and add sufficient water to mix. This pastry will keep good for a fortnight at least.

RICH SHORT PASTRY

(*For Tarts, Etc.*)

4 cups *Five Roses* flour
½ teaspoon baking powder
¼ teaspoon salt
½ cup butter
½ cup lard
Cold water to make stiff paste.

Mix all dry ingredients together in a bowl. Rub in butter and lard with the tips of the fingers until as fine as bread crumbs. About 3 tablespoons of water or cream are sufficient. The yolk of an egg added with the water improves the colour.

RICH SHORT CRUST

8 ounces *Five Roses* flour
5 ounces butter
1 egg (yolk)
Few drops lemon juice.

Sift the flour, rub the butter in lightly and quickly. Make a well in the centre, into which put the egg yolk, lemon juice and a few drops of water. Mix lightly, roll out once and it is ready for use.

PLAIN PASTRY

(*Contributed by a Confectioner's Daughter*)

1 pound *Five Roses* flour
¼ pound butter
½ pound lard
(Little more flour for rolling pin and board)
Cold water.

Work lard through flour with fingers. Use enough cold water to stick paste together, then turn out on board. Roll with rolling pin and spread on the butter a little at a time. Then fold over and roll again, repeating this process until all the butter is used up. If richer pastry is desired, use ½ pound of butter.

FLAKY PIE CRUST

Rub 1½ cups lard into 3 cups *Five Roses* flour, add a pinch of salt. Beat the white of 1 egg slightly. Add 5 tablespoons water to it and mix with the other ingredients into a soft dough. Do not mix more than necessary and do not use a lot of flour on the working board in making the dough, and the crust will be light and flaky.

PUFF PASTE

To every pound of *Five Roses* flour, allow 3 ounces butter and 3 ounces lard, and not quite ½ pint water.

Sift the flour and see that it is perfectly dry. Work the materials into a smooth paste, using a knife to mix with. Roll out to an equal thickness of about 1 inch. Break about 4 ounces more butter into small pieces and place on the paste. Sift over a little flour, fold it over and roll out again. Repeat the rolling and buttering until the paste has been rolled 4 times. Handle the paste as lightly as possible. Brushing the paste as often as rolled out and the pieces of butter placed therein with the white of an egg assist it to rise in leaves or flakes.

Note on Puff Paste—For the richest puff pastry, all butter is preferred by the best cooks—equal weights shortening and *Five Roses* flour.

ROUGH PUFF PASTRY

8 ounces *Five Roses* flour
6 ounces butter
½ teaspoon lemon juice
Pinch of salt
Cold water.

Chop the butter in the flour, not too fine, leaving it in pieces the size of a walnut. Make a pit in the centre, put in the lemon juice, sprinkle salt over. Mix rather more than a tablespoon of water slowly and lightly into the flour and butter, adding more water if necessary till it is a stiff paste. Roll out in long strips and fold in three, turning rough edges to right hand. Repeat this until it has been rolled four times.

NEW PIE CRUST

Scald 2 parts of fine oatmeal with 1 part of hot water. Mix well and roll fairly

[Pastry Baking and Crust Making]

thin. This bakes very quickly, so if using fruit which requires much cooking cook the fruit first. This crust is very tender and possesses the qualities of good short crust, and is healthier.

FARMERS' PIE CRUST

1 pint *Five Roses* flour
¾ cup butter or lard
1 cup buttermilk
1 teaspoon soda
1 teaspoon salt.

PASTRY FOR ONE PIE

½ cup lard and butter (mixed)
1½ cups *Five Roses* flour
3 tablespoons water
Pinch of salt.
    Roll thin.

YORKSHIRE THIN CAKES

½ pound light bread dough
½ pound *Five Roses* flour
½ pound pure lard, or butter, or both mixed.

Knead well, and let stand an hour or two. Roll out and cut into shapes with biscuit cutter or empty baking powder tin. The above makes an excellent crust for tarts, mince pies, etc., and is always fresh as if newly baked after being put into a hot oven for a few minutes.

USING UP LEFT-OVER PIE DOUGH

Cut into thin strips about 1 inch wide, sprinkle with butter, sugar and cinnamon, roll up like jelly roll, and bake a light brown.

◇ ◇ ◇

WELL-MADE bread or pastry baked from *Five Roses* flour possesses excellent keeping qualities. It surely is a great convenience and quite a saving in both fuel and labor to bake only once a week instead of twice. None but *Five Roses* flour has *so many* desirable features.

TARTS, PUFFS AND PATTIES

HOW TO MAKE PATTY CASES

(Adopted from "Gold Medal Cook Book")

Use puff paste for which recipe is given elsewhere. To shape the paste, roll to about ¼ inch in thickness and stamp out with 2¼ inch cutter twice as many pieces as you wish shells. Cut centres from one-half of them, leaving the rim about ½ inch wide. Lay these rings on the whole rounds, pressing them down that they may stick together. In very cold weather it may be necessary to wet the top of the large rounds near the edge to make sure that the rings will not slip. To make very deep shells, roll the paste about ⅛ inch thick and lay on two rings, or even three, but these are troublesome to make as they are apt to slip to one side. The oven should be as hot as for baking white bread.

Patty shells should rise in 10 minutes then take about 20 minutes longer to bake through and brown. There will usually be a little soft dough in the centre that should be picked out with a fork, taking great care not to break through the side or bottom crust. Large Vol-au-Vent cases should be rolled to the thickness of 1½ inches and may be round or oval in shape. Mark out an inner line about 2½ inches from the edge and with a thin, sharp knife blade (dipped first in hot water) cut from two-thirds to three-quarters of the way through the paste. These are much more difficult to bake than the smaller shells and there is always much uncooked paste to be removed from the centre. The filling gives the name to the dish.

BAKEWELL CHEESE CAKES

Weight of an egg in castor sugar, butter and *Five Roses* flour
Pinch of baking powder
1 egg
¼ teaspoon grated lemon rind
1 tablespoon jam
Rough puff pastry (rule given elsewhere)

Line a dozen small patty pans with rough puff pastry. Put in centre of each ½ teaspoon jam. Beat butter and sugar to cream, add the egg alternately with the flour. Lastly, add the lemon rind and baking powder. Put a teaspoon of this mixture on top of the jam. Bake in moderate oven 15 minutes. Serve with castor sugar sprinkled over. This **quantity will require ½ pound pastry.**

CANADIAN CHEESE CAKES

One pound of curd from scalded sour milk, drain and press dry; ½ pound sugar, ½ pound butter. Beat 8 eggs well. Add juice and grated rind of 2 lemons. Mix thoroughly. Bake in tart shells or in pies with under crust only.

COCOANUT PATTY PANS

2 ounces cocolanka
1 egg
1½ ounces castor sugar
½ pound pastry (short or puff)
1 tablespoon *Five Roses* flour
1½ ounces butter

Line a dozen patty pans, cream the butter and sugar, add the egg and flour. Lastly, add the cocoanut. Put a teaspoon of this mixture into each patty pan, and bake about 15 minutes.

MAIDS OF HONOUR

Line patty tins with nice rich pastry made with *Five Roses* flour.

FILLING

Melt piece of butter size of walnut, and add:

1 cup brown sugar
1 cup currants
1 tablespoon lemon peel
Yolk of 1 egg

LEMON PATTY CAKES

Beat well the yolks of 3 eggs. Add 1 cup white sugar and beat again. Add 1 tablespoon lemon juice and 1 tablespoon cold water, 1 cup *Five Roses* flour, into which 1½ teaspoons baking powder have been sifted, and the whites of the 3 eggs which have been well beaten. Beat all briskly, and bake in patty pans.

MOLASSES CAKES

Two dozen molasses cakes may be made in the following way:

1 cup molasses
1 cup brown sugar
½ cup lard
1 cup buttermilk
2½ cups *Five Roses* flour
2 teaspoons baking soda
2 tablespoons boiling water
1 egg
1 teaspoon ground ginger
1 teaspoon ground cloves
½ teaspoon cinnamon
Pinch of salt

Put molasses, sugar, lard, spices and a pinch of salt in basin to warm. Mix. Add the egg unbroken, also milk. Dissolve the soda in the boiling water and add to other ingredients. Then sift in the flour and beat all ingredients well together in basin. Bake in patty pans in moderate oven for 20 minutes.

OYSTER PATTIES

1 pint small oysters
½ pint sweet cream
1 tablespoon *Five Roses* flour
Pepper and salt to taste

Let cream just come to a boil. Mix flour in a little cold milk, and stir into the hot cream. Add salt and pepper. Let the oysters come to a boil in their own liquor, skim carefully and drain off all the liquor. Add the oysters to the cream and boil up at once. Fill patties.

RICE PATTY PANS

3 ounces ground rice
1½ pints new milk
3 ounces butter
4 ounces sugar
6 eggs (well beaten)
Pinch of salt
Flavor with nutmeg or lemon peel

Boil for 15 minutes the ground rice in the milk. When taken from the fire, stir in the butter and sugar. Add the well-beaten eggs, the salt and flavoring. When the mixture is nearly cold, line some patty-pans with thin puff paste made with *Five Roses* flour, and fill 3 quarters

full. Strew the tops thickly with currants (cleaned) and dried, and bake for 15 minutes or till done.

CREAM PUFFS

1 cup water
½ cup butter
1 cup *Five Roses* flour
3 eggs

Put the water in a granite saucepan to boil. When boiling, add butter and stir in the flour. Let cool. When cold, add the eggs well beaten. Beat all thoroughly and drop on to buttered tins. Bake 20 minutes in quick oven. When cool, slit with sharp knife. These may be filled with the following filling, but the whipped cream is much better.

FILLING

1 cup milk
½ cup sugar
1 egg
½ dessertspoon cornstarch

Boil milk, add sugar and cornstarch, lastly the well-beaten egg. When cool, flavor to taste.

If liked, one may brush the tops with a little beaten egg and milk before putting in oven. When cold, open and fill with whipped cream or custard filling, and dust tops with fine sugar.

GINGER PUFFS

1 cup sugar
½ cup butter
1 cup molasses (teacup)
1 egg
1 tablespoon ginger
Any other spice desired
1 teaspoon salt
1 teaspoon soda
1 cup milk
4 cups *Five Roses* flour

GINGER PUFFS
(*Eggless*)

½ cup butter
1½ cups brown sugar
¾ cup treacle
1 teaspoon ginger

[Tarts, Puffs and Patties]

1 cup sour milk
½ teaspoon soda
1 cup currants (well washed)
Five Roses to make medium stiff batter
    Bake in patty pans in quick oven.

CHOCOLATE ECLAIRS

¼ pint water
4 ounces *Five Roses* flour (sifted)
3 eggs
2 ounces butter
Sugar
Essence of vanilla or lemon
Pinch of salt

    Put the water, butter and salt into a saucepan. When boiling, draw from fire, stir in flour and sugar till it becomes a stiff paste—boil well. Add flavoring and eggs one at a time. Force into finger lengths. Bake in moderate oven to a pale brown. Fill with custard (or whipped cream) and cover with chocolate icing when cold. (See Eclair Custard.)

STRAWBERRY CREAMS

1 cup hot water
½ teaspoon salt
½ cup butter
1½ cups *Five Roses* flour
5 eggs

    Put hot water, salt and butter into a basin, and when boiling work in the flour until smooth. Let cool, and beat in one at a time 5 eggs. Spread into finger forms on tins, and bake in quick oven until light as a feather. Let cool, and cut open tops so as to fill with sweetened whipped cream and strawberries.

BUTTER TARTS

1 egg
1 cup brown sugar
1 cup currants
Butter size of a walnut
Flavor to taste

    Beat all until full of bubbles. Drop from teaspoon into lined patty tin, and bake in quick oven. One cup dates may be added if desired.

COCOANUT TARTS

1 quart milk
1 cup sugar
Yolks of 3 eggs
2 tablespoons cornstarch
¼ pound cocoanut

    Heat milk in double boiler, add other ingredients and stir in the cocoanut. While hot, fill tart shells with this mixture. Beat to a stiff froth the whites of the 3 eggs, in which beat ½ cup cocoanut and ⅓ cup sugar. Spread on tarts and tinge a delicate brown.

CREAM TARTS

1 cup sour cream
1 cup sugar
3 eggs
Flavor with lemon

    Bake in undercrust. Put a few currants on top of each tart, if desired.

MAPLE SYRUP TARTS

2 tablespoons *Five Roses* flour
1 egg (beaten light)
1 cup maple syrup
Butter size of walnut
1 teaspoon vanilla

    Moisten the flour with water. Mix ingredients together, and cook over hot water till slightly thickened. Cool, then pour into tart shells and bake. May be covered with whipped cream or meringue made with white of egg.

SNOWDEN TART

1 cup cornstarch
2 cups *Five Roses* flour
1 cup white sugar
½ cup lard or butter
2 eggs
1 teaspoon baking powder
Stewed apricots

    Mix thoroughly cornstarch, flour, sugar and baking powder. Separate yolks of eggs, beat well, mix with other ingredients, adding milk to make soft dough. Roll about ⅛ inch thick on floured board. Line pie plates, putting in crusts of bread or raw rice to keep in shape. Bake in moderate oven.

Meanwhile, beat up the whites of eggs to a stiff froth with a little sugar. Take out crusts and fill with stewed apricots. Then fill in roughly the beaten whites on top of fruit. Return to oven for a minute or two to set.

MACAROON TARTLETS

3 eggs (whites)
2 ounces castor sugar
2 ounces ground almonds
Pinch of salt.

Line 10 patty pans with short crust. Whip whites to a stiff froth, add castor sugar and almonds gradually. Fill prepared patty pans with mixture. Bake about 15 minutes.

FAIRY CREAMS

Line patty pans with good paste. Fill half full with red raspberries, fresh or preserved. Sprinkle on each a pinch of sugar and *Five Roses* flour. Bake and let cool. Before serving heap full with whipped cream. These are delicious.

—*Miss Nellie Barclay,*
Thamesville, Ont.

CREAM SLICES

Roll down some puff paste—preferably scraps—and cut into strips about 4 inches in width. Run over with a fork and let stand on the baking tins for a time, then bake in fairly quick oven.

[*Tarts, Puffs and Patties*]

When baked spread boiled custard over each strip, put 2 together and cover with "fondant" or water icing. Fondant is the best and smoothest eating. When thoroughly set, cut up into strips about 1 inch wide.

TART PASTE
(*Eggless*)

3 cups *Five Roses* flour
$\frac{2}{3}$ cup lard
1 tablespoon sugar
1 cup milk
$\frac{1}{2}$ teaspoon cream of tartar
1 teaspoon soda
Pinch of salt.

TARTS AND SHELLS
(*Makes 15 Large Tarts or 2 Shells*)

Into 1 large cup of *Five Roses* flour stir 1 teaspoon baking powder, $\frac{1}{2}$ cup butter and lard mixed. Fill cup up with boiling water and let stand. Beat stiff and dry white of 1 egg and put in the flour. Stir lightly. Add a little more flour (if needed) and roll as light and quickly as possible. Bake in a hot oven. These tarts are best with lemon or cream filling.

Notes on Tarts—Bake pie shells on outside of pan bottom up, and see how nice and even they will be.

Always put the sugar used in a tart in the centre of the fruit, not on the top, or it will make the paste sodden.

◇ ◇ ◇

DISCRIMINATING housewives have long since found *Five Roses* to be the best "*all purpose*" flour. For thickening soups and gravies, for rolling meats or dredging fruit, wherever flour comes into use, no matter how small the quantity, the fineness and uniform texture of *Five Roses* add class and quality.

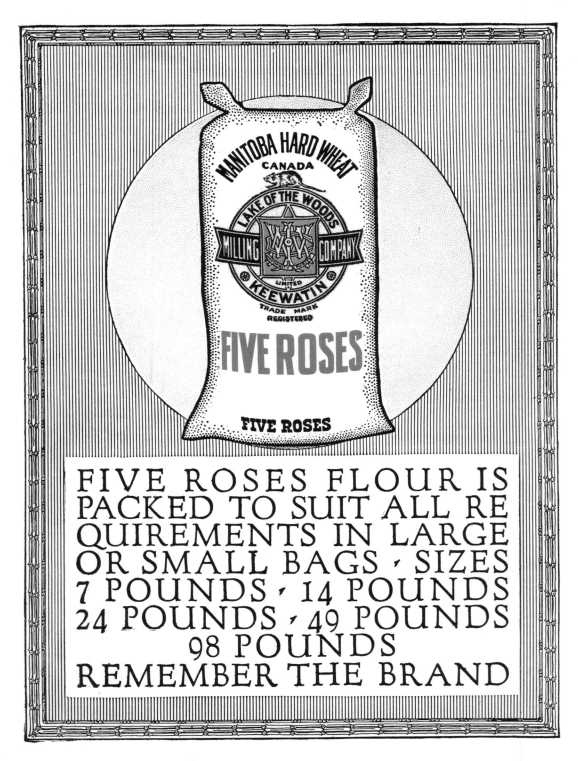

FIVE ROSES FLOUR IS PACKED TO SUIT ALL REQUIREMENTS IN LARGE OR SMALL BAGS · SIZES 7 POUNDS · 14 POUNDS 24 POUNDS · 49 POUNDS 98 POUNDS REMEMBER THE BRAND

PIES OF ALL KINDS

(*Specially written for the Five Roses Cook Book*)

IES are more of a luxury than a necessity, but, as Emerson said, "give me the luxuries of life and I will do without the necessities."

So that it is not worth while wasting time and materials unless you can make pies very good. The crust and fillings must be of the finest quality. Always adhere to the *Five Roses* standard.

Crust-making rules are given elsewhere. See page 71.

Never grease a pie tin: there is an old kitchen proverb which says "it's a poor crust that will not grease its own plate."

The crust should be cut and rolled exactly to fit the tin and cover the filling without stretching. Otherwise it may toughen and even break, letting out the filling, quite spoiling the appearance of the dish. Allowance should, however, be made for shrinkage.

Prick well the crust of all pies with fluid fillings. This will allow the steam to escape and also prevent the juice from running. To retain the juice, always put the sugar in first under the fruit on the bottom crust.

Pie crusts may readily be shaped and baked some days beforehand and reheated when required. If kept in a cool place, a well-made pie crust will keep for a long time. All air bubbles between crust and tin should be gently forced out, working from centre to sides.

All pastry requires a quick oven at the start, the smaller the shapes the quicker the oven. Once the puffing is over the heat may be reduced, especially for custard or egg fillings. Fruit pies should be allowed to cook slowly to avoid running over.

When only one crust is used, the paste may be made thicker.

After baking, pies should never be set on top of a hot stove, if you wish to avoid sogginess.

❖ ❖ ❖

SLICED APPLE PIE
(*1st Prize at County Fair, Picton, Ont.*)

First, have pie apples, say Wealthies, Greenings, Duchess, Red Astrachan. Line pan with light rich pastry and fill up with apples sliced thin and lengthwise. Sweeten to taste with granulated sugar. Add piece of butter size of butternut and sprinkle with a little cinnamon. When the top crust is put on, wet edges and rub together. Have a strip of cotton 1 inch in width, wet and draw around the edge. Remove this strip when pie is done.

Note on Apple Pies—A soda biscuit rolled fine and put in an apple pie will keep the juice from boiling over and prevent the oven from getting sticky and disagreeable. Bread dust could likewise be used.

APPLE SAUCE PIE

Beat the yolks of 2 eggs with ½ cup sugar until light. Then beat in 2 cups strained sweetened apple sauce. Flavour with wintergreen, and bake in one crust. Whip the whites of the eggs to a stiff snow. Add 2 tablespoons powdered sugar, spread over the pie. Brown lightly in oven.

PLAIN APPLE PIE

3 cups *Five Roses* flour
1 cup lard (or lard and butter mixed)
1 teaspoon cream of tartar
½ teaspoon soda
Pinch of salt
Sliced apples
½ cup sugar
1 nutmeg (grated)
Cinnamon to taste

Sift the flour, soda, cream of tartar and soda together. Rub the shortening in the flour, and use enough water to make it all stick together. Knead very little, roll thin, spread on plate. Fill plate nearly full with apples sliced very thin and

[*Pies of all Kinds*]

placed in smoothly. Spread half a cup of sugar over the apples, about a quarter of a nutmeg grated and cinnamon to taste.

 Dampen the edge all around about half an inch wide. Roll out top paste and lay it on. Mark around the edges with a pie-jigger or fork to press the pastes together and keep the juice from boiling over. Slit the top. Bake in quick oven about 20 minutes, or until the apples are done.

DRIED APPLE PIE

1 cup stewed apples
1 cup milk
1 cup sugar
1 egg and yolk of another
Nutmeg

Cover with meringue made of the white of the egg, after the above has been baked in under crust.

BACHELOR'S FRUIT PIE

1½ cups *Five Roses* flour
1 tablespoon (large) baking powder
Pinch of spice to suit taste
Pinch of salt
2 tablespoons brown sugar
½ cup raisins or currants
Fresh milk to make biscuit dough

Take a small deep granite pot or kettle, in which melt 2 tablespoons lard. Put in the dough so that it will cover bottom, then melt 1 tablespoon lard and pour over top. Bake 15 minutes in quick oven.

Note on Fruit Pies—Put soda in sour fruit and pies will require less sugar.

BACKWOODS PIE

1 cup brown sugar
1 cup syrup (maple syrup, if convenient)
½ cup sweet milk
Butter size of an egg
Yolks of 3 eggs
1 nutmeg.

Beat all together, lastly add the whites well beaten. Bake with one crust in moderate oven.

BANANA PIE

Line a deep pie tin with rich paste. Into this slice 1 large banana, or two small ones. Pour over it a boiled custard made with 1 pint rich milk, 2 beaten eggs (yolks) 2 tablespoons sugar and a little salt. Bake slowly in a moderate oven and finish with a meringue of whites of eggs, or stiffly whipped cream.

BANANA CREAM PIE

Slice 2 large bananas into a baked crust. Fill up with whipped cream, sweetened with vanilla. Drop a spoonful of red jelly on each piece.

NEW ENGLAND BLUEBERRY PIE

Wash and dredge blueberries with *Five Roses* flour; then scatter among them ½ cup sugar for each pint of berries. Fill paste shells with this, dot with butter, cover with another crust and bake.

These are richer than huckleberry or blueberry pies when made in the usual way, the flour thickening the juice slightly and the butter tempering the acid.

BUTTERMILK PIE
(*Makes 2 Pies*)

2 cups buttermilk
2 tablespoons *Five Roses* flour
2 tablespoons butter
2 eggs
1 cup sugar.

Bake with an undercrust.

BUTTER SCOTCH PIE

1 cup very dark brown sugar
1½ tablespoons *Five Roses* flour
1 tablespoon butter
Yolks of 2 eggs (whites for frosting)
1 cup sweet milk.

Cook in double boiler and put in baked crust.

CARAMEL PIE

Put in a pan to boil 1 cup brown sugar and butter the size of an egg, then thin out with 1 cup hot water. Mix 1 tablespoon cornstarch, 1 teaspoon vanilla, yolks of 2 eggs with water and stir in. Have crust ready and pour filling in, using the whites of eggs on top.

Not Bleached ~ Not Blended

[*Pies of all Kinds*]

CARROT PIE

1 cup cooked carrots (mashed)
½ cup sugar
2 eggs
1 pint sweet milk
2 tablespoons molasses
1 teaspoon cinnamon
½ teaspoon ginger.

Bake in one crust. Molasses may be omitted.

COCOANUT PIE

2 eggs
1 cup sugar
½ cup water
1½ teaspoons baking powder
1½ cups *Five Roses* flour
Small lump of butter.

Bake in 2 tins.

COCOANUT FILLING

1 egg
⅓ cup *Five Roses* flour
½ cup sugar
1 cup boiling milk.

Mix egg, flour and sugar together. Put in the boiling milk and boil until it thickens, stirring all the time. Use flavouring to taste and 1 tablespoon of shredded cocoanut.

CHICKEN PIE

Have a chicken of about 4 pounds. Remove all the fat, cut up and put into boiling water. Add a little pepper and salt to season. Cook until the meat can be picked from the bones quite easily. Skim out of the water, pick into small pieces and remove all the bones. There should be left about 3 cups of liquid for gravy. Leave this in the kettle and add *Five Roses* flour enough to make a thick gravy. Add about 1 tablespoon of butter, or more if required very rich. Pour over chicken and let cool.

CHICKEN PIE PASTE

3 cups *Five Roses* flour
2 teaspoons cream of tartar
1 teaspoon soda
¼ cup butter
¼ cup lard
Pinch of fine salt
Sweet milk to wet.

Sift flour, salt, cream of tartar and soda together. Rub in the butter and lard very fine, then wet with the milk to a dough like biscuit dough. Line a deep dish (a large pan does very well) with the cold mixture and cover with half the dough. Make some large holes in top crust for air. Bake 1 hour.

CRANBERRY PIES

Into a saucepan put one quart of nice clean cranberries and ¼ cup of water. Allow this to boil about ¾ hour, than add two full cups granulated sugar. After this has boiled about 15 minutes, stir in a piece of butter half the size of a nutmeg and one-half teaspoon of cassia. Then set to cool.

FOR CRUST

Take 2 cups *Five Roses* flour in the sieve with 1 teaspoon salt, ¼ soda and ½ cream of tartar. Sift this and mix well one small cup lard into it. Then mix with cold water soft enough to roll. Roll quite thin and cover well-greased pie plates. Fill the crusts with the berries. For top crusts roll remaining dough quite thin and cut in ⅛ inch strips. Cross the pies quite closely both ways, and bake until brown in a quick oven. These are delicious when served with whipped cream.

MOCK CHERRY PIE

1 cup cranberries (cut in halves)
1 cup sugar
1 teaspoon vanilla
1 tablespoon *Five Roses* flour dissolved in
½ cup water
1 egg

Mix well together and bake between 2 crusts.

CHOCOLATE PIE

1 pint milk
½ cup sugar
3 tablespoons *Five Roses* flour
1 square chocolate.

Grate chocolate, put in cold milk and let come to a boil. Mix flour and sugar well together, and stir gradually into boiling milk. This will make 1 pie. Serve with whipped cream.

[*Pies of all Kinds*]

CREAM PIE CRUST

(*No Butter or Lard*)

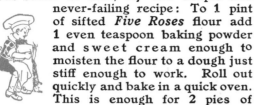

For a good cream pie crust made without butter or lard, try this simple and never-failing recipe: To 1 pint of sifted *Five Roses* flour add 1 even teaspoon baking powder and sweet cream enough to moisten the flour to a dough just stiff enough to work. Roll out quickly and bake in a quick oven. This is enough for 2 pies of single crust.

FRENCH CREAM PIE

1 cup currants
¾ cup granulated sugar
1 cup sour cream
2 eggs (keep whites for frosting)
½ teaspoon cinnamon
Pinch of salt
1 teaspoon baking soda (added last)

Bake a good rich pie shell and cook the filling on top of stove. Reserve whites of eggs to be beaten light and spread on top of pie and slightly brown.

CUSTARD PIE

Line a deep pie plate with good pie crust and grate a little nutmeg on the crust. Beat 3 eggs with ½ cup sugar, add ½ cup cream and milk enough to fill the crust (about 1 pint). Bake in moderate oven just to the boiling point. Serve cold. Or, reserve the whites of 3 eggs and, when the custard is done, beat the whites to a froth and spread on top. Add a little sugar to the whites and return to the oven and brown slightly.

Note on Custard Pies—For custard and fresh fruit pies, it is advisable to have paste very cold and firm and to have a quick oven; otherwise, the liquid will soak in and the crust be heavy or soggy.

MEXICAN DATE PIE

1 cup white sugar
Yolks of 2 eggs
1 cup sweet cream or milk
Chopped dates

Line pie plate with paste and put in a layer of chopped dates in bottom. Then add above mixture and bake. Beat whites of eggs stiff, sweeten with sugar and spread over top. Put in oven to brown.

LEMON PIE

Juice of 2 lemons
2 cups sugar
Yolks of 3 eggs
4 tablespoons *Five Roses* flour
Piece of butter

Stir all together with a little cold water. Add 3 cups boiling water and bring to a boil. Remove from stove and put in baked crusts. This will make 2 pies. Beat the whites of the eggs to a stiff froth. Add sugar and spread on top of pies.

MOCK LEMON PIE

3 eggs
1 cup sugar
1½ pints buttermilk
1 teaspoon extract of lemon
1½ tablespoons *Five Roses* flour

NEW MEAT PIE

Line a baking dish with biscuit dough rolled thin. Put in the chopped meat and thickened gravy hot. Instead of covering with a top paste, fill in the top with tiny biscuits about 1 inch in diameter. Cook 15 or 20 minutes.

MINCE PIE

1 quart fat beef (cooked well and chopped fine)
2 quarts green apples (chopped fine)
2½ cups raisins (seeded and chopped)
1½ cups currants
2½ teaspoons mixed spices
½ teaspoon grated nutmeg
3 cups brown sugar
4 tablespoons vinegar
1 cup hot water
3 tablespoons *Five Roses* flour (stirred in).

Fill crust and bake in moderate oven. Bake brown. Mince pies should be made with puff paste and 2 crusts. These pies will keep for several days. Should be reheated before serving.

[*Pies of all Kinds*]

RICH MINCE PIE

2 pounds lean beef boiled tender (minced fine when cold)
4 pounds apples (chopped fine)
2 pounds suet
2 pounds layer raisins
2 pounds sultanas
2 pounds currants
½ pound citron peel (shredded)
¼ pound orange peel
¼ pound lemon peel
¼ pound walnuts
¼ pound almonds

Put above over the fire with 3 pounds brown sugar made to a good syrup with a little water. While heating, add:

1 tablespoon cloves (ground)
1 tablespoon allspice (ground)
1 tablespoon salt
1 tablespoon ground ginger
1 tablespoon mace
1 nutmeg (grated)
Juice and rind of 2 lemons

Boil 15 minutes. Take from fire and, when cold, add 1 quart apple cider. Pack in a stone crock and pour over top ¾ pint of brandy. When properly sealed will keep for months, and grow more mellow with age.

PATENT OR MOCK MINCE PIE

4 eggs
4 cups water
1 cup sugar
1 cup molasses
1 cup *Five Roses* flour
1 cup vinegar
1 cup raisins
1 teaspoon cloves
1 teaspoon cinnamon
1 teaspoon soda
½ dozen crackers (very fine)

GREEN TOMATO MINCE

Chop very fine 1 peck of green tomatoes. Wash in a colander with a very weak brine to remove all juice. Boil a very little. Add 5 pounds brown sugar, 2 pounds raisins, cloves, cinnamon and allspice to taste, also a little candied peel.
—*Mrs. A. W. Fraser, Iron Springs, Alta.*

MAPLE SYRUP PIE
(No. 1)

1 cup maple syrup
1½ cups raisins
1 lemon (rind and juice)
2 tablespoons *Five Roses* flour
Bake with one or two crusts

MAPLE SYRUP PIE
(No. 2)

1 cup maple syrup
½ cup water
2 eggs (whites for frosting)
2 tablespoons *Five Roses* flour
Butter size of walnut

Cook in double boiler. Bake the crust, then fill up with custard. Cover with meringue.

SMALL PORK PIES
(*A Devonshire Recipe*)

Chop fine ¼ pound beef kidney suet and mix with it an equal quantity of butter. Rub both into a pound of *Five Roses* flour and set over the fire in a saucepan until the butter and suet are melted and the flour very hot. Knead together then into a stiff paste, cover with the cloth and put it near the fire while you make ready with the meat. There should be about 2 pounds of the neck of pork, and this should be cut into very small pieces, seasoned liberally with salt, pepper and a teaspoon of powdered sage, and cooked gently for 25 minutes before it goes into the pie. The paste must then be divided into as many pieces as you wish to have pies, and these must be made into round shapes—"built up" into the shape of round pies. The way to do this must be studied carefully, for it is a knack in itself. The fist is put into the middle of the piece of dough from which the pie is to be raised, and by working it in a circular fashion the hollow is formed which is to receive the meat. The process should really be seen to be adequately understood. When the pie is "raised" the meat is put into it, a round of paste laid on the top and its edge pinched to that of the lower crust. It is then baked in a steady, rather slow oven.
—*The New Home.*

[Pies of all Kinds]

RAISED, OR MELTON MOW-BRAY, PORK PIES

Put 2½ pounds of *Five Roses* flour in a bread pan. Set on stove in a saucepan ¾ pint cold spring water containing ½ pound good lard. When the water boils, make a hole or bay in the middle of the flour, and pour in the water and lard by degrees. When well mixed, knead with the hands, and roll out into sheets about ¼ inch thick. Line circular dishes or tins with the paste and then proceed with the filling. This should consist of lean and raw pork chopped up into dice, seasoned with pepper and salt. Roll out the covers, after wetting around tops of pies, and pinch covers and tops together with finger and thumb. Bake 1½ hours.

—*Mrs. A. Aspdin, Victoria, B.C.*

PUMPKIN PIE

Select a moderate sized pumpkin. Do not peel, as most of the sweet as well as color lies in the rind. Wash and cut into small pieces, after scraping out the stringy part. Put in a porcelain kettle with a pint of boiling water, and it will soon be covered with its own juices. It is necessary to evaporate these slowly, which will take six or eight hours. When the juice has nearly boiled off the pumpkin, lay a cloth in a colander, pour the pumpkin into it, fold the ends of the cloth over and place a plate and weights on same. Let drain in this way till morning.

To 4 cups of this strained pumpkin (measured after rubbing through a common flour sieve) add a teaspoon salt, 1 of mace, the same of nutmeg and a tablespoon of ginger or other desired flavoring. Add 4 eggs well beaten with 1½ cups of sugar. Now add slowly 4 cups of milk and a cup of rich cream. Taste the mixture, as some pumpkins require more sugar than others. This will make from 3 to 4 small pies. One moderate sized pumpkin will yield about 5 cups of strained pulp.

PUMPKIN PIE
(Eggless)

Cook pumpkin or squash tender. Rub through a fine sieve and measure off 3 cups. Over it grate half a nutmeg or its equivalent of orange peel. Add 1½ cups white coffee sugar. Moisten 4 heaping teaspoons cornstarch in ½ cup sweet milk and add to the pumpkin. Melt 1 tablespoon of butter, add a little salt and stir into the pumpkin. Now add 3 full pints of sweet milk. Stir well and pour the mixture into crusts. Bake in a hot oven until slightly browned on top. When cold, spread the top of one or two with tart jelly, and note the improvement. The custard in these pies will not leave the crust at the edge, nor will any water gather on top when allowed to stand a few hours, as is often the case with those made in the usual manner with eggs.

POT PIE

1 egg
½ cup sweet milk
2 teaspoons baking powder
Salt
Five Roses flour to make stiff batter

Drop from spoon into chicken gravy and boil 10 minutes.

RHUBARB PIE

2 cups rhubarb (stewed)
1 cup sugar
2 tablespoons *Five Roses* flour
1 egg

Bake with 2 crusts.

RHUBARB-DATE PIE

Line a pie tin with rich paste, and lay on this a layer of stoned dates. Fill up with stewed rhubarb, and bake with an upper crust.

SHEPHERD'S PIE

Peel and slice 2 pounds of potatoes. Cut up 1 to 2 pounds cold cooked beef, lean and fat together. Place potatoes in pie dish with ¼ pint beef gravy, and season with pepper and salt. Add 2 onions cut in 4 pieces. Place the meat over the potatoes and add more potatoes over the meat. Pour dripping over top layer of potatoes. Cover with paste and make hole in centre, through which pour a little beef stock once or twice while cooking. Bake in hot oven about ¾ of an hour.

SUGAR OR SHOO-FLY PIE
(1st Part)
3 cups *Five Roses* flour
1 cup sugar
¾ cup lard or butter

Rub thoroughly. This makes crumbs for the top.

(2nd Part)
1 cup molasses
1 cup hot water
1 teaspoon soda (dissolved in water)

Put water and molasses together and add soda. Divide into 4 plates, then add crumbs on top and bake with under crust only.

VENISON PIE

Wipe and cut the meat into nice pieces and dredge with *Five Roses* flour seasoned with salt and pepper. Place these pieces loosely in a pie dish and sprinkle over them 1 dessertspoon chopped parsley, pour in as much stock, diluted gravy or water as the dish will hold without the liquid touching the upper edges. Cover with pie crust, leaving a large opening in the centre. Bake for about 2 hours in good oven. When the crust is a nice, golden colour, cover the pie with clean greased paper to prevent burning.
—*Mrs. J. MacFarlane, Sunnywold, Okanagan Lake, Vernon, B.C.*

VINEGAR PIE

1 egg
1 tablespoon (heaping) *Five Roses* flour
1 cup sugar
1½ tablespoons sharp vinegar
1 cup cold water
Nutmeg to taste

Beat the egg, flour and sugar together. Add the vinegar and cold water. Flavor with nutmeg and bake with 2 crusts.

WASHINGTON PIE

1 cup white sugar
1 egg
1 cup sweet cream
1 teaspoon cream of tartar
½ teaspoon soda
½ teaspoon salt
Five Roses to make medium stiff batter
Nutmeg or lemon

Bake in 2 plates. Spread 1 cake with jelly and place the other on top. Serve cold.

❖ ❖ ❖

FROSTINGS AND FILLINGS

ALMOND ICING
½ cup butter
1 egg (white)
½ teaspoon almond extract
2 cups icing sugar

Cream butter, beat white of egg stiff, add almond flavouring and sugar. Stir in gradually. If too stiff, add a little milk. Use ½ pound almonds burnt and rolled. Cover cake with icing and roll in nutmeats.

BOILED ICING
1 cup granulated sugar
3 tablespoons cold water
1 egg (white)
1 teaspoon flavoring to taste

Put sugar and water in pan, stir and put on stove. When dissolved, let boil till it hairs, but do not stir. Beat the white of egg to a stiff froth, and add boiled sugar, beating all the while. When it begins to stiffen, add flavoring and beat. When quite thick and before it is cold, it is ready for use. Half a teaspoon of cream of tartar may be added. Sometimes, also, milk is used instead of water.

BUTTER ICING

Melt a little butter and mix with icing sugar. Flavor with vanilla.

Not Bleached - Not Blended

[*Frostings and Fillings*]

CARAMEL ICING
(No. 1)

2 cups granulated sugar
½ cup butter
½ cup milk

Boil for ¼ hour, cool a little, add vanilla to taste, and put on cake before it is cold.

CARAMEL ICING
(No. 2)

1¼ cups brown sugar
¼ cup white sugar
⅛ cup boiling water
2 eggs (whites)
1 teaspoon vanilla
⅛ cup English walnut meats

Mix sugar and water and let boil till syrup threads when dropped from spoon. Pour slowly, while beating constantly, on to the beaten whites, and continue beating until the mixture is nearly cool. Set in a pan of boiling water and cook, stirring constantly until mixture becomes slightly granular around the edge of dish. Remove from range and beat until mixture will hold its shape. Add vanilla and nutmeats broken in pieces. Pour on cake and spread with back of spoon, making a rough surface.

COCOA ICING

½ cup powdered cocoa
1½ tablespoons butter
1¾ cups white sugar
Pinch of salt
⅓ cup milk
2 teaspoons vanilla

To the milk and butter, add the cocoa, sugar and salt. Boil 8 minutes. Take off and beat until creamy. Add vanilla and pour over cake to depth of ⅛ inch.

CHOCOLATE ICING

¼ pound chocolate powder
1 tablespoon water
¼ pound icing sugar

Put chocolate and water into saucepan, and stir until melted. Add quickly icing sugar, and spread over cake with knife dipped in hot water.

CONFECTIONER'S FROSTING

Two tablespoons boiling water or cream and a little flavoring essence of vanilla, lemon, or almond. Add enough confectioner's sugar to the liquid to make of right consistency to spread.

LEMON ICING

1 egg yolk
1 cup sugar
1 lemon (grated rind and juice)

Mix all ingredients thoroughly and put in double boiler. Cook 15 to 20 minutes. Let cool and spread between cakes.

ORANGE ICING

In above recipe substitute grated rind and juice of 1 orange for the lemon, and add a little lemon juice.

MARSHMALLOW FROSTING

1 cup brown sugar
1 cup white sugar
1 cup water
1 tablespoon vinegar
2 eggs (whites)
¼ pound marshmallows (see marshmallow recipe).

Boil sugar, water and vinegar till thick like candy, then stir in the egg whites and marshmallows. Boil again and ice cake.

MOCHA FROSTING
(No. 1)

1 cup confectioner's sugar
¼ cup butter
2 tablespoons very strong coffee (hot)
1 teaspoon cocoa
1 teaspoon vanilla

Cream sugar and butter. Add other ingredients, mix together for 5 minutes and spread.

MOCHA FROSTING
(No. 2)

3 ounces fresh butter
6 ounces icing sugar (sifted)
2 tablespoons coffee extract

Put two layers of icing between cake layers and cover cake all over with the remainder, smoothing the sides with a warm knife and garnishing the top with a forcing pipe. Sprinkle with freshly chopped pistachio nuts.

MAPLE CREAM ICING

½ cup milk
Butter size of walnut
1 teaspoon vanilla
1 cup maple sugar
1 cup brown sugar

Boil till it forms a soft ball when dropped into cold water, then beat for a few minutes until it will spread nicely. Stir all the time it is boiling. Good made either wholly of brown or wholly of maple sugar.

PLAIN ICING

2 eggs (whites)
1½ cups powdered sugar
1 teaspoon flavoring

Beat eggs to stiff froth, add sugar and flavouring. Use at once or place in cool spot till required.

RAISIN ICING

1 cup sugar
½ cup water
1 cup raisins (stoned and chopped fine)
1 egg (white)
Vanilla

Boil sugar and water till it ropes, then add the raisins and fold in the white of egg. Flavor.

WALNUT ICING

1 egg
1 cup brown sugar
Butter size of walnut
1 cup chopped walnuts

Boil 5 minutes, stirring constantly. Flavor with vanilla.

APPLE FILLING

1 cup white sugar
1 cup water
1 cup grated apples
1 tablespoon *Five Roses* flour
1 lemon (juice and grated rind)
1 egg.

Cook in double boiler until clear. When cold spread on cake.

[Frostings and Fillings]

BANANA FILLING

Use above recipe, simply substituting sliced bananas for grated apples.

DATE FILLING

1 pound dates
1 cup sugar (white or **brown)**
1 cup boiling water
Flavor to taste

Boil till soft and tender. When cool, spread between cakes. Rind and juice of half an orange or lemon are sometimes added.

CHOCOLATE FILLING

4 tablespoons chocolate
1 pint boiling water
2 eggs (yolks)
2 tablespoons *Five Roses* flour
6 tablespoons sugar

Mix and boil till thick

COCOANUT CREAM FILLING

2 cups sweet milk
½ cup white sugar
2 tablespoons *Five Roses* flour
1 egg
½ cup cocoanut

If the cocoanut be dessicated, soak in hot milk.

LEMON FILLING

1 lemon (juice and grated rind)
1 cup cold water
1 cup sugar
1 egg
1 tablespoon *Five Roses* flour

Beat lemon rind and eggs together. Stir in sugar and lemon juice. Dissolve flour in cold water. Cook in double boiler till it jellies. Spread as usual.

MOLASSES FILLING

1 cup sugar
¾ cup molasses
4 eggs
1 nutmeg

Not Bleached - Not Blended

[*Frostings and Fillings*]

LEMON JELLY

Juice and rind of 2 lemons
1 cup sugar
3 eggs (well beaten)
¼ pound butter

Cook in double boiler, stirring until like thick cream. Put away in jars, in a cool place. Will keep for months.

ORANGE FILLING

Use same recipe as lemon filling, merely substituting rind and juice of 1 orange for lemon.

NUT FILLING

½ cup sugar
½ cup sweet cream
1 egg (white)
¼ cup chopped walnuts

Mix all well and boil slowly, stirring all the time. Any kind of nuts preferred may be used with above recipe. Egg may be omitted.

RAISIN CREAM FILLING

½ cup chopped raisins
¼ cup sugar
¼ cup water
1 tablespoon *Five Roses* flour

Cook until thick. When cold, whip half a pint of thin cream sweetened and flavored to taste. Add to raisin mixture. When cake is cold, put filling between layers and on top of cake.

STRAWBERRY ICING

4 tablespoons strawberry juice
1 cup sugar

Boil until it threads and **pour over** whipped white of 1 egg.

NOTES ON ICING

Instead of sprinkling chopped nuts, peel, shredded citron, etc., on small cakes, the mixture will adhere more satisfactorily if one side of each square is laid on the mixture before cakes are put in the pan to bake. White of egg, if kept closely covered and in a cool place, will keep over a week, and is as good for meringue as when fresh. Some people put the meringue on a pie or pudding while it is still hot. This causes the eggs to liquefy and quite spoils the effect. It is well to remember that anything to be mixed with white of egg must be done with a light lifting motion of the spoon, rather than stirring, which may liquefy the eggs.

A little *Five Roses* flour spread over the top of cakes before they are iced will prevent the icing from running.

◇ ◇ ◇

CANDIES

BUTTER SCOTCH

1 cup molasses
1 cup sugar
½ cup butter

Boil till it threads. Flavour with vanilla and pour on buttered pan.

CARAMELS

½ cup molasses
1 cup sugar
2½ cups milk
Vanilla extract

Boil 15 to 20 minutes. Pour in greased tin and cut into squares.

FUDGE NO. 1

1 cup white sugar
1 cup brown sugar
¼ cup syrup
½ cup sweet milk
¼ cup melted butter

Boil 2½ minutes, then add 2 teaspoons cocoa. Boil 5 minutes longer, then take from stove and add 1 teaspoon vanilla. Beat till creamy, then pour in buttered pan and mark in squares.

Not Bleached - Not Blended

FUDGE NO. 2

2 cups fruit sugar
¼ cake unsweetened chocolate
Small pinch of salt
Butter size of walnut.

Mix above together, then moisten with milk. Add a pinch of cream of tartar to make it light and foamy. Let boil until the soft ball stage. Then remove from fire and beat. One-third cake of chocolate may be used, depending on one's taste.

KISSES

Take the whites of 3 eggs well beaten, then stir in a cup of white sugar. Put on stove in a steamer or over water until light. Remove from stove and add 1 tablespoon cornstarch, 1 tablespoon vanilla, ½ pound cocoanut. Put on greased paper or tin. Bake until brown. Icing sugar may be used.

MAPLE CREAM

2 pounds brown sugar
½ pound almonds (blanched and cut in pieces)
½ pint sweet cream.

Boil sugar and cream together until it forms a firm ball when dropped in a little cold water. Add nuts, beat until cold or firm enough to spread on buttered tins.

SEAFOAM CANDY

3 cups light brown sugar
1 cup cold water
1½ tablespoons vinegar.

Boil to hard ball stage, beat whites of 2 eggs and pour in the candy. Beat quite stiff, add nuts and vanilla.

MARSHMALLOWS

2 tablespoons gelatine (rounded)
2 cups granulated sugar
Pinch of salt
Flavoring to taste.

Soak the gelatine in 8 tablespoons cold water. Heat the sugar with ½ cup water until dissolved. Add gelatine to syrup and just bring it to a boil, take off the stove and let stand in a bowl until partially cool. Add salt and flavoring, beat with a whip until soft, then with a large spoon until only soft enough to settle into a sheet. Dust granite pans thickly with fine powdered sugar, pour in the candy about ½ inch deep, and set to cool until it will not come off the finger. Turn out on powdered paper, cut in cubes and roll in sugar. Nuts, chocolate, or candied fruit may be beaten in, or the marshmallows may be rolled in grated cocoanut before being powdered.

—*Canadian Farm Cook Book.*

❖ ❖ ❖

*F*IVE ROSES *keeps better than any other flour we know of, because in milling all dirt and fermentable matter are carefully removed. No inferior portions of the wheat, no little pieces of the oily germ can escape the keen-eyed millers of* FIVE ROSES *to wreck your baking hopes. Now you know why* FIVE ROSES *keeps sweet and sound so long.*

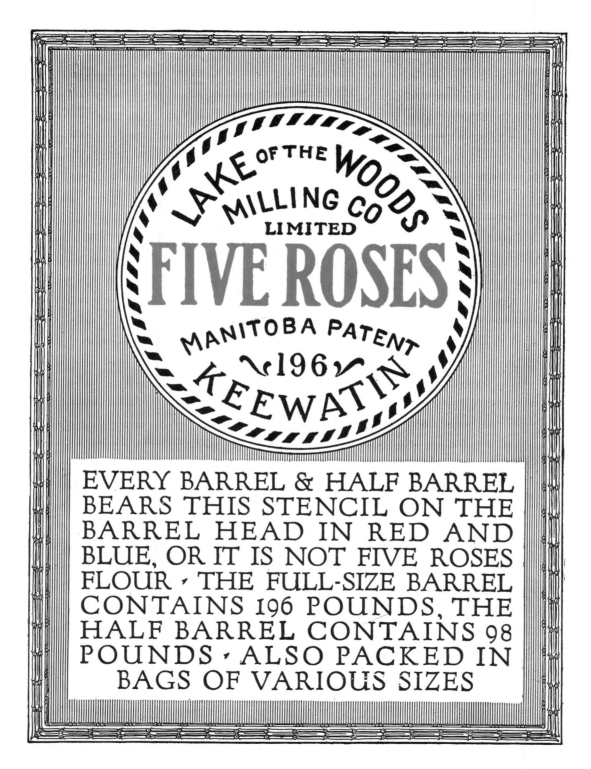

LAKE OF THE **WOODS**
MILLING CO
LIMITED
FIVE ROSES
MANITOBA PATENT
196
KEEWATIN

EVERY BARREL & HALF BARREL
BEARS THIS STENCIL ON THE
BARREL HEAD IN RED AND
BLUE, OR IT IS NOT FIVE ROSES
FLOUR · THE FULL-SIZE BARREL
CONTAINS 196 POUNDS, THE
HALF BARREL CONTAINS 98
POUNDS · ALSO PACKED IN
BAGS OF VARIOUS SIZES

CAKE MAKING AND BAKING

Specially prepared for the Five Roses Cook Book

MIXING

CLEAR the kitchen table of every non-essential. Perfect cleanliness should be observed in every detail. Have sleeves rolled up above the elbows, and have hands and nails in perfect condition.

Read the recipe thoroughly at least once. Collect all necessary ingredients and utensils beforehand.

All measurements are level, unless otherwise specified.

Have flour perfectly dry ; sift and measure. In fact, all **dry** ingredients should be measured *after* sifting.

Have pans ready greased. For this purpose fresh lard is preferred to butter. If the cake is large and requires long baking (for instance, a fruit or loaf cake), line the bottom with well-greased paper and sprinkle inside with a little flour, shaking out all loose flour before putting in the mixture.

The best utensil for mixing or beating is an earthen or stone bowl. It should be slightly warmed. A wooden spoon is also preferable.

Do not stir the cake ; always *beat* thoroughly, bringing the batter up from the bottom of the bowl at every stroke. A consistent upward motion tends to improve the texture considerably.

All ingredients should be the best obtainable, quite up to the *Five Roses* standard. Butter that is watery or oily and not well worked should never be used.

It is useful also to remember that too rich a cake breaks up easily ; that too much sugar makes a thick, hard crust ; too much egg a tough cake.

Sour milk makes a spongy, light cake ; sweet milk, one that cuts like pound cake. With sour milk, soda alone should be used ; with sweet milk, baking powder or soda and cream of tartar. Cream of tartar and soda are often substituted for baking powder, in which case allow 2 teaspoons of cream of tartar and a smaller one of soda to every 3 cups of *Five Roses* flour, and sift well together two or even three times.

◇ ◇ ◇

TEST FOR EGGS

As many of the recipes given on the following pages call for eggs, a good test is in order : Placed in a glass of water, an egg if fresh will remain resting at the bottom of the vessel ; if not quite fresh, it will rest with the big end raised higher than the small end, and the higher the big end is raised the older the egg. In warm weather, it is a good idea to place eggs in cold water before using, as they will froth finer if this is done. Be sure eggs are fresh, as no amount of beating will make a stiff froth if they are not.

To get a flat top on a cake, let the mixture come well up to the corners and sides of the pan, leaving a slight depression in the center. When baked, the cake will be perfectly flat.

BAKING

Be sure you understand your oven and the kind of oven each cake requires.

A good oven test is the following : if the hand can be held in from 20 to 35 seconds, it is a 'quick' oven ; from 35 to 45 seconds, it is a 'moderate' oven ; from 45 to 60, a 'slow' oven. Burning paper or flour is another test.

Never have anything else in the oven

[*Cake Making and Baking*]

while baking cakes, nor try to bake two different kinds at the same time. Do not open the door nor move the cakes for at

least 10 minutes. You may then peep into the oven to make sure they are baking nicely. Shut the door quietly without slamming.

Cake, like bread, rolls, etc., should bake gradually. It should bake inside before browning outside. Butter cakes should bake slowly in a moderate oven, while sponge cakes and their class should always bake quickly. It may be given as a general rule, that the thinner the cakes, the quicker the oven.

Cake is done when it leaves the sides of the pan, and when on inserting a straw or tooth-pick near the centre it comes out clean and dry.

When removing a cake from the oven, place the pan on a damp cloth for a moment; and it will then come out readily without sticking. When a layer cake burns at the bottom, however, leave the cake in the tin until cold before removing, and take a sharp knife and you can scrape off the burnt part without spoiling the cake.

CAKES WITHOUT EGGS

Owing to the high cost, and in some parts of the country great scarcity of eggs, alternate recipes are given in the following pages omitting the eggs. This is a feature which the editor has seen in no other cook book, and should prove very acceptable.

ANGEL CAKE OR ANGEL FOOD

No. 1

11 eggs (whites only)
1½ cups powdered sugar (sifted)
1 cup *Five Roses* flour
1 teaspoon cream of tartar
1 teaspoon vanilla
Pinch of salt

Sift flour, cream of tartar, sugar and salt together 4 or 5 times. Beat the egg whites in a large dish to a stiff froth. Add the sifted flour, etc., gradually, beating

all the time. Have pan ready—do not let the cake stand a minute after it is mixed. Bake 45 minutes, and do not open the oven door until the cake has been in at least 15 minutes.

Add 2 teaspoons rose water, if desired.

ANGEL CAKE

No. 2

1 cup sweet milk
1 cup *Five Roses* flour
1 cup fine granulated sugar
3 teaspoons baking powder
Pinch of salt
2 eggs (whites only)

Set milk in a pan of boiling water and heat to boiling point. Sift well together the dry ingredients five times. Into this, pour the cup of hot milk, stir smooth, then add the stiff whites of 2 eggs. Fold them in carefully. Do not grease the tin or flavor cake. Bake in moderate oven. Ice with water icing.

APPLE SAUCE CAKE

(*Eggless*)

No. 1

1 cup brown sugar
¾ cup butter
1 cup raisins
¼ pound peel
1½ cups hot apple sauce
1 teaspoon cinnamon
½ nutmeg
2½ cups *Five Roses* flour
2 teaspoons (level) soda dissolved in the hot apple sauce

Bake in a loaf. Three tablespoons molasses are sometimes added.

APPLE SAUCE CAKE

(*Eggless*)

No. 2

2 cups sugar
1 cup lard or butter
2½ cups apple sauce (unsweetened)
4 cups *Five Roses* flour
1 teaspoon ground cloves
1 teaspoon ground cinnamon
3 teaspoons soda
2 cups stoned raisins

DRIED APPLE CAKE
(Also Called "Farmer's Fruit Cake")

2 cups dried apples
2 cups molasses
1 cup butter
2 cups brown sugar
2 eggs (well beaten)
1 cup sour milk
4 cups *Five Roses* flour
1 teaspoon cassia
1 teaspoon allspice
Nutmeg to taste
2 teaspoons soda

Soak apples overnight in water. In the morning, simmer in molasses 1 hour, then add the butter. When cool, add brown sugar, well-beaten eggs, the sour milk, the flour, cassia, allspice and a little nutmeg, also the soda. A tried and true recipe.

DUTCH APPLE CAKE

1 pint *Five Roses* flour
½ teaspoon salt
½ teaspoon soda
1 teaspoon cream of tartar
¼ cup butter
1 egg
1 cup (scant) milk
4 sour apples
2 tablespoons sugar

Mix the dry ingredients, add the egg beaten and mixed with the milk. The dough should be soft enough to spread ½ inch thick on a shallow baking pan. Core, pare and cut the apples into eighths, lay them in parallel rows on the top of the dough, sharp edge down, and press enough to make the edge penetrate slightly. Sprinkle the sugar over the apple and bake ½ hour. Eat while hot with butter or with lemon sauce.
—*From Mrs. Lincoln's Boston Cook Book*

BANANA CAKE

1 cup granulated sugar
¼ cup butter
⅔ cup milk
2 eggs
2 cups *Five Roses* flour
1 teaspoon vanilla extract

Bake in layers, and put sliced bananas between. Any frosting.

BANANA CAKE
(Eggless)

1 cup white sugar
½ cup butter
1 cup sweet milk
2½ cups *Five Roses* flour
2 teaspoons baking powder
Lemon flavor
Banana

Cut banana in layer and place between layers of cake and on top of cake when baked.

MANITOU BLACK CAKE

3 ounces chocolate
Yolk of 1 egg (save white for frosting)
1 cup milk
2 tablespoons butter
1 cup sugar
1⅜ cups *Five Roses* flour
2 teaspoons baking powder
½ teaspoon soda
½ cup milk (making 1½ cups in all)
1 teaspoon vanilla
Pinch of salt

Melt the chocolate over hot water, and add gradually to it the well-beaten yolk of egg mixed with the 1 cup of milk (first mentioned above). Cook till it thickens slightly. Cream the butter and sugar, add the chocolate mixture and stir well. Add the mixed and sifted dry ingredients alternately with the remaining half cup of milk. Mix well. Flavor. The batter should be quite thin. Bake. When cool, frost with boiled frosting, using the left-over white of egg.

BLACK CAKE
(See Also Fruit Cake)

1 pound powdered white sugar
¾ pound butter
1 pound sifted *Five Roses* flour
12 eggs (whites and yolks beaten separately)
2 pounds seeded raisins (part of them chopped)
2 pounds currants (carefully cleaned)
½ pound citron (cut in thin strips)
¼ ounce each of cinnamon, cloves and nutmeg mixed
1 wineglass wine
1 wineglass brandy

[*Cake Making and Baking*]

Rub butter and sugar together, add the beaten yolks of eggs, part of the flour, then the spice and the white of eggs well beaten. Add remainder of the flour wine and brandy. Mix all together thoroughly. Cover bottom and sides of a four-quart milk pan with buttered white paper. Put in a layer of the mixture, then a layer of the fruit, which has been previously dredged with flour, alternating and using batter for last layer. A small cup of New Orleans molasses makes the cake blacker and moister, but for this it is not necessary to add more flour. Bake 3½ to 4 hours in a slow oven. This is excellent, and will keep for a long time. This black cake I have used for many years and find it most satisfactory for its keeping qualities, as it will improve with age if kept in air-tight tins.

BLACK HILL CAKE

1 cup sugar
Butter size of an egg
1 egg
1 cup sweet milk
2 teaspoons cream of tartar (level)
1 teaspoon soda
1 pint *Five Roses* flour

Beat sugar and butter together well. Add other ingredients. Pour into buttered tin two-thirds of mixture, and to remaining third add:

2 tablespoons molasses
½ teaspoon ground cloves
½ teaspoon allspice

Stir together and pour over top of first mixture. Bake in moderate oven.

BOILED CAKE

(*Eggless*)

1 cup cold water
1 cup raisins
1 cup sugar
½ cup butter
1 teaspoon cinnamon
1 teaspoon cloves
1 teaspoon baking powder
2 cups *Five Roses* flour

Pour the first seven ingredients into a saucepan and bring to boiling point, then cool. When cold, stir in the sifted flour and beat well. Turn into a buttered cake tin. Bake.

BREAD CAKE

1 cup sugar
2 eggs
3 tablespoons chocolate (melted)
½ cup butter
1 cup *Five Roses* flour
1 cup chopped raisins
1 teaspoon cinnamon
1 cup light bread sponge (see bread recipes)
½ teaspoon soda

Mix, beat well, and bake in moderate oven.

BRIDE'S CAKE

1½ pounds butter
1¾ pounds sugar
2 pounds eggs (18) beaten separately
4 pounds raisins (seeded and chopped)
5 pounds currants (well washed)
1 pound citron (cut fine)
1 pound almonds (blanched and chopped fine)
2 pounds *Five Roses* flour (sifted)
2 nutmegs
Mace (same bulk as nutmegs)
½ pint alcohol
1 teaspoon lemon essence (dissolved in the alcohol)
1 teaspoon soda

Weigh your butter and cut in pieces. Soften, but do not melt. Stir to a cream, then add the sugar and work until white. Beat the yolks of eggs and add. Beat again. Beat the whites to a stiff froth and also add. Sift the flour over the fruit. Mix well, then add to the other ingredients. Last of all, put in the citron and nuts and also a teaspoon soda dissolved in a little water. This makes a 3-story cake. Would cost $12 in a confectioner's —costs about $3.00. Lower story 1 foot in diameter.

See note appended to Groom's Cake recipe.

BRIDE'S CAKE

(No. 2)

½ cup butter
1½ cups fine granulated sugar
1 cup milk
3 cups *Five Roses* flour
2 teaspoons baking powder
6 eggs (whites)
Lemon and orange extracts
1 teaspoon almond extract

Cream the butter, add sugar and cream again. Add milk, flour and baking powder. Fold in the egg whites and 6 drops each of lemon and orange extracts, also 1 teaspoon almond extract. Bake slowly 45 minutes.

ALMOND ICING FOR BRIDE'S CAKE

Put 8 ounces almond paste into a bowl, and add 16 ounces of crushed and sifted sugar. Then add enough egg whites, unbeaten, to make a stiff paste. While working, add gradually 1 teaspoon rose water.

—*Mrs. A. W. Fraser, Iron Springs, Alta.*

BRIDEGROOM'S CAKE

1 cup butter
1 cup sugar
1 cup sweet milk
3 cups *Five Roses* flour
1 teaspoon baking powder
$\frac{1}{2}$ teaspoon vanilla
3 drops lemon extract
4 eggs
$\frac{1}{2}$ pound blanched almonds (shredded)
$\frac{3}{4}$ pound citron
$\frac{1}{2}$ pound candied cherries
$\frac{1}{2}$ pound candied pineapple (shredded).

Cream the butter, add sugar and cream again. Add extract, part of flour and mix well. Add egg yolks beaten until light-colored. Now add the remainder of the flour, into which sift the baking powder, and add the fruit. Then add the egg whites beaten until dry and stiff. Bake in moderate oven 1 hour. Ice the groom's cake in 2 colors to harmonize with color scheme of table decorations.

Note—The Bride's Cake is distributed only to the attendants of the bride. It usually contains a ring. The Groom's Cake is cut by him and given to *his* attendants. This distinction is given so that mistakes may not be made. The wedding cake should be at least 3 months old before being cut to be at its best.

—*Mrs. A. W. Fraser, Iron Springs, Alta.*

BROWN STONE FRONT

Mix together
$\frac{1}{2}$ cup grated chocolate
$1\frac{1}{4}$ cups sweet milk

1 cup brown sugar
1 beaten egg yolk

Boil and let cool before using, then add

$\frac{1}{2}$ cup butter
$\frac{3}{4}$ cup brown sugar
2 eggs (well beaten)
1 teaspoon soda dissolved in
$\frac{1}{4}$ cup sweet milk
1 teaspoon baking powder
1 teaspoon vanilla

Five Roses flour to make as stiff as ordinary layer cake.

Frost on top and between layers.

BUTTERMILK CAKE

1 cup butter
2 cups sugar
2 cups buttermilk
5 cups *Five Roses* flour
1 pound raisins
1 teaspoon soda
1 teaspoon cinnamon
1 nutmeg
Pinch of salt.

Cream the butter and sugar, add spices and salt. Then add the buttermilk with the soda dissolved in it. Lastly, add the flour mixed with raisins. Bake in moderate oven 1 hour. Other fruits and spices can be added to taste.

BUTTERNUT CAKE

1 cup sugar
$\frac{1}{2}$ cup butter
$\frac{1}{2}$ cup sweet milk
2 eggs
2 cups *Five Roses* flour
$\frac{1}{2}$ cup butternut meats (chopped)
$\frac{1}{2}$ cup raisins
2 teaspoons baking powder.

CARAMEL CAKE

3 teaspoons butter
1 cup sugar
3 eggs
$\frac{1}{2}$ cup milk
$1\frac{1}{2}$ cups *Five Roses* flour
2 teaspoons baking powder
Bake in layers. Caramel filling.

[*Cake Making and Baking*]

CHARLOTTE RUSSE

Lady fingers or stale sponge cake
2 cups cream
⅜ cup sugar
Flavoring to taste
1 teaspoon powdered gelatine
⅓ cup cold water or milk.

Note—Instead of gelatine above given, 1 ounce of sheet gelatine may be used.

Line a mould or dish holding about 6 cups with strips of the cake; the side next to the dish will be the outside when served. Trim the cake to fit the dish. The lady fingers may be stuck together with white of egg or dissolved gelatine. Put the gelatine to soak in cold water or milk. Whip the cream, beat in the sugar and flavor. Stand the gelatine over hot water and dissolve it. Then rapidly mix it with the whipped cream and pour into the cake-lined dish. Set away to cool before serving. This recipe came from MacDonald Institute.

CHERRY CAKE

2 eggs
¾ cup sugar
½ cup butter
2 tablespoons water
1 cup cherries
1 teaspoon soda
2 cups (small) *Five Roses* flour

Bake as usual. Ice with any frosting.

HILDA'S CHOCOLATE CAKE
(*The Most Delicious I ever ate*)

¾ cup butter
2 cups sugar
4 eggs (beaten separately)
¾ cup milk
2½ cups *Five Roses* flour
4 teaspoons baking powder
2 tablespoons vanilla
1 teaspoon allspice
½ teaspoon mace
3 tablespoons grated unsweetened chocolate

Cream butter and sugar until very light and white. Add well-beaten yolks, milk and flour (to which has been added and sifted 3 times the baking powder). While mixing in the flour, add gradually

the whites of the eggs which have been beaten dry and stiff. Add to this the vanilla flavoring. Beat briskly for one minute, then divide into 2 equal parts. To one part, add the allspice, mace and chocolate. Bake each part in 2 layers, making in all 4 layers.

FILLING

Boil ½ cup water and 1 cup sugar together, adding while boiling ¼ teaspoon cream of tartar until you can blow the syrup in feathers from a fork. Do not stir while boiling. Have ready the well-beaten whites of 2 eggs. Pour the liquid over this and beat until almost cool. Then add 4 tablespoons grated unsweetened chocolate and beat until cold. Add 1 teaspoon vanilla and spread between the layers and over the cake, alternating the light and dark layers.

CHOCOLATE COFFEE CAKE

1 cup sugar
1 egg
3 tablespoons butter
¼ cup milk
½ cup strong liquid coffee
¼ cup grated chocolate
2 cups *Five Roses* flour
2 teaspoons baking powder

Bake in a loaf or flat pan.

ENGLISH CHRISTMAS CAKE

(It is the best I have ever met. And everybody who has ever eaten the cake thinks it splendid.)

¾ pound butter
1 pound brown sugar
2 pounds currants
2 pounds raisins
1 pound dates
10 eggs (8 will do)
¼ pound almonds
¼ pound walnuts
½ cup molasses (or rose water)
½ teaspoon cloves
1 teaspoon allspice
1 teaspoon mace
1 teaspoon mixed spice
Vanilla
¾ teaspoon soda
5 cups *Five Roses* flour
¾ or 1 cup brandy

Not Bleached—Not Blended

Brandy may be mixed with other ingredients or poured over cake when baked. Bake in very slow oven 3 to 4 hours.

CHRISTMAS CAKE
(Prize Winner)

4 cups sugar
3 cups melted butter
4 cups molasses
2 cups sweet milk
10 eggs
2 teaspoons soda
2 teaspoons each cinnamon, cloves, allspice
2 nutmegs
8 cups *Five Roses* flour
3 pounds raisins
2 pounds currants
1 pound mixed peel
1 pound chopped nuts
    Bake in slow oven.

CHRISTMAS COCOANUT CAKE
(Four Layers)

2 cups sugar
$\frac{3}{4}$ cup butter
4 eggs
$\frac{1}{2}$ cup milk
$2\frac{1}{2}$ cups *Five Roses* flour
2 teaspoons baking powder
Vanilla
Cocoanut

Mix ingredients as usual, reserving the egg whites for filling. Beat whites with $2\frac{1}{2}$ cups sugar added gradually until stiff, white and smooth. Then add cocoanut, spread filling, and sprinkle thickly top and sides with cocoanut.

CITRON CAKE

2 eggs
$2\frac{1}{2}$ cups brown sugar
1 cup (heaping) butter and lard mixed
1 cup sour milk
1 cup citron
$1\frac{1}{2}$ cups currants
$1\frac{1}{2}$ cups raisins
A little lemon peel
Pinch of salt
1 teaspoon cinnamon
1 teaspoon nutmeg
1 teaspoon soda
4 cups *Five Roses* flour

COCOA CAKE

$\frac{1}{2}$ cup sweet milk
2 tablespoons cocoa
1 egg
1 cup white sugar
$\frac{1}{2}$ cup butter
$\frac{1}{2}$ cup sweet milk
1 teaspoon soda
2 cups *Five Roses* flour
Vanilla

Boil $\frac{1}{2}$ cup milk and cocoa till thick. When done, stir in the egg. When cold, add white sugar, butter and other half cup of milk, also soda dissolved in warm water. Add flour and flavoring. Bake in long pan.

COFFEE CAKE

2 cups brown sugar
1 cup molasses
1 cup butter
1 cup strong coffee
2 eggs
1 teaspoon baking soda
2 teaspoons ground cloves
1 teaspoon grated nutmeg
1 pound raisins
1 pound currants
4 cups *Five Roses* flour

COFFEE CAKE
(Eggless)

1 cup coffee
$\frac{1}{2}$ cup butter
1 cup sugar
1 cup molasses
3 teaspoons baking powder
1 teaspoon cloves
1 teaspoon cinnamon
1 nutmeg
$\frac{1}{2}$ pound raisins
$4\frac{1}{2}$ cups *Five Roses* flour

COONTOWN CAKE

2 eggs
$\frac{3}{4}$ cup brown sugar
$\frac{1}{3}$ cup sour milk
$\frac{1}{2}$ cup butter
$\frac{1}{2}$ cup molasses
$\frac{3}{4}$ cup washed currants
1 teaspoon soda
1 teaspoon mixed spice
2 cups (rounding) *Five Roses* flour

[*Cake Making and Baking*]

Bake in 2 layers. Date filling and chocolate icing sprinkled with walnuts.

COCOANUT LOAF CAKE

6 eggs (whites)
1½ cups powdered sugar
¾ cup butter
1 cup sweet milk
3 cups *Five Roses* flour
2 teaspoons baking powder
1 teaspoon lemon essence

Bake this as a loaf cake, and the next day cut off the upper and lower crusts. Trim off the sides, and slice in four layers. Grate 2 cocoanuts and put in the icing. Spread each layer top and sides with plenty of the icing. When cut, it will be perfectly white all through and a very handsome cake.

CORN MEAL CAKE

1 quart sweet milk
4 teaspoons baking powder
4 eggs
1 tablespoon salt
1 cup sugar
1 cup *Five Roses* flour
Corn meal to make stiff batter

Bake ½ hour

CORN CAKE

(*Eggless*)

1½ cups buttermilk
1 cup sour cream
1 cup sugar
3 cups corn meal
½ cup *Five Roses* flour
1 teaspoon soda
Pinch of salt

CORNSTARCH CAKE

1 cup white sugar
½ cup butter
3 eggs
¾ cup milk
1½ cups *Five Roses* flour
½ cup cornstarch
1 teaspoon vanilla
2 teaspoons baking powder

Cream butter and sugar, add eggs one at a time and beat well. Dissolve cornstarch in the milk, sift the baking powder in the flour 3 times. Add flavoring. Bake.

CREAM CAKE

1½ cups white sugar
1 cup sweet cream
¾ cup butter
4 eggs
1 cup sweet milk
1 teaspoon cream of tartar
½ teaspoon soda
3 cups *Five Roses* flour
Vanilla flavoring

Cream the sugar and butter. Break in the egg yolks. Add milk. Put soda and cream of tartar in the flour. Beat well. Add the well-beaten whites last. Beat the whole a little. Bake.

Note—An *Orange Cream Cake* is easily made by substituting 1 teaspoon of orange extract for vanilla in above recipe.

CRUMB CAKE

2 cups *Five Roses* flour
1 cup white sugar
¾ cup butter

Rub to crumbs. Take out 1 cup of the crumbs. Mix the rest with:

1 cup sour milk
1 teaspoon soda
1 teaspoon cloves
1 teaspoon cinnamon
1 egg
1 cup raisins
1 cup currants

Sprinkle the cup of crumbs on top of cake, then put in oven to bake.

CUP CAKE

2 cups sugar
¾ cup butter
3 eggs
3 cups *Five Roses* flour
1 teaspoon cream of tartar
½ teaspoon soda
1 cup milk (or water)
Pinch of salt

Beat the butter and sugar to a cream. Add the eggs well beaten, then the milk in which the soda has been dissolved. Add the flour with the cream of tartar and a little salt sifted together. Beat all together well, and flavour with lemon. Bake in fairly quick oven.

DATE CAKE

$\frac{1}{3}$ cup soft butter
$1\frac{1}{3}$ cups brown sugar
2 eggs
$\frac{1}{2}$ cup milk
$1\frac{3}{4}$ cups *Five Roses* flour
3 teaspoons cinnamon
$\frac{1}{2}$ teaspoon grated nutmeg
1 teaspoon soda
$\frac{1}{2}$ pound stoned dates (cut finely)

Mix in order given, and beat well together 3 minutes. Turn into buttered cake pan, and bake in moderate oven for 40 minutes. Remove from pan and sprinkle top with powdered sugar.

DATE OAT CAKE

1 cup rolled oats
$2\frac{1}{2}$ cups *Five Roses* flour
1 cup brown sugar
$\frac{1}{2}$ cup butter
$\frac{1}{2}$ cup lard
$\frac{1}{2}$ cup sour milk
$\frac{1}{2}$ teaspoon soda (dissolved in milk)

Roll paste quite thin and spread date filling between 2 layers. Cook together and let cool.

DELICATE CAKE

1 cup butter
2 cups sugar
1 cup sweet milk
$\frac{1}{2}$ teaspoon soda
1 cup cornstarch
$2\frac{1}{2}$ cups *Five Roses* flour
1 teaspoon cream of tartar
7 eggs (whites)

Cream butter and sugar, dissolve soda in sweet milk and add. Sift together flour, cornstarch and cream of tartar and turn in to butter and sugar. Beat well, and add whites beaten to a stiff froth. Flavor to taste. Bake in moderate oven. This cake never fails of being good, if made with *Five Roses* flour.

DEVIL CAKE

CUSTARD

1 cup grated chocolate
$\frac{1}{2}$ cup sweet milk
1 cup brown sugar
1 egg (yolk only)
1 teaspoon vanilla

Stir in saucepan, cook and cool

CAKE

1 cup brown sugar
$\frac{1}{2}$ cup butter
2 cups *Five Roses* flour
$\frac{1}{2}$ cup sweet milk
2 eggs (beaten separately)
1 teaspoon soda

Cream butter, sugar and yolks of eggs. Add milk. Sift flour and whites of eggs beaten stiff. Beat all and add custard. Add last 1 teaspoon soda dissolved in little warm water.

Ice with marshmallow frosting.

EAGLE CAKE

1 cup brown sugar
$\frac{1}{2}$ cup butter
1 egg
1 cup sour milk
1 cup raisins
2 cups *Five Roses* flour
1 teaspoon soda (dissolved in the milk)
1 teaspoon cinnamon
$\frac{1}{2}$ teaspoon each cloves and nutmeg

FIG CAKE

(*Eggless*)

1 pound figs
1 pound brown sugar
$\frac{1}{2}$ teaspoon salt
$1\frac{1}{2}$ teaspoons cream of tartar
$1\frac{1}{2}$ teaspoons soda
4 tablespoons melted butter
Five Roses flour

Boil separately for 2 hours figs and brown sugar with enough water to cover. When cool, add the salt, cream of tartar and soda. Dissolve both the cream of tartar and soda in milk. Add melted butter and enough *Five Roses* flour to make a soft dough.

[*Cake Making and Baking*]

EAGLE CAKE
(*Eggless*)

1 cup sugar
⅓ cup butter
1 cup sour milk
1 teaspoon cinnamon
½ teaspoon cloves
½ nutmeg
1 teaspoon soda
1 cup raisins
2 cups *Five Roses* flour

ECONOMY CAKE

1 teacup sugar
1 egg
1 tablespoon shortening
2 teaspoons baking powder
Enough *Five Roses* flour to make it drop
    easy from the spoon
    Beat well. Bake ½ hour

FAVORITE CAKE

½ cup milk
1 cup pulverized sugar
½ cup butter
1 egg (whole) and whites of 2 more
2 cups (scant) *Five Roses* flour
1 teaspoon (large) baking powder
1 teaspoon vanilla
1 cup seeded raisins (well-floured)

    Bake in square tin. Frost with plain
or chocolate icing. Cut in squares.

FIG LOAF

½ cup butter
1 cup granulated sugar
½ cup sweet milk
2 cups *Five Roses* flour
    (sifted)
3 teaspoons baking pow-
    der
1 teaspoon vanilla extract
3 eggs (whites)
Figs

    Beat butter to a cream. Gradually
beat in sugar, then alternately milk and
sifted *Five Roses* flour with baking powder. Flavor with vanilla extract and beat
in whites of 3 eggs beaten stiff.

    Have ready about ½ pound table figs,
cut in two or three pieces, and drop these

pieces in batter here and there as it is
being poured into buttered pan. Bake in
moderate oven, and ice when it becomes
cold.

PLAIN FRUIT CAKE

½ pound currants (well washed)
½ pound raisins
1 cup butter (beaten to a cream)
1 cup white sugar
1 cup milk
3 cups *Five Roses* flour
3 eggs (beaten separately)
3 teaspoons baking powder
    Paper a dish and bake 1 hour

NOTES ON FRUIT CAKES

1. Heavy cakes are often the result of
using damp fruit. After washing, currants and raisins should be left in colander in a slightly warmed place for
some time. Should also be dredged
with flour before mixing with other ingredients.

2. Fruit cakes, generally speaking, should
bake in from 2 to 4 hours.

3. It is well to remember that dried fruits
added to doughs make them stiffer, as
they absorb the moisture in the dough,
while with fresh fruits the contrary is
the case.

4. Pan should not be more than two-thirds
full.

5. To enrich the colour, housewives sometimes brown the flour before making a
spice or fruit cake.

WHITE FRUIT CAKE

1 cup butter
1 cup sugar
1 cup milk
2½ cups *Five Roses* flour (more or less)
2 teaspoons baking powder
1 pound dates
¼ pound shelled almonds
¼ pound citron peel
Juice and rind of 1 orange
2 tablespoons brandy
Whites of 7 eggs
1 pound raisins

    Mix butter and sugar together. Add
milk and flavoring. Dredge the fruit
with flour, mix all together, and add the

whites of the **7** eggs beaten stiff. Bake in a slow oven **2** hours.

FRUIT CAKE
(*Without Eggs or Butter*)

1 cup brown sugar
½ cup molasses
1 cup sour cream
1 tablespoon soda (put in cream when dissolved)
1 tablespoon boiling water (to dissolve soda)
3½ cups *Five Roses* flour
2 pounds raisins
½ pound currants
Citron
1 cup preserves
Pinch of salt
Spices
Almond flavor

If made **1** month before using, this will be found a very moist cake and may be kept any length of time.

OATMEAL FRUIT CAKE
(*Eggless*)

1 cup brown sugar
½ cup butter
1 teaspoon allspice
1 cup sour milk
1½ teaspoons soda
1¾ cups *Five Roses* flour
1½ cups oatmeal
1 cup chopped raisins

RIBBON FRUIT CAKE
(*Also Called "Checkerboard Cake"*)
No. 1
DARK PART

1½ cups sugar (white or brown)
1 cup butter
2 cups browned *Five Roses* flour
Yolks of 6 eggs
1½ pounds raisins
½ pound currants
½ pound citron peel
1 pound dates
¼ pound nuts
1 teaspoon soda (dissolved)
½ teaspoon cloves, cinnamon, nutmeg and allspice

[*Cake Making and Baking*]
LIGHT PART

1 cup white sugar
½ cup butter
½ cup sweet cream
2½ cups *Five Roses* flour
2 teaspoons baking powder (**heaping**)
1 pound almonds (chopped fine)
½ pound citron peel
½ pound grated cocoanut
1 teaspoon rose water
1 teaspoon lemon extract
1 small slice orange peel
Whites of 6 eggs

RIBBON FRUIT CAKE
No. 2
LIGHT PART

1½ cups white sugar
½ cup butter
½ cup sweet milk
2 cups *Five Roses* flour
Whites of 4 eggs
½ teaspoon soda
1 teaspoon cream of tartar

DARK PART

1 cup brown sugar
½ cup butter
½ cup sweet milk
Yolks of 4 eggs
1 square grated chocolate
Flavor with cinnamon
Cloves and nutmeg
2 cups *Five Roses* flour

Mix and bake in two layers. Put lemon cheese between.

STEAMED FRUIT CAKE

4 eggs
1 cup butter
1 cup sugar
½ cup molasses
½ cup strong coffee (or tea)
1 pound raisins
1 pound currants
½ pound walnuts
¼ pound citron
1 teaspoon each kind of spice
1 teaspoon soda
¼ pound dates (optional)
Five Roses flour to make rather stiff dough.
Steam 2½ hours.

[*Cake Making and Baking*]

FUDGE CAKE

1¾ cups *Five Roses* flour
1½ cups sugar
½ cup butter
½ cup sweet milk
2 eggs
1 teaspoon vanilla
2 ounces grated chocolate
1½ teaspoons cream of tartar
1 teaspoon soda (dissolved)

Just before adding the soda, add to ingredients ¾ cup boiling water. Bake in 2 layers.

FILLING FOR FUDGE CAKE

⅛ cup grated chocolate
1 cup sugar
½ cup sweet milk
Butter size of ½ egg

Boil until thick enough to spread on cake without running. Add 1 teaspoon vanilla before spreading on cake. This is really a fine cake for cutting and will keep several days. Walnuts may be added.

GOLD AND SILVER CAKE

GOLD PART

8 yolks of eggs
1 cup butter
2 cups sugar
4 cups *Five Roses* flour
1 cup sour milk
1 teaspoon soda
1 teaspoon cornstarch
Lemon or vanilla extract

SILVER PART

2 cups sugar
1 cup butter
4 cups *Five Roses* flour
1 cup milk
1 teaspoon soda
1 teaspoon cornstarch
8 whites of eggs
Almonds

Put in alternate spoonfuls of each part.

Note—The above recipe may be made separate, and called gold cake, and the second part called silver cake.

HANDY CAKE

1 egg
1 cup sugar
Butter size of egg
½ cup sweet milk
2 small teaspoons baking powder
Five Roses flour to make stiff batter
Flavor with vanilla

Bake in 1 large tin or 2 small ones. Ice with chocolate.

HICKORY NUT CAKE

½ cup (scant) butter
1 cup granulated sugar
1 cup sour cream or milk
1 teaspoon soda
2 teaspoons cream of tartar
Pinch of salt
1 cup hickory nut meats (chopped finely)
2 eggs
1½ cups (heaping) *Five Roses* flour

ICE CREAM CAKE

1 cup sugar
½ cup butter
½ cup milk
1¾ cups *Five Roses* flour
1 teaspoon baking powder
3 eggs
½ teaspoon vanilla

Cream the sugar with the butter. Add milk, then the flour sifted with the baking powder. Beat well and fold in whites of eggs. Add vanilla. Bake in 2 tins from 20 to 30 minutes. Frost with yolks of eggs and white sugar.

ROLL JELLY CAKE

(*Jelly Roll*)

3 eggs (beaten separately)
1 cup sugar
2 tablespoons sweet milk
2 teaspoons baking powder
1 cup *Five Roses* flour
Lemon flavoring

Beat the yolks with the sugar and sweet milk. Beat the whites to a stiff froth, then thoroughly with the yolks and sugar. Mix the flour and baking powder and add to other ingredients. Flavor with lemon and bake immediately in moderately hot oven.

Not Bleached-Not Blended

Note for Jelly Rolls—While hot, remove from pan and lay on cloth wrung out of cold water. Sprinkle a little sugar on cloth, and while cake is still warm spread with jelly and roll quickly, putting your hands under the cloth. This helps to keep cake from cracking. If there are any crusty edges that might interfere with proper rolling, these should be trimmed off with a sharp knife while still hot.

JERSEY LILY CAKE

½ cup butter
1 cup granulated sugar
1 cup sweet milk
2 eggs (whites)
1 teaspoon vanilla
2 teaspoons baking powder
2 cups *Five Roses* flour
Raisins
Chopped walnuts.

Cream butter and sugar. Add whites beaten stiff, also milk, vanilla, baking powder and sifted flour. Put half the batter in a small dripping pan, then put a layer of seeded raisins and a layer of chopped walnuts, and finally the balance of the batter. Bake in moderate oven. Ice and put whole walnut meats on top.

JUNE CAKE

1 cup pulverized sugar
½ cup butter (small)
2 eggs (well beaten)
1½ cups *Five Roses* flour
½ cup milk
1½ teaspoons baking powder
1 teaspoon vanilla.

When nearly cold, frost with pulverized sugar mixed with a little cream or rich milk, flavored with vanilla or almonds.

KENTISH CAKE

¼ pound butter
¼ pound castor sugar
¼ pound *Five Roses* flour
3 eggs
1 ounce grated chocolate
1 ounce ground almonds
1 ounce dessicated cocoanut
¼ teaspoon vanilla.

[Cake Making and Baking]

Cream butter and sugar Add gradually flour and the 3 eggs, beating the mixture for several minutes after each egg is added Stir in the grated chocolate, almonds and cocoanut. Flavor with vanilla or other flavoring. Butter a flat round cake tin, line with buttered paper and put cake mixture into it spreading it evenly over tin. Bake 30 or 40 minutes. When cold, cover with chocolate icing.

KING EDWARD CAKE

½ cup butter
1 cup brown sugar
3 eggs well beaten
2 cups *Five Roses* flour
½ cup sour milk
1 teaspoon soda
1 teaspoon cinnamon
2 tablespoons molasses
1 cup raisins (boiled in hot water).

Mix as usual. Put raisins in last of all.

PLAIN LAYER CAKE

1 cup white sugar
½ cup butter
½ cup sweet milk
3 eggs
1 cup *Five Roses* flour
½ cup cornstarch
3 teaspoons baking powder.

Bake in 3 tins, and when cool spread with jelly.

Note on Layer Cake—Ordinary layer cakes should bake in from 15 to 20 minutes.

LEMON CAKE

2 cups white sugar
1 cup sweet milk
½ cup butter
2 teaspoons baking powder
3 cups *Five Roses* flour
2 eggs (beaten separately).

Mix as usual, sifting the baking powder and flour together before adding. Add the eggs last of all, the whites and yolks beaten separately. Bake in layers, and spread with filling preferred.

[Cake Making and Baking]

LIGHT CAKE

1 cup sweet cream
1 egg
1 cup sugar
1½ cups *Five Roses* flour
3 teaspoons baking powder
Pinch of salt.

Bake in 2 layers.

RAISIN LAYER CAKE

1 cup brown sugar
½ cup butter
3 eggs
2 tablespoons syrup
2 cups chopped raisins
½ teaspoon cloves
½ teaspoon cinnamon
Little nutmeg
½ cup sour milk
2 teaspoons cream of tartar
1 teaspoon soda (scald the soda)
1½ cups *Five Roses* flour.

Bake in 2 layers.

DARK LAYER CAKE

(*Eggless*)

¾ cup brown sugar
½ cup molasses
½ cup warm water
1 tablespoon butter
1 teaspoon soda
2 cups *Five Roses* flour.

Bake in 2 layers. Nut filling.

DARK LAYER CAKE

½ cup sugar
1 egg
1 tablespoon butter
1 cup syrup
1 cup boiling water
1 teaspoon soda in hot water
1 teaspoon mixed ginger, cloves
and cinnamon
⅔ cup *Five Roses* flour.

Use nut filling.

QUICK LAYER CAKE

2 eggs
1 cup sugar
1 cup (scant) milk
2 tablespoons melted butter
2 teaspoons baking powder in
2 cups *Five Roses* flour.

Mix and bake as usual. Put any filling between layers.

MADEIRA CAKE

½ pound white sugar
½ pound *Five Roses* flour
¼ pound butter
1 tablespoon baking powder
1 teacup milk
2 eggs.

Beat eggs and butter separate, then add sugar. Beat well together, then stir in the flour, milk and baking powder. Put in a well-greased tin and bake about 1½ hours in moderate oven.

MARBLE CAKE

LIGHT PART

1 cup white sugar
½ cup butter
½ cup sweet milk
½ teaspoon soda
1 teaspoon cream of tartar
3 eggs (whites beaten stiff)
2 cups *Five Roses* flour.

Mix all together and beat.

DARK PART

1 cup brown sugar
½ cup butter
½ cup molasses
½ cup sour milk
¾ teaspoon soda (dissolved in milk)
1 teaspoon cloves
½ teaspoon nutmeg
3 eggs (yolks beaten stiff)
2½ cups *Five Roses* flour.

Mix all together and beat dark part stiffer than white part.

When each part is ready, drop a spoonful of dark, then a spoonful of light batter over the bottom of baking dish; and proceed so until you fill the pan. Be quick or cake will be heavy. Bake in hot oven.

CHEAP MARBLE CAKE

1 egg
1 cup sugar
1 cup milk
2½ cups *Five Roses* flour (sifted)
2 teaspoons baking powder
4 tablespoons butter.

Take ½ the mixture and add 2 table-spoons molasses, 1 (small) teaspoon cloves, cinnamon and allspice. Drop first a spoonful of dark, then a spoonful of light batter. If desired, 2 tablespoons chocolate may be added to the dark part.

CHOCOLATE MARBLE CAKE

½ cup butter
1 cup sugar
½ cup sweet milk
1½ cups *Five Roses* flour
1 teaspoon cream of tartar
4 eggs (whites only).

Take 1 cup of the above mixture, and add to it 5 tablespoons powdered choco-late. Wet with 2 tablespoons milk and flavour with vanilla. Put a layer of white and then of dark batter in baking pan. Bake in hot oven. Ice with chocolate icing.

MARGUERITE CAKE

1 cup brown sugar
¼ cup butter
2 eggs
½ cup buttermilk
½ cup black syrup
1 teaspoon (small) mixed spice
1 teaspoon soda
2 cups *Five Roses* flour.

Bake in 2 layers.

MOCHA CAKE

No. 1

½ cup butter
½ cup sugar
½ cup milk
2 eggs
2 cups *Five Roses* flour
2 teaspoons baking powder.

Spread in square pan, and cut in squares. Cover with almond icing and roll in nuts.

[Cake Making and Baking]

MOCHA CAKE

No. 2

½ cup butter
1 cup sugar
1½ cups *Five Roses* flour
Yolks of 3 eggs
1 teaspoon baking powder
Grated rind of 1 lemon and
1 teaspoon of juice
1 tablespoon warm water.

Have whites well beaten and add al-ternately with the flour. Add the warm water last.

ICING

1 cup icing sugar
½ cup butter
3 tablespoons cream
1 teaspoon vanilla.

Put all in a bowl, and set in hot water until melted. Cut the cake in squares, dip in icing, then in rolled peanuts that have previously been browned. See Coffee Icing.

MOLASSES LAYER CAKE

No. 1

1 egg (or yolks of 2)
1 cup molasses
1 tablespoon melted butter
½ cup boiling water
1 teaspoon soda
1 teaspoon cinnamon
½ teaspoon cloves
2 cups *Five Roses* flour.

Make 2 thick layers. Put together with any kind of jelly, and frost top.

MOLASSES CAKE

(No. 2)

4 eggs
1 cup sugar
1 cup molasses
1 cup butter
4 cups *Five Roses* flour
1 cup sour milk
1 teaspoon soda
Spice of all kinds
Fruit (if desired).

[Cake Making and Baking]

MOLASSES CAKE

(*Eggless*)

2 cups molasses
1 cup lard
2 teaspoons soda dissolved in
1 cup hot water
4 cups *Five Roses* flour
Flavor
Pinch of salt.

MOUNTAIN CAKE

1 cup rich sour cream
1 cup sugar
2 eggs
1 teaspoon soda
½ teaspoon cream of tartar
2 cups *Five Roses* flour
½ teaspoon lemon extract
Pinch of salt.

Stir cream and sugar together, add the eggs beaten, then the soda dissolved in a little warm water, then the flour gradually (with the cream of tartar and pinch of salt mixed in it). Add the lemon extract, beat well, and bake for ½ hour in moderate oven.

NATIONAL CAKE

WHITE PART

Cream together 1 cup white sugar and ½ cup butter, then add ½ cup sweet milk, beaten whites of 4 eggs, ½ cup cornstarch, 1 cup *Five Roses* flour (into which have previously been mixed 1 teaspoon cream of tartar and ½ teaspoon soda). Flavor with lemon extract.

BLUE PART

Cream together 1 cup blue sugar sand and ½ cup butter; then add ½ cup sweet milk, the beaten whites of 4 eggs, 2 cups *Five Roses* flour (into which have previously been mixed 1 teaspoon cream of tartar and ½ teaspoon soda). No flavor.

RED PART

Cream together 1 cup red sugar and ½ cup butter; then add ½ cup sweet milk, the beaten whites of 4 eggs and 2 cups of *Five Roses* flour in which mix ½ teaspoon cream of tartar and ½ teaspoon soda. No flavor.

Place in a baking pan, first the red, then the white, and last the blue mixture. Bake in moderate oven.

WATER MELON CAKE

By taking the white and red parts as given above, what is called a watermelon cake is readily obtained by baking in layers and putting the red between two white parts.

PEANUT CAKE

½ cup butter
¾ cup milk
1 cup (small) sugar
1 teaspoon (heaping) baking powder
2 eggs (beaten separately)
Flavoring
Enough *Five Roses* flour to make stiff batter.

ICING

Pulverized sugar and milk, enough to moisten 10 cents worth of peanuts. Butter size of a hickory nut chopped fine. Flavoring.

Bake cake in a shallow tin. When done, cut in small triangles. Take each piece and cover all over, except bottom, with icing. Then sprinkle with the peanuts and set away to harden.

PEANUT LOAF

4 tablespoons butter
1 cup sugar
1 egg
1½ cups *Five Roses* flour
1½ teaspoons baking powder
½ cup milk
1 cup peanuts (cut fine).

Bake in a loaf.

OATMEAL CAKE

3 eggs
½ cup butter
1½ cups brown sugar
2 cups oatmeal
1¼ cups *Five Roses* flour
1 teaspoon soda
1 teaspoon baking powder
1 cup boiling water.

Ice with boiled icing.

Not Bleached - Not Blended

OATMEAL CAKES
(*Eggless*)

3 cups oatmeal
2 cups *Five Roses* flour
1 cup sugar
1 cup shortening
$\frac{3}{4}$ cup buttermilk
$\frac{1}{2}$ teaspoon soda.

Roll the paste out thin, spread date filling on half, then turn the other half over and cut with cake cutter.

ORANGE CAKE

4 eggs
6 ounces sugar
$\frac{1}{2}$ pound *Five Roses* flour
1 orange
1 teaspoon baking powder
$\frac{1}{2}$ teacup milk
$\frac{1}{2}$ cup butter.

Put the eggs and sugar into a basin, and beat for 10 minutes. Add the rind of the orange grated. Sift in the flour and baking powder. Pour in the milk and mix all together. Butter a cake tin and bake in a moderate oven for $\frac{1}{2}$ hour. Use the juice of the orange for the icing.

1-2-3-4 CAKE

1 cup butter
2 cups sugar
3 cups *Five Roses* flour
4 eggs
1 cup cold water (or milk)
2 teaspoons cream of tartar
1 teaspoon soda
1 teaspoon vanilla.

Sift the cream of tartar and soda with the flour twice before adding. The addition of 1 cup raisins makes a pleasing variety.

PEEL CAKE

$1\frac{1}{2}$ cups brown sugar
$\frac{1}{2}$ cup butter
3 eggs (well beaten)
$\frac{1}{2}$ cup sour milk
2 cups chopped raisins
$\frac{1}{2}$ cup peel (orange or lemon)
$\frac{1}{2}$ nutmeg
1 teaspoon cinnamon
1 teaspoon soda
Five Roses flour to mix stiff
Bake in slow oven.

PEPPER CAKE

1 cup raisins (stoned)
1 cup baking syrup
2 eggs
$\frac{1}{2}$ cup butter
$\frac{1}{2}$ cup sour cream
$\frac{1}{2}$ cup sugar
2 cups *Five Roses* flour
1 teaspoon soda
1 teaspoon cinnamon
Nutmeg
1 teaspoon black pepper

Bake about 40 minutes.

CHEAP PLUM CAKE

$\frac{1}{2}$ pound *Five Roses* flour
$\frac{1}{4}$ pound currants
$\frac{1}{4}$ pound mixed raisins
1 ounce candied peel
6 ounces brown sugar
6 ounces butter
2 eggs
$\frac{1}{2}$ teaspoon allspice
$\frac{1}{2}$ teaspoon baking powder
$\frac{1}{4}$ teaspoon carbonate of soda.

Rub butter and flour together, and add other ingredients. Mix lightly with warm milk. Bake in a slow oven $1\frac{1}{2}$ hours.

PORK FRUIT CAKE
(*Eggless*)

1 pound solid fat pork (chopped very fine)
Pour over this 1 pint boiling water, then add:
2 teaspoons baking soda
2 cups sugar
1 cup molasses
1 pound currants
1 pound seeded raisins
$\frac{1}{2}$ pound citron peel (cut fine)
1 cup chopped nuts
$\frac{1}{2}$ glass brandy
1 teaspoon cloves
1 teaspoon ginger
2 teaspoons cinnamon
1 grated nutmeg
4 cups (even) *Five Roses* flour.

Pour into a pan lined with buttered paper, and bake for 2 hours in moderate oven.

[*Cake Making and Baking*]

PORK CAKE

1 pound pork (chopped fine), boil 2 minutes in half pint of water
1 cup molasses
2 cups sugar
3 eggs
2 teaspoons soda
1 pound raisins (chopped fine)
1 pound dates (chopped)
Cinnamon
Cloves
Nutmeg
Five Roses flour to make stiff batter.

This makes 3 loaves.

POOR MAN'S CAKE

2 cups brown sugar
½ pound lard
1 teaspoon (scant) salt
2 teaspoons cinnamon
1 teaspoon cloves
1 teaspoon nutmeg
1 teaspoon soda
½ cup currants
1½ cups water
3½ cups *Five Roses* flour

Bake 50 minutes in moderate oven.

OLD-FASHIONED POTATO CAKE

(*Eggless*)

2 cups *Five Roses* flour
1 teaspoon salt
2 teaspoons baking powder
1 cup finely mashed potatoes
Milk or water.

Mix the flour with the salt and baking powder. Then add the finely mashed pota-toes and water or milk enough to make a soft dough. Turn the whole into a well-greased frying pan and cook slowly, turning occasionally, adding a little more lard to the pan each time until the cake is a nice brown on each side and well cooked through. This should take about 30 minutes. Spread with butter and eat while hot. Very cheap and a nice change for supper.

POUND CAKE

1 pound sugar
1 pound butter
1 pound eggs (10 eggs, shelled)
1 pound *Five Roses* flour (4 cups).

Cream the butter and sugar together, then add beaten whites of eggs, after the yolks, ½ teaspoon soda in a tablespoon milk. Put 1 teaspoon cream of tartar in flour, also a little salt. Add lastly lemon essence. Bake 30 minutes in moderate oven.

PRUNE CAKE

1 cup sugar
⅔ cup butter
3 eggs (reserve whites of 2 for icing)
1 cup cooked prunes (chopped)
1 teaspoon (small) soda
4 tablespoons sour milk or hot water
1 teaspoon cinnamon
1 teaspoon nutmeg
1 teaspoon cloves
1½ cups *Five Roses* flour.

RASPBERRY CAKE

1 cup white sugar
½ cup butter
2 eggs
2 tablespoons buttermilk
1½ cups *Five Roses* flour
1 teaspoon cinnamon
1 teaspoon soda
Nutmeg
1 cup raspberries (to be added last).

Bake in layers.

RIBBON CAKE

2 cups sugar
1 cup butter
4 eggs
1 cup milk
3½ cups *Five Roses* flour
1 teaspoon cream of tartar
½ teaspoon soda
Flavor with lemon.

Bake ⅔ of above mixture in 2 pans. To the remainder, add 1 tablespoon molasses, 1 cup chopped raisins, ½ cup currants, a piece of citron chopped fine, ¼ teaspoon each of cinnamon, cloves and nutmeg. Bake in pan. Then put the sheets alternately with a little jelly between. Ice the top layer.

Not Bleached ~ Not Blended

RAILWAY CAKE

1 pound *Five Roses* flour
6 ounces butter and lard mixed
6 ounces sugar
2 eggs
½ pint milk
1 teaspoon carbonate of soda
1 teaspoon cream of tartar
1 ounce caraway seeds
2 ounces candied peel.

This cake requires no beating. Put into a quick oven at once, and bake 1 hour.

RICE CAKE

1 cup white sugar
1 cup rice flour
5 eggs
1 teaspoon flavoring.

Beat all together 20 minutes. Bake ½ hour in moderate oven.

RYE MEAL CAKE

2 eggs
1 cup brown sugar
1 cup sour cream
1 cup *Five Roses* flour
1 cup rye meal
1 teaspoon soda
1 teaspoon cream of tartar.

Currants may be added, if desired.

SCRIPTURAL CAKE

4½ cups *Five Roses* flour, 1 Kings iv, 22
1 cup butter, Judges v, 25
2 cups sugar, Jeremiah vi, 20
2 cups raisins, 1 Samuel xxx, 12
2 cups figs, Nahum iii, 12
2 cups almonds, Numbers xvii, 8
½ cup sour milk, Judges iv, 19
3 tablespoons honey, 1 Samuel xiv, 25
Pinch of salt, Leviticus ii, 13
6 eggs, Jeremiah xvii, 11
2 teaspoons soda, Amos iv, 5
Season with spices to taste, 2 Chronicles ix, 9.

Follow Solomon's prescription for making a good boy (Proverbs iii, 12) and you will have a good cake. Bake in slow oven.

[*Cake Making and Baking*]

SHINGLES

½ cup butter
1½ cups sugar
½ cup boiling water
½ teaspoon soda
Five Roses flour to stiffen
Vanilla.

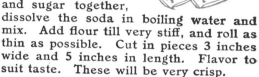

Beat the butter and sugar together, dissolve the soda in boiling water and mix. Add flour till very stiff, and roll as thin as possible. Cut in pieces 3 inches wide and 5 inches in length. Flavor to suit taste. These will be very crisp.

SHORT CAKE

1 quart *Five Roses* flour
1 teaspoon salt
4 teaspoons baking powder
½ cup butter and lard
1¼ cups milk.

Sift together four times dry ingredients. Rub in butter and lard. Add milk. Bake in sheets in quick oven. Double the shortening if cake is wanted very crisp and short. Place fresh fruit between layers, and serve with sugar and cream.

PEACH SHORT CAKE

Make a rich baking powder crust and roll to ¼ inch thickness. Cut with cooky cutter, and butter ½ the resultant small cakes. Place the unbuttered ones on top. Bake them, then split open and fill each one with fresh peaches cut in thin slices, and sprinkle with powdered sugar. Serve hot with whipped cream. Cream is nicer if flavored with almond extract and filled with chopped almonds.
—*Miss Rea Moon, Oakwood, Ont.*

STRAWBERRY SHORT CAKE

(No. 1)

2 cups *Five Roses* flour
2 teaspoons baking powder
½ teaspoon salt
2 teaspoons sugar
¾ cup milk
¼ cup butter
Strawberries.

[*Cake Making and Baking*]

Mix the flour, baking powder, salt and sugar, and sift twice. Work in the butter with the tips of the fingers, and add the milk gradually. Toss on floured board,  divide into two parts. Pat and roll out. Bake in pie tins in a hot oven 15 minutes. Split and butter. Sweeten strawberries to taste, crush slightly and put between and on top of the short cake. Cover the top with whipped cream. Decorate top with whole raw berries. Serve at once.

To Cut a Short Cake—Take a firm hold of a piece of silk thread at either end as you would a knife. It will not make it soggy like using a knife. Especially good for splitting hot shortcake.

STRAWBERRY SHORT CAKE
(No. 2)

4 cups *Five Roses* flour
2 teaspoons cream of tartar
1 teaspoon soda
1 tablespoon sugar
1 teaspoon salt
½ cup butter
1 egg
1 cup (large) milk
Strawberries (hulled and cleaned).

Sift together the flour, cream of tartar, soda, sugar and salt. Rub the butter into the dry ingredients. Beat the egg and add the milk. Stir lightly and quickly into the prepared flour. Roll in two sheets ½ inch thick, laying one sheet on top of the other. Bake in a hot oven. While hot, separate layers and spread with chopped strawberries and sugar between layers and over top.

RHUBARB SHORT CAKE

Use same recipe as above for layers. When cake is done instead of spreading with chopped strawberries, spread stewed rhubarb between layers sandwich fashion. Sprinkle sugar on top and serve hot.

BOSTON SHORT CAKE

4 cups *Five Roses* flour
4 teaspoons baking powder
Shortening enough to make better than pie paste

1 handful granulated sugar
1 egg (well beaten in cup)
Fill balance of cup with sweet milk or cream.

Roll crust and spread with desired filling. Roll up and slice about 1 inch thick and bake.

SHREWSBURY CAKES

Sift 1 pound sugar, some pounded cinnamon and a nutmeg grated into 3 pounds of *Five Roses* flour (sifted). Add a little rose water to 3 eggs (well beaten) and mix with the flour, etc. Then pour into it as much melted butter as will make it of a good thickness to roll out. Mould well and roll thin. Cut into desired shapes with a biscuit cutter.

SPICE CAKE

3 eggs
1½ cups sugar
1 cup butter
½ cup milk
½ cup hot water
1 teaspoon baking powder
½ teaspoon soda
1 teaspoon grated nutmeg
1 teaspoon cinnamon
1 teaspoon cloves
1 cup raisins
¼ pound chopped walnuts
3 cups *Five Roses* flour.

SPONGE CAKE
(No. 1)

6 eggs
3 cups sugar
4 cups *Five Roses* flour
1 cup cold water
2 teaspoons cream of tartar
1 teaspoon soda
Flavoring.

Beat eggs until very light. Add sugar and beat again. Sift the flour and cream of tartar together. Dissolve soda in the water, and add to the eggs and sugar, mixing in the flour at once. Flavor to taste, and bake in a moderate oven for 30 minutes or more.

To Brown Sponge Cakes—Do not paper the tins, but rub with melted suet and then sprinkle with fine sugar.

[*Cake Making and Baking*]

SPONGE CAKE
(No. 2)

4 eggs (6 sometimes used)
1 cup granulated sugar
1 cup *Five Roses* flour
¼ teacup water
1 teaspoon baking powder
Pinch of salt
Vanilla.

Beat eggs separately. Bring sugar and water to a boil, pour boiling syrup slowly on eggs after mixing them. Then beat for 10 minutes before adding the flour, which you sift 4 times with the baking powder. Then stir in lightly. Add salt and flavoring. Bake in a pan with a funnel in centre. Sprinkle the top lightly with sugar before putting in oven. Bake very slowly for 40 minutes. Don't open oven for first 15 minutes.

CHILDREN'S SPONGE CAKE

1½ cups *Five Roses* flour
2 teaspoons cream of tartar
1 cup sugar
2 eggs (broken in a cup)
Fill cup up with milk or cream.

Stir all together in a mixing bowl. Beat hard for 5 minutes. Bake about 10 minutes in muffin pan.

BURNT SUGAR CAKE

1 cup sugar
2 eggs
½ cup butter
1 cup white sugar
1 teaspoon vanilla
1 cup cold water
2 cups *Five Roses* flour
2 teaspoons baking powder.

Take 1 cup white sugar and set on stove to burn until quite brown. Then add ½ cup boiling water and stir well. When cool, add half to the cake mixture. Mix the rest with icing sugar and put on top.

SUNSHINE CAKE

Whites of 7 eggs beaten to a stiff froth with ½ teaspoon cream of tartar. Add 1 cup sugar, yolks of 5 eggs well beaten, 1 cup *Five Roses* flour and 1 teaspoon flavoring. Bake in a loaf.

SULTANA CAKE

¼ pound butter
2 eggs
¼ pound sugar
¼ pound sultanas
2 ounces peel
2 cups *Five Roses* flour
1 teaspoon baking powder.

Cream butter and sugar. Add separately and unbeaten. Beat well. Then add flour and other ingredients. Bake 1 hour.

STRAWBERRY CAKE

½ cup butter
1 cup (large) sugar
3 eggs (save white of 1 for icing)
1½ cups *Five Roses* flour
1 cup canned strawberries (equal quantity fruit and juice)
1 teaspoon soda.

Note—Raspberries or cherries may be used.

Cream butter and sugar. Add beaten eggs, then strawberry fruit and juice (cold). Sift soda with flour and add last. Strawberry icing.

TIC-TAC-TOE CAKE

4 eggs
2½ cups sugar
1 cup butter
1 cup sweet milk
2½ cups *Five Roses* flour
2 teaspoons baking powder.

Mix and divide into 3 parts. In one part put:

½ cup raisins
½ cup currants
½ teaspoon nutmeg or cinnamon.

In another part put:

2 tablespoons grated chocolate
1 teaspoon vanilla extract.

In remaining part put:

1 teaspoon lemon extract.

TRIFLE CAKE

Line a glass bowl with a layer of sponge cake. Cover with red currant jelly or raspberry jam, then more cake. Sprinkle over this a handful of cocoanut and ½ cup chopped almonds. Saturate with ½ cup brandy. Pour over all a custard made of

[Cake Making and Baking]

1 pint milk, 2 eggs, 2 tablespoons sugar, pinch of salt, vanilla. When cold, serve with whipped cream.

TUMBLER CAKE

2 tumblers of brown sugar
1 tumbler butter

1 tumbler molasses
1 tumbler sweet milk
5 tumblers *Five Roses* flour
2 teaspoons (small) soda
1 teaspoon cloves
1 teaspoon cinnamon
1 teaspoon nutmeg.

Above makes a good fruit cake by adding 1 pint raisins and 1 cup currants.

WALNUT CHOCOLATE CAKE

Yolks of 2 eggs
1 cup sugar
½ cup butter
¼ cup sweet milk
⅔ cup grated chocolate
1 cup walnut meats
2 cups *Five Roses* flour
1 teaspoon soda
2 teaspoons cream of tartar
1 teaspoon vanilla.

Sift the soda and cream of tartar with the flour. Bake in 2 layers, and ice with white boiled icing. Use orange filling.

WASHINGTON LOAF CAKE

3 cups light brown sugar
2 cups (scant) butter
1 cup sour milk
Little nutmeg
1 teaspoon cinnamon
5 eggs
1 teaspoon soda
4 cups *Five Roses* flour
1 cup currants
2 cups raisins
1 cup almonds.

Mix as usual, stirring fruit in last, well dredged with flour.

BOILING WATER CAKE

3 eggs (well beaten)
1 cup sugar
1 cup *Five Roses* flour
3 teaspoons (small) baking powder
4 tablespoons *boiling* water.

Have oven at good baking heat and water boiling before starting to make this cake, as it must be made quickly. Pans should be oiled ready to receive it. It will be found good either as a layer, plain, or roll jelly cake. Beat eggs well, and beat in the sugar. Have ready the flour with the baking powder sifted in. Add 4 tablespoons boiling water to eggs and sugar, stirring constantly. Add the flour, beat well and bake at once from 10 to 15 minutes, according to heat of oven and size of baking pan. The thinner it is spread, the shorter time it takes to bake. Handy when milk is scarce.

WEDDING CAKE
No. 1

12 eggs
4 cups brown sugar
2 pounds butter
2 cups molasses
½ cup sour milk
6 cups currants
6 cups raisins (seeded)
½ pound mixed peel
2 teaspoons cinnamon
½ nutmeg
½ teaspoon pepper
2 teaspoons soda
2 teaspoons cloves
2 teaspoons mixed spice
1 teaspoon mace
10 cents worth almond nuts (cut fine)
Five Roses flour to stiffen.

Note—Some cooks add 1 pint brandy. (See also recipes for Bride's Cake (2) and Groom's Cake, with note.)

WEDDING CAKE
No. 2

12 eggs
2 pounds sugar
2 pounds butter
5 pounds raisins
5 pounds currants
1 pound dates
1 pound mixed peel
1½ pounds almonds (blanched and chopped)
2 nutmegs
1 teaspoon mace
2 teaspoons cinnamon
2 teaspoons soda
1 pint rich cream
Five Roses flour to thicken.

Note—Rose water may be added, if desired.

WHEAT SHORTS CAKE

1½ cups wheat shorts
1 cup *Five Roses* flour
½ cup sugar
Pinch of salt
2 teaspoons (small) soda
4 teaspoons (small) cream of tartar
1 cup milk
½ cup water.

Mix together quickly and bake in hot oven.

WHITE CAKE

½ cup butter
2 cups granulated sugar
3 eggs (beaten separately)
½ cup sour milk
2 teaspoons (heaping) baking powder
¼ teaspoon saleratus
2 cups *Five Roses* flour.

Cream butter, then mix in the sugar next add the beaten yolks, to which a little of the beaten whites has been added. Then add sour milk to which has been added the saleratus. Add the sweet milk and flour. Put in little milk, then little flour, till everything is used up. Flavoring may be put in the sour milk. Hot oven for 20 minutes.

YORKSHIRE PARKIN

1 pound coarse oatmeal
½ pound lard
½ pound cooking sugar
2 teaspoons mixed spice
1 pound *Five Roses* flour
1 pound molasses
2 teaspoons ground ginger
1 teaspoon baking powder
Juice of 1 lemon
3 eggs
Milk to stiffen.

Mix well and bake in a slow oven in dripping tin.

[*Cake Making and Baking*]

LANCASHIRE PARKIN

1½ pounds fine oatmeal
½ pound butter
1 teaspoon ginger
1 teaspoon baking soda
½ pound *Five Roses* flour
½ pound cooking sugar
1 pound molasses.
1 egg
2 cups milk.

Dissolve the soda in the milk. Melt the butter and molasses together. Beat the egg in, and add the soda last. Mix well. Bake in slow oven in dripping tin.

PARKIN

(*Without Eggs*)

No. 1

1 pound *Five Roses* flour
¼ pound sugar
3 ounces butter
3 ounces lard
½ gill syrup
A little milk
1 teaspoon ginger
1 teaspoon bicarbonate soda.

Roll out thin and bake 20 to 30 minutes in a moderate oven.

PARKIN

(*Without Eggs*)

No. 2

1¼ pounds fine oatmeal
1 ounce ground ginger
10 ounces moist sugar
½ pound *Five Roses* flour
½ pound syrup
A little milk

Warm the milk with the syrup and add enough to the dry ingredients to make a stiff paste. Pour into a greased tin, and bake slowly for about 1 hour.

◇ ◇ ◇

FIVE ROSES is packed to suit the convenience of housewives in clean, new bags of 7 pounds, 14 pounds, 24 pounds, 49 pounds, 98 pounds; also in barrels of 196 pounds and half-barrels of 98 pounds.

Not Bleached—Not Blended

GINGERBREAD

(*This recipe won 1st Prize with
Five Roses Flour*)

1½ cups *Five Roses* flour (sifted)
½ cup sour milk
½ cup sugar
½ cup molasses
⅓ cup butter
1 egg (not beaten)
1 teaspoon soda
1 teaspoon ginger.

Don't beat very much. Bake 20
minutes in moderate oven in shallow pan.

GINGERBREAD

No. 2

½ cup butter
1 cup granulated sugar
1 tablespoon ginger
2 eggs (well beaten)
1 cup molasses
Pinch of salt
1 teaspoon baking soda (dissolved in mo-
    lasses)
1 cup cold water
3 cups *Five Roses* flour.

Mix in the order named, and bake 20
or 30 minutes. Icing may be used, if
preferred.

GINGERBREAD

(*Eggless*)

2 cups molasses
2 teaspoons ginger
⅔ cup butter
3 teaspoons soda
1 cup buttermilk
Five Roses flour to thicken.

Stir the molasses and butter together,
add ginger. Put the soda in a cup and
pour a little boiling water over it, then fill
up cup with buttermilk. Mix thick with
flour, but not too thick. Quick oven.

SOFT GINGERBREAD

1 egg
½ cup brown sugar
½ cup sour milk
2 teaspoons soda
½ cup molasses
1½ cups *Five Roses* flour
1 teaspoon mixed spices
1 teaspoon ginger
2 tablespoons shortening.

Note—One cup raisins sometimes
used.

Measure the flour and spices into a
sieve. Measure brown sugar and egg into
mixing bowl and stir until the sugar is
dissolved. Measure sour milk and dissolve in it half the soda. Heat the molasses, and add remaining soda. Stir the
egg and sugar until the latter is dissolved,
then add sour milk and molasses with the
dissolved soda. Sift in the flour and spices.
Lastly stir in the shortening, which has
been melted in baking tin. Bake about
25 minutes in quick oven. Bake either in
gem pans or in a ginger cake tin.

HONEYCOMB GINGERBREAD

(*Eggless*)

1½ pounds treacle
1½ ounces ground ginger
½ ounce ground caraway seeds
2 ounces allspice
4 ounces orange peel (shredded fine)
½ pound sweet butter
6 ounces blanched almonds
1 pound honey
1½ ounces carbonate of soda
Five Roses flour to make moderately thick
    dough
¾ ounce tartaric acid.

Make a pit in 5 pounds *Five Roses*
flour, then pour in the molasses and all
the other ingredients, creaming the butter. Then mix them altogether into a
dough. Work it well, then put in ¾ ounce
tartaric acid. Put dough in buttered pan,
and bake for 2 hours in a cool oven. To
know when it is ready, dip a fork into it;
if it comes out sticky, put in oven again.
Otherwise, it is ready.

GINGERBREAD

(*Without Butter, Milk or Eggs*)

1 cup brown sugar
1 cup blackstrap
1 tablespoon meat fryings
1 cup boiling water
1 teaspoon soda dissolved in boiling water
1 teaspoon ginger
Five Roses flour to make thin batter.

Bake slowly in moderate oven. Any desired frosting may be used.

SCOTCH SHORTBREAD

(No. 1)

1 pound *Five Roses* flour
2 ounces sugar (sifted)
1 ounce candied peel (sliced small)
8 ounces butter (more or less).

Mix the flour and sugar together, and add the candied peel. Make into a paste with 8 to 10 ounces of good butter sufficiently warm to be liquid. Press the paste together with the hands and mould upon tins into large cakes nearly 1 inch thick. Pinch the edges and bake the shortbread in a moderately warm oven for 20 minutes or longer if it should not be crisp, but do not allow it to become deeply colored.

[Gingerbread]

SHORTBREAD

(No. 2)

¾ pound *Five Roses* flour
½ pound butter
¼ pound light brown sugar.

Cream butter and sugar, add flour, mixing thoroughly with the hands. Roll not too thin and cut into small-sized cakes with a fork and bake in moderate oven.

SCOTCH SHORTBREAD

(No. 3)

¼ pound fresh butter
2 ounces fine sugar
½ ounce cornstarch
6 ounces *Five Roses* flour.

Knead cornstarch and sugar into the butter, then gradually knead in flour. Roll out into a round. Pinch the edges with fore-finger and thumb, prick over top with fork, cut in eight. Place on baking dish and bake in moderate oven 20 minutes. Leave on tin to harden.

◇ ◇ ◇

*N*O *other flour has received such emphatic commendation. No other flour has such enthusiastic advertisers among Canadian housewives.*

Not Bleached - Not Blended

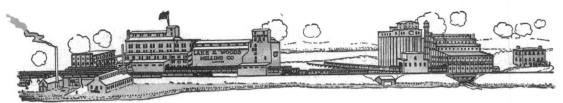

KEEWATIN. "A" and "C" Mills—Combined Daily Capacity 10,000 Barrels

Also "D" Mill at MEDICINE HAT—Daily Capacity 2,200 Barrels

THE daily capacity of the mammoth mills of Lake of the Woods Milling Company is **13,700** barrels. Every working day the hungry rolls grind into *Five Roses* flour about 62,000 bushels of the splendid wheat that has made Canada famous throughout the world.

Wherever the best baking is done, the product of these mills is known and appreciated. In Canada, the West Indies, South Africa, the United Kingdom and elsewhere, discriminating housewives insist upon *Five Roses* and will have no other. In less than one generation *Five Roses* flour has become the standard by which others are judged.

PORTAGE LA PRAIRIE. "B" Mill—Daily Capacity 1,500 Barrels

Not Bleached - Not Blended

DOUGHNUTS, CRULLERS AND OTHER FRIED CAKES

THE fat should be ready when the doughnuts are cut. All lard or other fat to fry doughnuts, crullers or fritters *must* be sizzling hot.

Heat your fat gradually and test by dropping into it a small spoonful of batter. If it rises at once to the surface, swells rapidly and browns quickly, the fat is ready. Another test is to sprinkle the smallest quantity of water when it should give off a crackling sound. It is not at all necessary that the fat should smoke like a factory chimney.

Always have a large quantity cut before beginning to fry, and so avoid the danger of fat cooling or smoking.

Avoid putting too many cakes into the fat at once, else the heat will be reduced and, instead of becoming crisp and toothsome, the outer surfaces will absorb the grease. Care must be taken at this stage, or you may get "dough" nuts in the full sense of the word—brown outside and uncooked dough within.

Doughnuts and fritters should fry in from 3 to 5 minutes. When crisp and golden brown, remove from kettle with perforated spoon and set in heated colander or on brown unglazed paper to drain free from grease. Roll while still hot in powdered sugar.

When properly made (and carefully hidden) these dainty goodies will not only keep several weeks, but improve with age. Pack in a stone crock, sprinkling each layer with powdered sugar.

If doughnuts be put into the oven and thoroughly re-heated before serving, they will taste marvellously like pastry that has just been made.

❖ ❖ ❖

PLAIN DOUGHNUTS
No. 1

1 egg
1 cup sugar
1 teaspoon (small) soda
1 cup fresh sweet milk
2 cups *Five Roses* flour
2 teaspoons (small) cream of tartar
Nutmeg to taste.

Beat the eggs and sugar together. Dissolve soda in the milk and mix with above. Sift flour and cream of tartar together, beat well and add nutmeg. Roll out as soft as can be handled. Cut with doughnut cutter and fry in hot lard. If skimmed milk be used, add 1 teaspoon melted butter. These are excellent. I double the rule, which makes 5 dozen.

DOUGHNUTS
No. 2

1 cup sugar
2 eggs
2 tablespoons melted butter
⅔ cup sweet milk
2 teaspoons (heaping) baking powder
Five Roses flour to roll
Flavor with spice or lemon.

DOUGHNUTS WITHOUT EGGS

6 cups *Five Roses* flour
2 cups sugar
1 cup cream
1 cup skim milk
2 teaspoons cream of tartar
1 teaspoon soda
1 teaspoon salt.

Not Bleached - Not Blended

[Doughnuts and Crullers]

Sift the cream of tartar, soda and salt with the flour. Dissolve the sugar in the cream and skim milk. Add the nutmeg and pour into the flour, forming all into a dough. Roll out, cut and fry.

MOLASSES DOUGHNUTS

1 cup molasses
2 cups buttermilk
2 eggs
1 teaspoon ginger
2 teaspoons melted butter
Five Roses flour to make soft dough.

Do not knead, but pat lightly with the hands. Roll out and fry in hot lard. These are delicious.

POTATO DOUGHNUTS
(Eggless)

2 cups hot mashed potatoes
2 cups sugar
1 cup sweet milk
2 tablespoons butter
5 teaspoons (level) baking powder
1 teaspoon vanilla
Five Roses flour to make soft dough.

Mix as usual. Roll out $\frac{1}{2}$ inch thick. Fry in hot grease. The potatoes keep the doughnuts soft. These keep fresh much longer than if made with eggs.

RICH RAISED DOUGHNUTS
(With Yeast)

1 cup butter
2 cups sugar
4 cups scalded milk
1 yeast cake dissolved in
$\frac{1}{2}$ cup lukewarm water
Five Roses flour
3 eggs (beaten).

Cream the butter. Add 1 cup sugar and beat again to a cream. Add the scalded milk and yeast cake dissolved in lukewarm water. Mix with *Five Roses* flour to make a thick batter. Cover and let rise over night. In the morning, add to the sponge the 3 beaten eggs, another cup sugar and $\frac{1}{2}$ nutmeg grated. Mix with *Five Roses* flour to make a smooth dough than can be kneaded. Let rise, turn out on a board and roll half an inch thick.

Cut into shape, and let rise again for about $\frac{1}{2}$ hour. Then fry and roll in powdered sugar, after draining a minute on paper.

SOUR CREAM DOUGHNUTS

1 cup thick sour cream
$1\frac{3}{4}$ cups sour milk
2 eggs
1 cup lightest yellow sugar
1 teaspoon salt
1 teaspoon soda (dissolved in little hot water)
1 teaspoon cream of tartar
Five Roses flour to roll.

Set dough aside in cool place for 3 hours. Then roll and cut quickly. Fry in hot fat. Do not mix too stiff.

CRULLERS

$\frac{1}{2}$ pound sugar
3 eggs
1 tablespoon sweet milk
$1\frac{1}{2}$ ounces butter
Five Roses flour
1 teaspoon soda
Salt.

Mix the ingredients with enough *Five Roses* flour to make thick dough. Roll this out and stamp little cakes which drop into hot lard.

CRULLERS WITHOUT EGGS

1 pint sugar
$\frac{2}{3}$ pint cold water
2 tablespoons lard
2 teaspoons cream of tartar
1 teaspoon soda
1 teaspoon salt
Flavor with lemon or vanilla
Five Roses flour.

FRITTERS
No. 1

3 eggs (beaten separately)
3 cups *Five Roses* flour
2 cups sour milk or buttermilk
1 teaspoon soda
1 teaspoon salt.

Not Bleached - Not Blended

Dissolve the soda in the milk, stir in the egg yolks, then the sifted flour and salt, lastly the whites beaten stiff. Have kettle of boiling fat ready, drop the batter in by spoonfuls, and cook the fritters to a light brown.

Note—Sliced bananas or chopped apples can be added, if desired.

Fat in which fritters are fried should be very deep and boiling hot. When done, remove like doughnuts and drain from grease. Transfer to hot platter covered with folded napkin and serve at once.

FRITTERS

No. 2

2 tablespoons butter
6 tablespoons sweet milk
1 teaspoon baking powder
Five Roses flour to roll.

Roll thin, cut into small squares, and fry in hot lard. Serve with maple syrup.

PARSNIP FRITTERS

Make ordinary fritter batter. Have boiled 4 or 5 parsnips (whole). Put fritters on pan and slice parsnips lengthwise. Lay 2 or 3 slices on top of each fritter. The number of slices to use on each fritter will depend on size of the fritters. Brown nicely, and serve with any good syrup or honey.

PUMPKIN FRITTERS

Boil the pumpkin, then pour off the water. Let it get quite cold. Take a plate and press the pumpkin down, so as to squeeze out all watery particles still left. Stir in 2 eggs and some *Five Roses* flour (well dried) to make a batter. From a spoonful of the batter you will have a fritter which must be baked in a pan with boiling fat. Let the pot not be too sparing, the deeper the pot you fry them in the less you use and the nicer the cake. Mix pounded cinnamon and sugar and serve with the cakes.

[Doughnuts and Crullers]

JERSEY WONDERS

1 pound *Five Roses* flour
¼ pound butter
¼ pound sifted sugar
4 eggs
2 teaspoons baking powder (more, if desired).

Beat eggs light and mix with sugar and butter. Sift in the flour and baking powder. Allow to rise. Then roll out thin and cut out about 3 inches square. Make 3 slits across each, and fry until brown in hot lard.

BEEF CROQUETTES

4 cups minced meat
1 egg
4 tablespoons home-made tomato catsup
2 tablespoons salad dressing
⅓ cup *Five Roses* flour
1 medium-sized onion (chopped).

Mix all together. Moisten with gravy, season to taste. Make into cakes and fry.

CHICKEN CROQUETTES

½ pint cold chicken (cut fine)
1 tablespoon parsley (chopped fine)
1 teaspoon salt
½ teaspoon pepper
1 tablespoon butter
2 tablespoons *Five Roses* flour
¼ pint milk
Pepper and salt
1 egg
Bread crumbs.

Mix the chicken with the parsley and season with salt and pepper. Make a sauce with 1 tablespoon butter, 2 of flour, Add the milk, also season to taste. Add the chicken mixture to this and make into rolls. Beat the egg and add 1 teaspoon water. Roll the croquettes in the egg, flour well and roll in sifted bread crumbs. Shape into cutlets by flattening with knife and fry in hot lard.

[*Doughnuts and Crullers*]

POTATO CROQUETTES

1 quart mashed potatoes (cooked)
Butter size of an egg
1 teaspoon salt
¼ teaspoon pepper
1 egg
1 cup milk or cream.

Mould into small balls. Fry in lard.

BEEF AND POTATO CAKES

Mix with a cup of cold roast beef 2 cups mashed potatoes seasoned as for the table. Add a beaten egg. Mix and shape into balls and flatten like cakes. Roll in bread crumbs. Fry a golden brown. Nice for breakfast or tea.

Note on Breading Fried Things—The reason many fried things have a flat taste, though the mixture may be highly seasoned, is that the seasoning of the bread crumbs has been neglected. Try mixing the bread crumbs with salt, pepper, and, if desired, a drop or two of any desired seasoning, before moulding.

For frying or covering the tops of entrees, use bread crumbs instead of cracker crumbs, as they have less of a flat taste.

TWIST CAKES

½ pint sour milk or buttermilk
2 cups sugar
1 cup butter
3 eggs (well beaten)
1 teaspoon soda
1 teaspoon nutmeg
Five Roses flour to make smooth dough.

Roll out and drop in boiling fat.

MENNONITE TOAST

3 eggs
1 pint sweet milk
Pinch of salt.

Beat eggs well, and add sweet milk and salt. Cut slices 1 inch thick from a loaf of bread made with *Five Roses* flour. Remove crust. Dip slices into the egg and milk. fry like doughnuts in hot lard or dripping till a delicate brown. Sprinkle with powdered sugar and serve hot.

◇ ◇ ◇

*D*AINTY, disappearing doughnuts; light, digestible crullers and fried things—how quickly *Five Roses* accustoms one to quality. It has the knack of producing just the right kind of dough that tastes like nuts, that bobs deliciously in the rich, deep fat. And yet *Five Roses* is the sturdy, glutinous flour that resists fat absorption, taking barely enough to brown becomingly, to crisp quickly without greasiness, heaviness or sogginess. Never an outraged stomach with *Five Roses* doughnuts and crullers. Golden to the hungry eye, tooth-teasing, able-bodied nuts of dough that improve with age when carefully concealed from busy little milk teeth.

SMALL CAKES OF ALL KINDS

Commonly called "Goodies"

TO PROVIDE VARIETY IN SMALL CAKES

IT is sometimes desirable to make from the same dough a wide variety of small cakes. To provide this and at the same time get various flavours, you might collect extracts and spices, a lemon, an ounce or so of chocolate, whole and chopped walnuts, shelled peanuts, nuts of all kinds, chopped raisins, citron, candied cherries, some of the macaroni alphabets and some sugared caraway seeds. Other things which might be used in the same way are candied peel, angelica, preserved ginger, almond paste, shredded cocoanut, cardamon seeds, and any other materials used to give colour or flavour to candies.— *Selected.*

◆ ◆ ◆

JAM-JAMS

SANDWICH CAKES

2 cups white sugar
1 cup butter
1 cup cream
1 egg
Five Roses flour to make soft dough
2 teaspoons cream of tartar
1 teaspoon soda
Flavour with spice, nutmeg or cinnamon.

Roll out, cut into small cookies and bake. Put two together with icing sugar and peach, quince or any jelly you please.

JAM-JAMS
No. 1

2 eggs
1 cup brown sugar
1 cup shortening
6 tablespoons syrup
2 teaspoons (small) soda
1 teaspoon lemon or vanilla
Five Roses flour to roll thin.

Roll thin, cut and bake. While warm, put two together with jam.

JAM-JAMS
No. 2

2 quarts *Five Roses* flour
1 teaspoon soda
2 teaspoons cream of tartar
1½ cups lard
1½ cups yellow sugar (rolled smooth)

3 eggs
1 tablespoon vanilla
Milk.

Wet the soda with milk. Add lard, flour, sugar. Then add the eggs. Knead well and roll thin. Cut long with knife and put jam in between. Ice or not, according to taste. Good either way.

SNOWBALLS

2 cups sugar
1 cup sweet milk
½ cup butter
3 cups *Five Roses* flour
3 teaspoons baking powder
5 eggs (whites).

Mix and beat well. Bake in deep square tin. Cut in 2 inch squares. Remove outside. Frost on all sides, then roll in freshly grated cocoanut.

GINGER JAM-JAMS
(*Eggless*)

1 cup sugar
1 cup molasses
1 cup shortening
½ cup hot water
1 teaspoon soda
1 tablespoon vanilla
1 teaspoon ginger
Pinch of salt
Five Roses flour to mix stiff.

Not Bleached - Not Blended

[*Jam-Jams*]

OATMEAL JAM-JAMS

¾ cup butter (or half lard)
½ cup sweet milk
1 egg
1 cup sugar
½ teaspoon soda
1 cup *Five Roses* flour
2 cups rolled oats.

If not stiff enough, add a little more flour and oatmeal maintaining proportions. Turn a large dripping pan upside down and roll out on the bottom covering the whole pan, and bake in a quick oven. When done, cut in halves and spread jam between the halves. Then cut in squares. Date, or raisin or fig fillings may be used instead of jam, if desired. These are really delicious.

OATMEAL JAM-JAMS

(*Eggless*)

2 cups *Five Roses* flour
2 cups rolled oats
1 cup dripping
1 cup sugar
¼ teaspoon salt
½ teaspoon cinnamon
1 teaspoon soda
Sour milk.

Rub all ingredients together with the exception of the soda, which should be dissolved in enough sour milk to hold other ingredients together. Roll thin. Have ready 1 pound of figs cooked soft with 1 cup sugar and a little water. Cut cakes into shapes and put a spoonful of figs on top then put another cake on and press edges firmly together and bake in a hot oven. These are delicious. Filling may be altered to suit taste.

LEMON CHEESE CAKES

Whites of 4 eggs (or whites of 4
    and yolk of 1)
1½ cups of sugar
½ cup butter
½ cup milk
2 teaspoons baking powder
2 cups *Five Roses* flour
    Use lemon filling.

JUMBLES

2 cups sugar
1 cup lard
2 eggs
1 cup sweet milk
1 teaspoon soda
½ teaspoon cream of tartar
Five Roses flour to mix stiff
Lemon extract (optional).

Beat lard and sugar to a cream, and add the eggs. Dissolve the soda in milk and add the cream of tartar. Stir in flour till about as stiff as pound cake. Put plenty of flour on the board, and dip out the dough with a spoon. Flour rolling pin well and roll to about ¼ inch thick. Sprinkle sugar over top, cut out and bake in quick oven. When done, set on edge. The softer these jumbles are rolled out, the better they will be.

FRUIT JUMBLES

No. 1

1½ cups white sugar
½ cup butter
1 pound chopped dates
¼ pound chopped walnuts
3 cups *Five Roses* flour
3 eggs
1 teaspoon vanilla
1 teaspoon soda (dissolved).

Stir butter and sugar together, then add the beaten eggs. Add flour, fruit and vanilla, and last of all the soda. The dough should be very stiff. Dip spoon into hot water and spread each spoonful into the shape of cake.

FRUIT JUMBLES

No. 2

1 quart *Five Roses* flour
1 pint granulated sugar
1 cup butter
4 eggs
4 tablespoons canned berry or cherry
    juice
1 teaspoon cinnamon
2 teaspoons baking powder.

ALMOND MACAROONS

Blanch dry ½ pound almonds, and make into a paste with 1 teaspoon rose water. Beat 3 egg whites with ½ cup powdered sugar, adding slowly ½ teaspoon almond extract. Then add the almonds, chopped fine. If very soft, add 1 tablespoon *Five Roses* flour. Roll in balls size of walnuts with wet hands. Flatten a little and place apart on buttered paper. A pastry tube is very useful in shaping the cakes. Bake 15 or 20 minutes in a moderate oven.

COCOANUT MACAROONS

No. 1

½ pound sugar
½ pound cocoanut
4 eggs (whites)
1 tablespoon *Five Roses* flour.

Mix all together, and make into small cakes. Bake slowly.

COCOANUT MACAROONS

No. 2

3 eggs (whites only beaten stiff)
½ pound desiccated cocoanut
¾ cup granulated sugar.

Drop from teaspoon on buttered baking sheet. Cook in moderate oven till slightly brown.

OATMEAL MACAROONS

3 cups rolled oats
1 cup sugar
2 eggs
2 tablespoons butter
2 teaspoons baking powder
1 tablespoon milk.
Five Roses flour to make into small balls.

Bake in hot oven on greased pan.

BROWNIES

2 eggs
1 cup white sugar
⅔ cup butter
1½ cups *Five Roses* flour
1 teaspoon cinnamon
1 teaspoon allspice
1 pound dates
½ pound shelled walnuts.

[*Jam-Jams*]

Stone the dates, chop dates and nuts fine. Bake in slow oven for 20 minutes. Put dates and nuts in last. Grease pan well.

GRAHAM BROWNIES

1 cup butter (melted)
2 cups brown sugar
2 eggs
2 tablespoons buttermilk
2½ cups *Five Roses* flour
2½ cups graham flour
1 teaspoon soda.

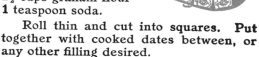

Roll thin and cut into squares. Put together with cooked dates between, or any other filling desired.

LADIES' FINGERS

1 egg (or 2 eggs)
1 cup sugar
½ cup butter
¼ cup sweet milk
1 pint *Five Roses* flour
2 teaspoons baking powder
1 teaspoon vanilla.

Beat the butter, sugar and egg together until very light. Add the vanilla and milk. Last, add the baking powder and flour sifted together. Cut in little strips about ¼ inch thick, roll in sugar and bake in quick oven. Use your hands to roll, instead of rolling pin.

GERMAN LADY FINGERS

5 eggs (yolks)
½ pound sugar
½ pound blanched almonds
Grated rind of 1 lemon
½ pound *Five Roses* flour.

Beat the yolks and sugar for 15 minutes. Add almonds cut fine and grated lemon rind. Mix well, and add the flour gradually. Roll out and cut into strips length and size of your forefinger. Bake in moderate oven.

CHEESE FINGERS

Cut puff paste into strips length and size of forefinger, sprinkle with a layer of grated cheese, press upon this another strip of pastry, sprinkle again with cheese and bake in quick oven.

[*Jam-Jams*]

CHEESE STRAWS

(*Eggless*)

1 cup *Five Roses* flour
2 cups chopped cheese

1 tablespoon butter
1 teaspoon (scant) baking powder
Pinch of salt.

Mix with water and roll out like pie crust. Cut in strips and bake light brown.

CHEESE STRAWS

$\frac{3}{4}$ cup grated cheese
$\frac{1}{2}$ cup butter
1 teaspoon sugar
$\frac{1}{2}$ teaspoon salt
Pinch of cayenne pepper
1 teaspoon nutmeg
1 egg
2 tablespoons sweet cream
1$\frac{1}{4}$ cups *Five Roses* flour.

Mix all other ingredients, then add flour. Roll out and cut 6 inches long by $\frac{1}{4}$ inch wide. Bake in moderate oven.

❖ ❖ ❖

DROP CAKES

HERMITS

No. 1

2 eggs
1 cup (large) sugar
$\frac{3}{4}$ cup shortening
$\frac{3}{4}$ cup sour milk
$\frac{3}{4}$ teaspoon soda
$\frac{1}{2}$ teaspoon cinnamon
1$\frac{1}{2}$ cups *Five Roses* flour
1$\frac{1}{2}$ cups oatmeal
$\frac{1}{2}$ cup chopped raisins
1 cup walnuts (chopped).

Drop from spoon onto buttered pan and bake. They should spread out like cookies.

Note on Drop Cakes—This class of cake bakes very well on buttered paper in baking pan.

HERMITS

No. 2

1$\frac{1}{2}$ cups sugar
$\frac{1}{2}$ cup molasses
1 cup butter
$\frac{1}{2}$ cup milk
3 eggs (not beaten) added separately
1 cup chopped raisins
$\frac{1}{2}$ cup currants
$\frac{1}{2}$ teaspoon nutmeg
$\frac{1}{2}$ teaspoon cloves
$\frac{1}{2}$ teaspoon cinnamon
1$\frac{1}{2}$ teaspoons baking powder
Five Roses flour for medium stiff dough.

Drop from fork onto a pan and bake in moderate oven. If *Five Roses* flour is used, it does not need to be made as stiff as with ordinary flour.

BRAN DROPS

1 cup bran
1$\frac{1}{2}$ cups *Five Roses* flour
2 teaspoons baking powder
1 egg
Butter size of egg
1 cup sugar
Milk or water.

Mix with milk or water until of about the consistency of fruit cake. Drop by spoonfuls on a greased dripping pan. Bake in quick oven.

BROWN BETTIES

1 cup sugar
2 cups *Five Roses* flour
1 egg
2 tablespoons butter
$\frac{1}{2}$ teaspoon soda
1 teaspoon cream of tartar
$\frac{1}{2}$ teaspoon salt
4 tablespoons milk
$\frac{1}{2}$ cup chopped nuts
$\frac{1}{4}$ cup chopped raisins.

Drop from a teaspoon and bake in quick oven.

COCOANUT DROPS

3 eggs (whites only) beaten stiff
1 cup icing sugar
2 cups grated cocoanut
2 tablespoons *Five Roses* flour.

Drop from spoon on buttered pan, and bake in quick oven.

GINGER DROPS

3 eggs
1 cup butter
1 cup brown sugar
1 cup molasses (or syrup)
1 tablespoon ginger
1 tablespoon soda dissolved in
1 cup boiling water
5 cups *Five Roses* flour (unsifted).

Drop from tablespoon into well-greased pan, 3 inches apart. Bake in slow oven.

HONEYCOMB DROPS

1 pound syrup
½ pound brown sugar
4 ounces butter
11 ounces *Five Roses* flour
2 teaspoons ground ginger (or more to taste)
6 drops oil of lemon.

Drop from spoon on greased pan. Give plenty of room to spread. Bake in moderate oven to golden brown. Syrup made from sugar is best.

OATMEAL DROPS

3 cups oatmeal
3 cups *Five Roses* flour
2 cups brown sugar
1 cup raisins (seeded and chopped)
1 teaspoon cinnamon
1 cup melted butter
2 eggs (well beaten)
1 teaspoon soda dissolved in
½ cup sour milk.

Mix all dry ingredients together, then add other materials. Drop by teaspoons on greased tin and bake in moderate oven. One cup walnut meats may be added, if desired.

DROP TEA CAKES

6 cups *Five Roses* flour
1 cup sugar
1 cup butter
1 cup lard
1 cup currants
1 egg (beaten)
Pinch of salt
3 teaspoons baking powder.

Mix all together with milk enough to make a stiff batter. Drop into buttered pans and bake in quick oven.

[*Drop Cakes*]

TEA KISSES

Sift together 2 cups *Five Roses* flour, 2 teaspoons baking powder, ½ teaspoon salt Then rub in ½ cup butter, 1 cup white sugar, 2 eggs, scant ⅓ cup of sweet milk and 1 teaspoon lemon flavouring. Drop on buttered tin. Sprinkle with granulated sugar, and bake in hot oven.

NUGGET CAKES

1 cup brown sugar
½ cup butter and lard mixed
2 eggs
3 cups wheat flakes or rolled oats
1 cup (large) *Five Roses* flour
1 cup chopped nuts
1 teaspoon soda
2 teaspoons cream of tartar
1 teaspoon vanilla.

Drop in tiny balls on pan, and bake in quick oven.

ROCKS

1 cup butter
1½ cups white sugar
3 eggs (yolks)
½ teaspoon ground cloves
¾ teaspoon ground cinnamon
1 pound chopped dates
1 cup broken walnuts (not too fine)
1 teaspoon baking soda dissolved in
1 tablespoon hot water
2¾ cups *Five Roses* flour.

Cream butter and gradually add and beat in the sugar. Add the beaten yolks. Mix in other ingredients in order given. Lastly, add the whites of the three eggs beaten dry. Drop into buttered pans and bake in fairly quick oven.

COCOANUT ROCKS

½ cup butter
2 eggs
½ pound cocoanut
½ cup white sugar
1 teaspoon baking powder
Five Roses flour to make stiff.

Mix with hands. Roll out like cookies, and bake.

[*Drop Cakes*]

OATMEAL WAFERS

1 cup sugar
1 cup butter
½ cup sour milk
¼ teaspoon cinnamon and nutmeg
⅓ cup walnuts (chopped fine)
1 teaspoon soda
4 cups oatmeal
2 cups *Five Roses* flour.

Roll thin, cut in squares, and bake in quick oven.

PEANUT WAFERS

1 pint chopped peanuts
3 eggs (well beaten)
1 cup white sugar
1 teaspoon salt
2 tablespoons butter
2 tablespoons sweet milk
Five Roses flour to stiffen.

Roll and cut in strips like lady fingers.

ROSETTE WAFERS

2 eggs
1 teaspoon sugar
¼ teaspoon salt
1 cup milk
1 cup *Five Roses* flour (more or less).

Beat the eggs slightly with sugar and salt; add milk and flour, and beat until smooth.

CHOCOLATE WAFERS

2 ounces chocolate

1 cup brown sugar
1 cup white sugar (granulated or powdered)
1 cup butter
1 egg (beaten)
2 cups *Five Roses* flour
1 teaspoon vanilla.

Grate the chocolate and set the cup into hot (not boiling) water to melt. Mix together the brown sugar and the white and rub in the butter. When creamy, add the beaten egg and then the melted chocolate, stirring briskly. Finally, add the flour and bake in quick oven.

OYSTER PATTIES

A good oyster patty shell may be obtained by merely omitting the sugar from recipe for Rosette Wafers.

BUTTER CRACKERS

Rub 4 ounces butter into 1 pound *Five Roses* flour. When well mixed, add enough cold water to dampen and add 1 teaspoon salt. Beat with rolling pin until smooth, then roll thin, cut into small cakes, and bake on tins in quick oven for 15 minutes. Let each cracker be about the size of a dollar piece and nearly ½ inch thick.

OATMEAL CRACKERS

4 cups oatmeal
2 cups *Five Roses* flour
1 cup sugar
1 teaspoon soda
1 cup shortening
Sour milk to roll out.

SWEET CRACKERS

3 cups sugar
1 cup lard
1 cup sweet milk
2 eggs
2 ounces baking ammonia
Five Roses flour to make stiff dough
Pinch of salt.

Dissolve ammonia in 1 cup hot water and add salt. Use lemon flavour to taste. Mix stiff with *Five Roses* flour. Roll thin and bake in hot oven.

❖ ❖ ❖

DON'T *risk disappointing the children. Always use FIVE ROSES flour for small cakes of all kinds. Packed in barrels or bags—the same good flour.*

JAMS   JELLIES   CONSERVES

(Favourite Home Recipes of Five Roses Flour Users)

SPICED CRANBERRIES

5 pounds cranberries
3½ pounds brown sugar
2 cups vinegar
2 tablespoons ground cinnamon and all-
    spice
1 tablespoon cloves.

Boil all together for 2 hours. Serve with hot or cold meats.

CITRON PRESERVES

Cut 1 large citron in small pieces. Use same weight of citron and sugar, add 1½ pounds raisins and 4 large lemons sliced thin. Cook 2 or 3 hours until clear.

PICKLED DATES

One pound of dates. Separate and put in bottle. Take enough vinegar to cover, add a little whole allspice and bring all to a boil. Pour over dates, let stand for a few days and they are ready for use.

TO HAVE FRESH FRUIT THE YEAR ROUND

Use raspberries (red or black), red currants or long blackberries. Mash the fruit well and take 1 cup of fruit and 1 cup of granulated sugar alternately. Put in porcelain kettle, stir well several times during the 48 hours it should stand, then put in cans and cover. Do not cook. Keep in coolest place you have. I have prepared this every year for four years and have not had any spoil.
—*Mrs. David Soper, Straffordville, Ont.*

GRAPE CONSERVE

To every 5 pounds of grapes, take 3 pounds of sugar, 2 pounds seedless raisins and ½ pound English walnuts. Separate pulp from skins, heat pulp scalding hot, put through colander and sieve, then add skins to pulp with the sugar. Boil slowly for 20 minutes, add the rasins and boil for 15 minutes, then add chopped nut meats and seal.
L. A. M., Indian Head, Sask.

HOW TO PRESERVE GINGER

Wash and thoroughly scrape the rhizomes (or root stock); throw quickly into cold water to prevent discoloration. Cover with fresh cold water; bring to boiling point and drain. Cover again with boiling water and cook slowly until the ginger is tender; drain, this time saving the water to use for the flavouring of other preserves, or it may be put aside for a ginger extract. Weigh the ginger, and to each pound allow a pound of sugar and half a pint of boiling water. Put the sugar and water in a preserving-kettle; bring to boiling point and skim. Put in the ginger and cook slowly until each piece is perfectly transparent. The ginger may now be put away the same as other preserves, or drained free from the syrup, cut into thin slices and rolled in granulated sugar. The syrup may be used for flavouring preserves.

—The New Home.

PINEAPPLE JAM

To 1 pound of grated pineapple and ¾ pound of loaf sugar. Boil 10 minutes.

STRAWBERRY JAM

1 heaping bowl strawberries
1 bowl (scant) sugar.

Set on hot stove and stir to dissolve the sugar. Let boil hard for 10 minutes. Skim and bottle.

CRAB APPLE JELLY

Put the crab apples into preserving-kettle. Pour in enough water to cover and boil until quite soft. Put into cheese-cloth bag and strain over night. To every pint of juice add 1 pound of sugar. Boil juice 20 minutes and add the sugar. Stir well, and let boil up once, then remove from fire and put in glass jars.

[*Jams, Jellies, Conserves*]

SPICED GRAPE JELLY

Crush and strain the juice of grapes that are turned but not ripe. Use equal quantities of juice and sugar and to each quart add ½ teaspoon ground cloves, 1 tablespoon cinnamon. Boil rapidly 20 minutes. Put in glasses.

PEAR MARMALADE

12 pounds of pears (chopped middling fine)
9 pounds sugar
1 pound raisins
3 oranges (juice and rind)
3 lemons (juice and rind)
½ pound shelled walnuts (chopped).

Cook till of right consistency.

RHUBARB MARMALADE NO. 1

Wash and cut rhubarb into small pieces, weigh and put in preserving kettle. Over this put 1 pound of sugar to every pound of rhubarb, and to every 2 pounds of rhubarb slice thinly 1 lemon and half an orange. Let stand 24 hours, then place over fire and boil 1 hour, or until thick, being careful to stir, as it easily burns. When thick, place in jars while hot and seal.

RHUBARB MARMALADE NO. 2

4 pounds rhubarb
6 pounds sugar
4 lemons (juice and rind)
¾ cup walnuts.

Cook very carefully for a few minutes, stirring all the while till there is some juice formed. Add walnuts just before taking from fire. Cook 15 minutes.

◇ ◇ ◇

Do You Buy Flour in "Wood"?

The only barrel fit to hold *Five Roses* flour is made by expert coopers in our own good factory at Keewatin from the finest western poplar.

It is the strongest, most durable flour package made; proof against sifting, loss of flour, free from knot holes.

Reinforced with wooden, likewise sturdy wire hoops.

The *Five Roses* barrel or half barrel, when empty, supplies a very useful receptacle suited to a thousand varied purposes about the home.

Accept no substitute, make no compromise, see that you always get *Five Roses* flour in a *Five Roses* barrel, stencilled in red and blue.

Not Bleached - Not Blended

BEVERAGES

GRAPE WINE

Take **1** gallon of grapes and add **1** gallon of water after bruising the grapes. Let stand for **8** days and then draw it off. To each gallon of wine add **3** pounds of white sugar, stirring it in. Let stand **10** or **12** hours, when it can be bottled.
—*Miss Josie Jones, Oxford Mills, Ont.*

GINGER BEER

Put in a kettle **2** ounces whole ginger, ½ ounce cream of tartar, **2** lemons cut in very thin slices, **2** pounds white sugar, **2** gallons boiling water. Simmer slowly for about **20** minutes. Take from fire and when nearly cold stir in **1** yeast cake (dissolved). After it has fermented—which will be in **24** hours—bottle for use.
—*Mrs. A. St. Laurent, Heffley Creek, Kamloops, B.C.*

HOP BEER

Boil and strain one handful of hops, and add **1** pint of molasses and enough water to make **2** gallons. When lukewarm, add **1** cake of yeast and let stand over night. Skim and pour off from the yeast carefully, add **1** tablespoon wintergreen and bottle for use.
—*Mrs. Wm. Holdsworth, Hanbury, Ont.*

LEMONADE SYRUP

2 pounds brown sugar
6 lemons
1½ pints water
2 ounces tartaric acid.

Boil sugar and water to **a** thin syrup, then add lemon juice. Let boil a little, and while boiling add acid and remove from stove. Bottle when cold. Will keep well. For drinking purposes in hot weather, take **1** tablespoon to **1** glass of water. Sweeten to taste.
—*Mrs. A. J. Allen, Sr., Reids Mills, Ont.*

ORANGEADE

4 oranges
3 lemons
4 pounds white sugar
2 ounces citric acid.

Grate the yellow skin (not the white part) of the oranges, add the acid and sugar, and scald with **2** quarts boiling water. When cool, add the juice of oranges and lemons. Let stand **24** hours, strain and bottle. For drinking purposes, take **1** tablespoon to a cup of water.
—*Mrs. John Brydone, Milverton, Ont.*

◇ ◇ ◇

*T*HE *housewife can effect considerable saving in her flour bill by using such a* thirsty *flour as FIVE ROSES. It not only absorbs more water in the dough, but it retains more water in the oven, thus producing more bread.*

" *We have been using FIVE ROSES flour and can gain a loaf of bread on every baking.*"—Miss H. R., Brougham, Ont.

" *Where I use seven quarts of FIVE ROSES flour, I have used nine quarts of other flour.*"—A. P., Marshville, Ont.

" *Have tried others, and always go back to FIVE ROSES, as I have more bread with same amount of flour.*"
—*Mrs. C. H. McN., Englehart, New Ont.*

"*FIVE ROSES is both better and cheaper than any other.*"
—Mrs. A. B., Brock Road, Ont.

"*Economy to use the best, which we think FIVE ROSES is.*"
—Mrs. A. W. McC., Mountain View, B.C.

"*No waste bread at all while using your flour.*"—Mrs. D. S., Straffordville, Ont.

(NAMES ON REQUEST)

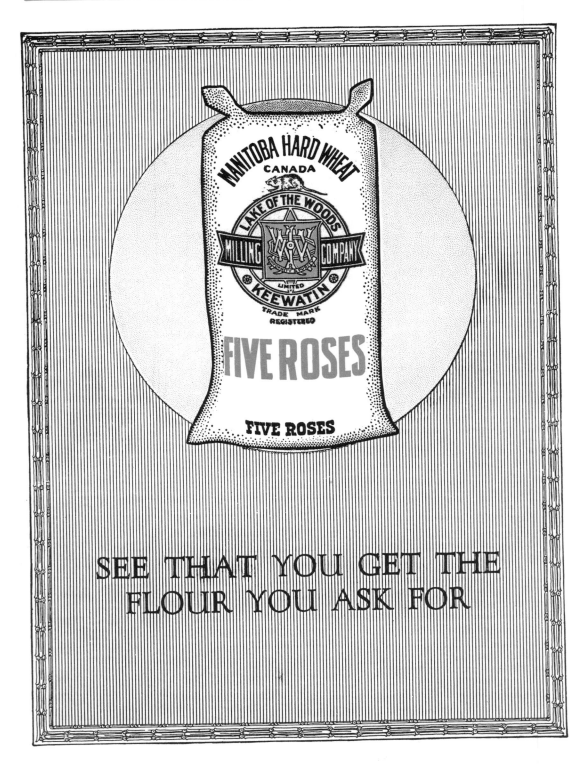

SEE THAT YOU GET THE
FLOUR YOU ASK FOR

FILLING THE COOKY JAR

(Specially prepared for the Five Roses Cook Book)

COOKIES are the children's everlasting delight, in which case it is well to remember that "men are but children of a larger growth."

The following recipes will supply toothsome cookies that require careful concealing if they are to "keep" well.

Cookies, like pastry—because of the large proportion of fat they contain—should be thoroughly chilled before any attempt is made to roll out the dough. To ensure the best results, the dough should be left standing in a cold place for a short time before rolling and cutting.

Use as little flour as possible. Avoid a stiff cooky dough, and roll rather thin. Use a pancake turner for lifting the cookies into the pan for baking, also in removing the cakes after baking.

Cookies should bake in about 10 minutes. The oven should be rather quick, not too hot, however, as these cakes burn very easily. Cookies are at their best when two or three days old.

The cooling and proper packing of these small cakes have much to do with their keeping qualities. Cookies put into an earthen or stone jar, lined with a clean cloth, while still hot, and kept closely covered will be much more melting and will keep their aroma much longer than if allowed to cool exposed to the air.

❖ ❖ ❖

ALMOND COOKIES

Beat to a hard sauce ¼ pound sweet butter and ¼ pound pulverized sugar (sifted). Add the yolks of 3 well-beaten eggs. When a smooth cream, add 4 ounces blanched and sliced almonds, and 6 ounces *Five Roses* flour (in which has been sifted 1 teaspoon baking powder). Stir with a wooden spoon until a smooth paste. Use sugar in making the dough into balls, and set these 1 inch apart in greased pan. Wet the tops lightly and sprinkle with sugar and place an almond in the centre of each. Bake to a light straw color.

AMMONIA COOKIES

1 ounce pulverized ammonia
2 cups milk or sweet cream
3 cups white sugar
1 cup butter
2 eggs (beaten light)
Five Roses flour to roll thin
Flavouring to suit.

Put ammonia into milk and warm till it is thoroughly dissolved. Mix ingredients as usual and roll out thin. Sprinkle with sugar and bake in fairly hot oven.

AUNT MARY'S COOKIES

2 cups white sugar
2 cups butter
4 eggs (well beaten)
5 cups *Five Roses* flour
2 teaspoons soda
4 teaspoons cream of tartar
1 teaspoon salt
Flavour to taste (nutmeg or ratafia).

Roll not too thin and sprinkle with white sugar. Bake 10 minutes in quick oven. For a change, press a raisin or nut-meat in centre of each. A piece of peel could likewise serve.

BOSTON DROP COOKIES

1 cup butter
½ cup sugar
3 eggs
1 teaspoon soda
1½ teaspoons hot water
1¼ cups *Five Roses* flour
½ teaspoon salt
1 teaspoon cinnamon
1 cup currants.

Drop on buttered tins and bake quickly.

[*Filling the Cooky Jar*]

BUTTERMILK COOKIES

2 eggs
2 cups dark brown sugar
2 lumps butter size of an egg
1 cup buttermilk
1 teaspoon cream of tartar
1 teaspoon (level) soda
Five Roses flour to stiffen
Pinch of salt.

Don't mix too stiff. Roll out and cut into desired shapes. Sprinkle granulated sugar over dough before cutting. Quick oven.

Note—For a change, brush with milk and sprinkle with granulated sugar or stick a large raisin in centre of cooky.

CARAWAY COOKIES

2 cups (small) sugar
1 cup butter
½ cup sweet milk
1 egg
2 teaspoons baking powder
1 teaspoon caraway seed
Five Roses flour to make soft dough.

Mix very soft, roll out, sprinkle with sugar on top. Cut in shapes, bake in quick oven. The caraway seed may be left out, substituting with 2 teaspoons vanilla.

COCOANUT COOKIES

Cream ½ cup butter and 1 heaping cup sugar. Add 1 well-beaten egg, ½ cup sour milk, 1 level teaspoon soda and 1 teaspoon baking powder. Add gradually 3 cups *Five Roses* flour and ½ cup shredded cocoanut. Roll thin and sprinkle with sugar. Bake in quick oven. Flavour or not, as desired.

SWEET CREAM COOKIES

1 cup cream
1 cup sugar
1 egg
1 teaspoon cream of tartar
½ teaspoon soda
½ teaspoon salt
Five Roses flour to make soft dough.

Roll thin and bake in quick oven. Flavour with nutmeg, lemon or ratafia.

COFFEE COOKIES

1 cup molasses
1 cup sugar
1 teaspoon spice
1 cup lard and butter (mixed)
1 cup hot strong coffee
1 teaspoon soda
Five Roses flour to roll stiff.

SOUR CREAM COOKIES
(*Eggless*)

2 cups granulated sugar
2 cups sour cream
2 teaspoons soda (dissolved in hot water).
½ teaspoon salt
1 teaspoon vanilla extract
Five Roses flour to make soft dough.

Roll out, cut and bake in hot oven. Fine and economical when eggs are scarce.

SOUR CREAM COOKIES
(*Eggless*)

⅔ cup softened butter
1½ cups sour cream
2 cups sugar
1 teaspoon soda
4 cups *Five Roses* flour.

Stir butter and sugar together. Add the cream, then the flour in which the salt and soda have been well sifted together. Add more flour if necessary. Keep materials all cold while rolling out and the cookies will require less flour.

COOKIES WITHOUT EGGS
CREAM

1 cup sugar
½ cup butter
1 cup water
2 teaspoons cream of tartar
1 teaspoon soda
Flavour with nutmeg
Five Roses flour to stiffen.

DATE COOKIES
(*Oatmeal*)

1 cup brown sugar
½ cup shortening
2 cups *Five Roses* flour
½ cup sour milk
1 teaspoon soda
1 tablespoon molasses.

[Filling the Cooky Jar]

Roll pastry very thin and cut with small cake cutter. Bake. When cool, spread with date filling and press two together in jam-jam style.

FAVORITE COOKIES

2 cups sugar
1 cup (heaping) butter
2 eggs (well beaten)
Nutmeg or other flavouring
1 cup sweet milk
3 cups *Five Roses* flour
2 teaspoons (rounded) baking powder.

Cream together in a large bowl sugar and butter. Add the eggs well-beaten. Grate in a little nutmeg or use any other flavouring preferred. Gradually pour in the sweet milk and *Five Roses* flour which has been sifted 3 times with the baking powder. Roll out quite thin and use a small cutter (I could not get a small enough cutter and punched some holes in the bottom of a very small baking-powder can). Bake in rather quick oven, and let the cookies get cold and hard before putting away. These will keep good and remain crisp almost indefinitely, and therefore are good to make up in large batches.

Note—Above recipe makes splendid lemon cookies by the simple addition of the rind and juice of 1 lemon, omitting all other flavouring.

FRUIT COOKIES
No. 1

1 cup raisins
1½ cups brown sugar
1 cup shortening
1 egg (beaten)
4 tablespoons sweet milk
1 teaspoon baking soda
Pinch of salt
Five Roses flour
Nutmeg or mixed spice.

Seed and chop raisins finely, flour and set aside. Beat together sugar and shortening (butter and lard mixed). When creamy, add beaten egg, sweet milk, baking soda, salt, and enough *Five Roses* flour to make a stiff batter. Add floured raisins with grated nutmeg (or mixed spice) and enough flour to make a stiff dough. Roll rather thin and bake in quick oven.

GINGER COOKIES

1 cup molasses
1 tablespoon soda
1 cup sugar
1 egg
1 tablespoon ginger
1 teaspoon cinnamon
1 tablespoon vinegar
Pinch of salt
Five Roses flour to roll.

Bring molasses to a scald and pour in soda dissolved in a little warm water. Pour while foaming over sugar, egg, ginger, cinnamon and salt beaten together. Then add vinegar and flour enough to roll stirred in as lightly as possible.

HICKORY NUT COOKIES

½ cup butter
½ cup sugar
½ cup milk
3 eggs (well beaten)
1 teaspoon baking powder
1 cup hickory nuts (chopped)
Five Roses flour to roll thin
   Quick oven.

HONEY COOKIES

2 eggs
1 cup sugar
1 cup honey
1 teaspoon soda
1 tablespoon ginger
1 tablespoon cinnamon
Five Roses flour to roll.

SOFT HONEY CAKES

1 cup butter
2 cups honey
2 eggs
1 cup sour milk
2 teaspoons soda
1 teaspoon ginger
1 teaspoon cinnamon
4 cups *Five Roses* flour.

LEMON COOKIES

5 cents worth baking ammonia
5 cents worth oil of lemon
2 cups butter
2½ cups sugar
1 pint sweet milk (warmed)
3 eggs
Five Roses flour to make soft dough.

[*Filling the Cooky Jar*]

Beat together eggs, sugar and butter. Add oil of lemon, then baking ammonia dissolved in the warmed milk. Mix to a soft dough with *Five Roses* flour. Roll thin, and bake as other cookies.

MOLASSES COOKIES
(*Eggless*)

1 cup lard
2 cups molasses
1 teaspoon soda
1 dessertspoon ginger
1 teaspoon cloves
1 teaspoon spice
Pinch of salt
Five Roses flour to roll.

MAPLE SUGAR COOKIES

1 cup sugar
1 cup maple sugar (crushed)
1 cup butter
2 eggs (well beaten)
2 tablespoons water
2 teaspoons baking powder
Five Roses flour to make soft dough.

OATMEAL COOKIES

3 cups oatmeal
1½ cups cream
2 eggs
2 cups sugar
1 cup lard
1 teaspoon soda
Pinch of salt
1 teaspoon cinnamon
Essence of peppermint
Five Roses flour.

Soak the oatmeal ½ an hour in the cream. Add the eggs, sugar, lard, soda, salt and cinnamon. Flavor with essence of peppermint to taste. Roll out thin with *Five Roses* flour. Spread in tins and bake in moderate oven. Cut into squares while warm. Let stand in tin until cool, then lift out.

PRIZE SUGAR COOKIES

(At one of the fall fairs when there was a mixed competition of cookies made from all kinds of flour, this recipe with *Five Roses* flour took first prize.
—*Leonard H. Bishop, Golden, B. C.*)

2 cups sugar
1 cup butter
3 eggs
½ cup milk
1 teaspoon soda
2 teaspoons cream of tartar
Pinch of salt
Five Roses flour to roll.

Cream butter and sugar, add eggs, then milk. Add enough flour to roll out, sifting soda, cream of tartar and salt into the flour.

PEANUT COOKIES

1 cup peanuts (chopped not too fine)
2 tablespoons butter
1 cup sugar
3 eggs
2 tablespoons milk
¼ teaspoon salt
2 teaspoons baking powder
Five Roses flour to roll.

Note—This will also make almond or walnut cookies by changing the nuts.

TEN-EGG COOKIES

10 eggs
1 pound butter
2 pounds sugar
3 pounds *Five Roses* flour
1 nutmeg
1 tablespoon soda.

If not stiff enough to roll, add more flour. They should be stiff enough not to run in the pan while baking. These will keep a long time.

TRILBYS

4 cups rolled oats
2 cups *Five Roses* flour
1 cup (large) brown sugar
1 egg
1 teaspoon soda
1 cup butter or lard
Buttermilk to moisten.

Roll thin. Cut into small squares. Bake in quick oven. When cooked, put together with date dressing.

Not Bleached - Not Blended

COFFEE SNAPS

$\frac{1}{2}$ cup molasses
$1\frac{1}{2}$ cup sugar
$\frac{1}{2}$ cup lard and butter (mixed)
$\frac{1}{2}$ teaspoon soda dissolved in
$\frac{1}{4}$ cup strong coffee
Five Roses flour to roll.

Bake in quick oven. Roll thin and while warm put 2 together with jam or jelly.

GINGER SNAPS WITHOUT EGGS

(*Without Eggs*)
"*Like We Buy*"

1 cup molasses
1 cup sugar
1 cup shortening (lard or butter)
1 teaspoon (heaping) soda
1 teaspoon (level) ginger
1 teaspoon salt
$\frac{1}{2}$ cup boiling water
Five Roses flour to stiffen.

Do not roll out. Pinch off pieces size of marbles and roll with hands. Place about 1 inch apart in pans and bake in moderate oven until right shade is obtained.

Note on Ginger Snaps—If gingersnap dough be mixed at night and left standing in a cool place till morning, it can be handled far more easily and with less flour (especially when *Five Roses* is used) than in the usual way. Moreover, it utilizes the first oven heat. Ground ginger may be omitted, and finely chopped preserved ginger used instead.

RICH GINGER SNAPS

2 cups sugar
2 cups molasses
2 eggs (well beaten)
2 tablespoons butter
2 tablespoons ginger.

Mix above ingredients and set pan on stove until contents are as hot as the finger can bear. Then add the following:

3 teaspoons soda dissolved in
2 tablespoons vinegar
Five Roses flour to roll.

[*Filling the Cooky Jar*]

Add the flour quickly and cut. Use only as much flour as is necessary and leave the pan in a warm place and take only part of the dough onto the board to roll at one time. Bake in very quick oven.

GINGER SNAPS

(*Without Shortening*)

2 eggs
1 cup molasses
1 cup sugar
2 teaspoons lemon extract
2 teaspoons soda
1 teaspoon cream of tartar
1 tablespoon ginger
Five Roses flour to stiffen.

Mix together and let stand $\frac{1}{2}$ hour. Then stiffen, roll and bake. These will suit people with delicate stomachs.

GINGER BALLS

$\frac{1}{3}$ cup melted lard
$\frac{1}{3}$ cup sugar
1 cup light molasses
1 egg (beaten)
1 teaspoon cinnamon
$\frac{1}{2}$ teaspoon cloves, ginger, and salt
1 teaspoon soda dissolved in
1 teaspoon hot water
3 cups *Five Roses* flour.

Mould into balls, roll in granulated sugar and bake.

FRUIT SNAPS

$\frac{1}{2}$ cup milk
1 cup butter
1 teaspoon soda
$1\frac{1}{2}$ cups sugar
$\frac{1}{2}$ cup molasses
3 eggs
1 cup raisins
1 cup currants
1 teaspoon cloves
1 teaspoon ginger
1 teaspoon cinnamon
1 teaspoon allspice.
Five Roses to roll soft as can be cut.

These snaps will keep several months when properly made—*and safely hidden.*

[*Filling the Cooky Jar*]

LEMON SNAPS

Juice of 2 lemons and grated rind of 1
1 cup sugar
½ cup butter
1 egg
3 teaspoons milk
½ teaspoon soda
1 teaspoon cream of tartar
Five Roses flour to make rather stiff.

Roll out thin and cut. Bake in fairly hot oven.

SUGAR SNAPS

1 cup butter
2 cups sugar
4 cups *Five Roses* flour
1 egg
1½ teaspoons baking powder.

EVERY time you fold and butter a pastry dough, every time you roll it, you add an extra flake. When the heat expands the cold air between the buttered flakes, each layer puffs and springs in the oven. This is how puff paste is made. Because *Five Roses* flour has elasticity to spare, you can fold and roll your pastry much thinner without snapping. Because *Five Roses* resists fat absorption, your pastry is never soggy, nor do the layers stick together—the shortening acts as an impenetrable coating between the flakes. Because *Five Roses* is ground to a uniform fineness, your pastry puffs evenly in the oven, and you get that even flakiness of texture so much desired—thin as tissue paper. If you really desire crisp, melting pie crust with that nutty flavor peculiar to Manitoba wheat kernels alone, follow the lead of the best pastry makers in Canada. Follow their recipes. Use *Five Roses* flour.

Not Bleached ~ Not Blended

CATSUP PICKLES SAUCES SALADS

CRAB APPLE CATSUP

Scald crab apples and put through colander. Take 8 pounds crab apples, 3 cups sugar, 3 cups weak vinegar, 1 teaspoon pepper, 1 teaspoon cinnamon, 1 teaspoon cloves, 1 tablespoon salt. Boil until it is like jam.

TOMATO CATSUP

One peck ripe tomatoes, 6 onions, Boil together till done, then put through, colander. Add $\frac{1}{2}$ ounce allspice, $\frac{1}{2}$ ounce cloves, $\frac{1}{2}$ ounce ginger, 1 ounce black pepper, 4 ounces salt, 4 ounces mustard, 1 pound sugar (brown), 1 quart cider vinegar, 2 or 3 red peppers. Boil $1\frac{1}{2}$ hours.

CORN RELISH

One dozen corn (evergreen or sweet corn), 1 small cabbage, 2 large red peppers, $\frac{1}{4}$ pound mustard, 3 pints white vinegar, 3 cups granulated sugar, $\frac{1}{2}$ cup salt, 2 tablespoons celery seed. Boil 30 minutes and can hot.

HORSERADISH SAUCE

Put $\frac{1}{2}$ pint of milk or cream in double boiler. Rub together a tablespoon cottolene, lard or butter, and 1 even tablespoon *Five Roses* flour. Stir into boiling milk, add 1 ounce young horseradish finely grated, $\frac{1}{2}$ teaspoon salt and $\frac{1}{2}$ teaspoon sugar. Nice with boiled, fresh or salted meat.

CHOW-CHOW

One bushel green tomatoes, 2 dozen onions, 2 cups salt. Chop finely and let stand over night. Drain and boil in weak vinegar 2 hours, then drain again. Make a syrup of 8 pounds brown sugar, 2 tablespoons each of cloves, cinnamon and allspice, 1 teaspoon black pepper, $\frac{1}{2}$ teaspoon cayenne pepper, 3 quarts vinegar. Let boil, then pour over the tomatoes.

TOMATO RELISH
(*Not Cooked*)

One peck ripe tomatoes chopped finely and drain over night, 2 cups chopped celery, 4 large onions, 2 peppers cut finely, 3 cups sugar, 2 ounces white mustard seed, 1 quart good vinegar. Put in sealers without cooking.

PURPLE CABBAGE PICKLE

Chop finely 1 gallon purple cabbage. Add $\frac{1}{2}$ cup salt, and then put in stone jar. Over this pour boiling water, cover and let stand until cold. Drain well through a cloth. Again pour over with boiling water and drain as before. Add 1 cup grated horseradish, and over this 2 quarts boiling vinegar to which have been added 2 cups sugar. Cover and let stand until cold.

CUCUMBER PICKLES

Nine green cucumbers and 4 onions chopped finely. Let stand 3 hours in brine. Drain cucumber out of brine, add the following dressing and boil 2 or 3 minutes.

DRESSING

One-half cup *Five Roses* flour, $\frac{1}{2}$ cup sugar, 2 tablespoons mustard, a little cayenne pepper, 1 tablespoon celery seed, pinch of salt, nearly 1 quart of vinegar.

FRENCH PICKLES

Two quarts cucumbers, 1 quart onions, 1 small head of cabbage, 1 small head of cauliflower, 2 bunches of celery. Add green peppers to taste. Cut all in small pieces, but do not chop finely. Sprinkle with salt, let stand 2 hours, then drain. Scald in equal parts vinegar and water, and then remove from this. Make a paste of 2 cups sugar, 5 tablespoons mustard, 1 cup *Five Roses* flour, $\frac{1}{2}$ gallon vinegar. Boil this until it comes to a paste, and then pour over the pickles.

HOW TO CAN GREEN CORN
No. 1

Nine cups of corn cut from cob, 1 cup sugar, $\frac{1}{2}$ cup salt, 1 pint hot water. Boil 5 minutes, put in scalded cans and seal at once. When ready to use, drain off all liquid, rinse in cold water, set where it will heat gradually, then boil 5 minutes. Drain again, then season.

[*Catsup, Pickles, Sauces, Salads*]

HOW TO CAN GREEN CORN
No. 2

Cut ripe sweet corn from the cobs and pack in glass jars, pressing the corn down as tightly as possible. A little wooden mallet that exactly fits the jar is useful to press it down with. To each quart can, add 1 teaspoon salt. Place the cans in a wash boiler, on the bottom of which has been placed a thick folded cotton cloth. Have the covers of the cans screwed down very tightly. Fill the wash boiler to the neck of the cans with cold water, cover and let boil for 3 hours and a half. Take cans out and screw down air-tight. When cool, set in the cellar and you have lovely sweet corn all winter for all purposes. I have tested this several times and never had one can spoil yet.
—*Mrs. H. J. B., Craighurst, Ont.*

CANNED BEETS

Boil the beets till tender, drop in cold water, remove and skin. If too large for jars, cut lengthwise in halves or quarters. Warm the jar and, as fast as the beets are skinned, drop them in until the jar is nearly full. To 1 pint vinegar add 2 cups sugar, set on stove and let come to a boil. While boiling, pour over the beets until the jar is running over. Drop in a few cloves and allspice, then seal.

APPLE SALAD

Chop an equal quantity of apples and cabbage and stir into them a cream dressing. The juice of the apples will greatly dilute the dressing, so do not use too much. The apples should be chopped only a short time before using. A few minced nut meats sprinkled over the top are a pleasing addition.

CREAM DRESSING

One cup cream, ¼ cup vinegar, 1 teaspoon mustard, pinch of salt and a dash of pepper.

BEET SALAD

Boil 6 beets and chop finely 1 head of celery, add pepper and salt.

DRESSING

One half cup white sugar, 2 teaspoons mustard, 1 cup vinegar, 1 egg, a little butter and salt.

CABBAGE SALAD

One quart cabbage cut finely, 1¼ cups vinegar, 1 teaspoon mustard, 1 egg, 1 teaspoon butter, ¼ cup *Five Roses* flour, ½ cup sugar. Boil all together until thick, then add cabbage.

FRENCH SALAD

To 1 pint canned peas add 1 pint celery cut finely, ½ cup walnuts chopped finely, ½ cup chopped orange. Serve with mayonnaise dressing on shredded lettuce.

IRISH POTATO SALAD

Boil 6 potatoes until very soft, peel and mash. While hot, season to taste with salt, pepper and spice, and add 1 teaspoon butter. Boil 2 eggs and dissolve the yolks in 2 tablespoons vinegar. Pour over potatoes and mix well. Put in dish, slice the egg whites and put over potatoes.

POTATO SALAD DRESSING

Two eggs, butter size of egg, 1 teaspoon mustard, 1 tablespoon cornstarch or *Five Roses* flour, 2 cups water, 1 cup vinegar. When cold, add sour cream. Let cool before adding the eggs.

SALAD DRESSING
No. 1

Four eggs (beaten separately), 2 even tablespoons mustard, 4 tablespoons white sugar, 4 tablespoons butter, ½ cup vinegar, dash of cayenne pepper and salt. Mix well together butter, sugar, mustard, salt. Add beaten yolks of eggs. Stir in vinegar and beat well. Cook in double boiler till soft like custard. When done, add whites of eggs well beaten. When ready to serve, add cream.

SALAD DRESSING
No. 2

One-half cup sour cream, 1 cup vinegar, pinch of salt, 1 teaspoon *Five Roses*

Not Bleached - Not Blended

flour, 1 egg, 2 teaspoons mustard. Cook well together.

MAYONNAISE DRESSING

Blend the yolks of 2 raw eggs with 1 teaspoon of mustard, pinch of salt and a

[Catsup, Pickles, Sauces, Salads]

dash of paprika. Add slowly a few drops of olive oil, stirring rapidly, then more at a time. When thick, add a little vinegar or lemon juice, then more oil and vinegar until $\frac{1}{2}$ a cup of oil and 2 tablespoons of lemon juice and the same of vinegar have been used.

◇ ◇ ◇

SOME OLD HOME FAVOURITES

HOME-MADE BAKING POWDER
No. 1

$\frac{1}{2}$ pound tartaric acid
$\frac{1}{2}$ pound best baking soda
1 quart *Five Roses* flour.

Procure the first two ingredients from a trustworthy druggist. Sift the three ingredients thoroughly together as many as half a dozen times, and put the powder in air-tight cans or bottles, excluding the light. Use an *even* instead of a *heaping* teaspoon ordinary baking powder. This recipe has been tried four years by
—*Mrs. John Jones, Surge Narrows, B.C.*

HOME-MADE BAKING POWDER
No. 2

$8\frac{1}{2}$ ounces cream of tartar
4 ounces of soda
2 ounces cornstarch.

Best quality of each should be purchased. Sift all together at least a dozen times, the last time into baking powder tins. Seal up all cracks by pasting strips of paper over them. About one half as much of this is required as of the average powder sold. The cornstarch is added to take up the moisture and keep the powder dry.
—*Miss Ruth Aykroyd, Kingston, Ont.*

CORN VINEGAR

Cut off cob 1 pint of corn. Take 1 pint brown sugar or molasses to a gallon of rain water and add the corn. Put in jar, cover with thin cloth and set in sun. In 3 weeks it will be vinegar.
—*Mrs. J. H., Orangeville, Ont.*

EGG OMELETTE
(*For Six*)

Six eggs beaten separately. Mix in with the yolks 1 cup of milk in which 6 teaspoons cornstarch have been blended, and season with $\frac{1}{2}$ teaspoon salt. Fold the whites in lightly and turn in hot frying pan, in which 1 tablespoon butter has been placed. Let it set nicely in bottom, and when nearly done set in oven to brown. Fold over and serve.

PICKLE FOR CORNING MEAT

Four pounds coarse salt, 8 quarts water, 2 pounds brown sugar, 1 ounce saltpetre. Stir till dissolved, boil and skim. Let cool before pouring over meat. Turn the meat every day for a week. During the summer this may be boiled with an addition of a cup of salt and sugar. A plate or flat stone should be used to keep the meat beneath the pickle. Apply the above recipe to each 100 pounds of meat. Repeat the application 3 times for hams and shoulders, and twice for bacon, rubbing in well. The meat should be cured in 3 weeks.

SUMMER BREAKFAST SAUSAGE

Take equal parts of beef, pork and breadcrumbs. Fresh pork, salted pork or bacon may be used. Put all through the mincing machine. Season with salt and pepper. Beat up an egg and add to the mixture.

[Some Old Home Favourites]

Press into a firm roll, tie in a thickly floured cloth, plunge into boiling water and cook for 2½ hours. Turn out when cooked, and drain. Nice cold or hot.

—*Mrs. R. A. Sim, Rathmullen, Sask.*

POTATO PUFFS

Take 2 cups mashed potatoes and stir in 2 tablespoons melted butter. Beat to cream, and add 2 eggs beaten very light, 1 teacup milk or cream and salt to taste. Bake in deep dish in quick oven till nicely browned.

POTATO SCALLOP

Take a deep baker and put on top of stove with a little butter in it. Slice 1 small onion in it and let it fry a few minutes. Take it from the stove and put 6 potatoes sliced thin in the pan in layers, putting pepper, salt and a little butter on each layer. Sprinkle a few breadcrumbs on top and pour ½ pint of milk over all. Bake in moderate oven 1 hour.

—*Miss Grace Jackson,*
North Sydney, N.S.

EGG PRESERVATIVE

1 pint salt.
2 pints fresh lime.
3 gallons cold water.

Mix well, giving it 2 days to dissolve, stirring often. Pour off the liquid after the lime settles. Put in the eggs without cracking shell, and keep covered with brine. If brine falls short, make more in same way and add to the eggs. Do not put the eggs in a wooden vessel. Get a stone of lime, slack with boiling water, then measure the lime for eggs. This will cover 14 dozen eggs. I have used this formula for years and my eggs are as good the next spring as when I put them away. I always put up my eggs for the winter in May when they are cheapest.

—*Mrs. A. L. Hornby, Gilbert Plains,*
Man.

STICKFAST PASTE
(*Will Keep Twelve Months*)

Always handy, inexpensive, and when dry can readily be softened with water. Dissolve 1 ounce of alum in a quart of water. When cold, add as much *Five Roses* flour as will make it of the consistency of cream. Then add a thimbleful of resin and 2 or 3 cloves. Boil to right consistency, stirring all the time.

*H*ELP *the cause of better baking. Make housekeeping easier for your friends by telling them how to get a copy of the FIVE ROSES cook book. For coupons and instructions, see beginning of book.*

FOR ADDITIONAL RECIPES

❖ ❖ ❖

FOR ADDITIONAL RECIPES

◇ ◇ ◇

FOR ADDITIONAL RECIPES

❖ ❖ ❖

FOR ADDITIONAL RECIPES

❖ ❖ ❖

Not Bleached - Not Blended